Public purpose or private benefit?
The politics of energy conservation

MANCHESTER
UNIVERSITY PRESS

Issues in Environmental Politics

series editors Tim O'Riordan, Arild Underdal *and* Albert Weale

As the millennium approaches, the environment has come to stay as a central concern of global politics. This series takes key problems for environmental policy and examines the politics behind their cause and possible resolution. Accessible and eloquent, the books make available for a non-specialist readership some of the best research and most provocative thinking on humanity's relationship with the planet.

Public purpose or private benefit?

The politics of energy conservation

Gill Owen

Manchester University Press
Manchester and New York
distributed exclusively in the USA
by St. Martin's Press

Published by Manchester University Press
Oxford Road, Manchester M13 9NR, UK
and Room 400, 175 Fifth Avenue, New York, NY 10010, USA
http://www.man.ac.uk/mup

Distributed exclusively in the USA by
St. Martin's Press, Inc., 175 Fifth Avenue, New York,
NY 10010, USA

Distributed exclusively in Canada by
UBC Press, University of British Columbia, 6344 Memorial Road,
Vancouver, BC, Canada V6T 1Z2

British Library Cataloguing-in-Publication Data
A catalogue record for this book is available from the British Library

Library of Congress Cataloging-in-Publication Data applied for

ISBN 0 7190 5025 1 *hardback*

First published 1999

06 05 04 03 02 01 00 99   10 9 8 7 6 5 4 3 2 1

Typeset in Sabon
by Special Edition Pre-Press Services, London
Printed in Great Britain
by Bookcraft (Bath) Ltd, Midsomer Norton

Contents

Tables

Abbreviations

CCGT	combined-cycle gas turbine
CFL	compact fluorescent lamp (low-energy light bulb)
CHP	combined heat and power
DSM	demand-side management
EC	European Commission
EST	Energy Saving Trust (UK)
EU	European Union
GDP	gross domestic product
GNP	gross national product
HEAS	Home Energy Advisory Service (Victoria, Australia)
IEA	International Energy Agency
IRP	integrated resource planning
LCP	least-cost planning
LNG	liquefied natural gas
LPG	liquefied petroleum gas
MITI	Ministry of International Trade and Industry (Japan)
NEA	National Energy Action (UK)
NGO	non-governmental organisation
OECD	Organisation for Economic Co-operation and Development
OPEC	Organization of Petroleum Exporting Countries
RPI	retail price index
SEDA	Sustainable Energy Development Authority (New South Wales, Australia)
TFC	total final consumption (also referred to as 'delivered energy')
TPES	total primary energy supply
UNFCCC	United Nations Framework Convention on Climate Change

Units

GWh	gigawatt-hour
kJ	kilojoule
kWh	kilowatt-hour
MtC	million tonnes of carbon
Mtoe	million tonnes of oil equivalent
toe	tonnes of oil equivalent

Preface and acknowledgements

This book is a development of a PhD thesis on energy conservation policy which I undertook on a part-time basis at Birkbeck College, University of London, in 1991–94. However, its history goes back rather further – to my involvement in the energy conservation field since 1979, working initially for the City of Newcastle upon Tyne in the UK's first Energy Advice Unit, my subsequent role as one of the co-founders, in 1981, of Neighbourhood Energy Action (NEA) and my work since 1988 as an independent energy policy consultant.

The PhD thesis dealt solely with the United Kingdom, Denmark and Japan, but for this book I have included three other countries – the United States, Australia and the Netherlands – and brought the story up to date by examining developments up to early 1998. Together the six countries studied provide some interesting comparisons and contrasts in their approaches to the development of energy conservation policy.

There are many people who have provided inspiration or practical help who I wish to thank. First, my PhD supervisor, Professor Paul Hirst, for all his advice and support, and I am grateful to him and my PhD examiners, Professor Gavin Drewry and Dr Jim Tomlinson, for encouraging me to publish a book based on my thesis. Also Professor Timothy O'Riordan of the University of East Anglia, who, while I was writing a paper on the UK's Energy Saving Trust for him, suggested that I should approach Manchester University Press about writing a book on the politics of energy conservation.

My thanks go to the many people in the UK and elsewhere who, over the years – but particularly while I was writing the thesis and this book – stimulated thoughts and ideas. I particularly want to mention the following by name: Clive Bates, Stewart Boyle, David

Crossley, David Green, Michael King, Eoin Lees, Hugh Outhred, Ben Pimlott, Stephen Tindale and Andrew Warren.

I am grateful to those who helped with information while I was writing the book, particularly Stephen Evans, Mark Ellis, Annette Gydesen, Wilhelma Kip, Alan Pears and Linda Taylor. I also wish to thank the various officials past and present in government departments in the UK and elsewhere who have helped with ideas and information.

Finally, I thank my editor, Nicola Viinikka, and her assistant, Pippa Kenyon, for all their help and, of course, my publishers, Manchester University Press.

Gill Owen

Introduction

Energy conservation is a policy area which attains high profile only infrequently. After the Second World War it featured to a limited extent in Europe and Japan as they struggled to cope with coal supplies that were insufficient to meet demand. In 1973 and 1979 the oil crises thrust it into the limelight worldwide for probably the first time and led many countries to adopt their first energy conservation policies and programmes. During the 1980s interest in conservation waned as oil prices fell, but many governments took on board the energy efficiency message of getting the most out of every cent or penny spent on energy. Since the Rio 'Earth Summit' in 1992 energy conservation has once again become a focus of policy debate as it is seen as a key means of reducing greenhouse-gas emissions.

Yet, while few people would argue against using energy wisely, or against minimising the use of fossil fuels to reduce greenhouse-gas emissions, most people and most governments would agree with the environmental lobby that energy conservation is not taken seriously enough. This raises a number of questions that are explored in this book.

It has become accepted wisdom that people will not invest in energy saving themselves and will not choose energy-efficient appliances, buildings, etc.; thus, it is argued, governments have to provide incentives and regulate. But is this so largely because energy prices have been low and falling since the early 1980s? Is the problem largely due to unwillingness on the part of politicians to raise energy taxes?

In a number of countries during the 1980s there was a change of terminology from *energy conservation* – associated with the public interest 'save it' message during the oil crises of the 1970s – to *energy efficiency*, emphasising the private value, to households and businesses, of using energy more wisely. Is there a difference between energy efficiency and energy conservation or is this change purely semantic? Does the change of terminology affect the choice of policy instrument and the way in which energy conservation is 'sold' to the public?

Is part of the problem that there has never been any serious attempt to sell energy conservation, particularly to the householder? It has been assumed that government subsidies are required, which may be true when energy prices are low and falling. However, perhaps the energy conservation industry would have been more successful if it had devoted more effort to marketing its products instead of spending time trying, largely unsuccessfully, to get subsidies.

The liberalisation of energy markets could open up new opportunities for energy saving. Hitherto, large monopolistic energy suppliers (whether state-owned or private) have had no interest in energy conservation, which might reduce the number of units they sell, and no need to offer particular services or products to their captive customers. In the new environment energy suppliers will have to compete with each other for customers, and there is the potential for such competition to include energy-saving services – better to have customers using fewer units than to lose them to competitors. But, for such competition to work, suppliers have to feel that customers will value energy saving – again this may depend on energy prices. Competition in energy supply reduces prices (one of the main reasons for introducing it), so if governments expect this to boost energy conservation they may have to raise energy prices or impose energy taxes.

Liberalisation of energy markets thus raises again the question of whether energy conservation can compete with energy supply on the basis of its private benefits, or whether only government intervention can ensure that it achieves its public purpose of reducing greenhouse-gas emissions.

Several factors make energy conservation interesting from the general perspective of public policy and politics.

- It forms part of the broader area of energy policy and, as such, touches every area of activity, energy being essential to both businesses and households.

- It provides an interesting study of the nature of the state (interventionist versus non-interventionist), policy networks and policy communities – in particular the links between the broader energy policy community and the energy conservation policy community.
- It is a complex policy area which, in many countries, straddles several central government departments as well as local and regional government. For this reason, problems of co-ordination are often cited as a reason why its implementation is frequently ineffective.
- At various times and in various countries energy conservation has been advocated by enthusiasts and developed by governments to meet a wide range of policy objectives, including conservation of finite resources, alleviating fuel poverty, job creation, business efficiency, and reduction of emissions associated with energy production and use.
- New environmental imperatives – particularly concerns about climate change – have heightened interest in energy use and how growth in demand can be contained.
- Energy conservation would seem to conflict with the interests of powerful industries – oil producers, electricity and gas utilities, coal producers, etc. – who wish to sell more units of energy.
- Recent trends in public policy of privatisation and market liberalisation and the introduction of specialist industry regulators, which have had profound effects on governance and the role of the state, have been developed particularly in the field of energy policy.
- The privatisation and liberalisation of energy markets is leading some commentators to question whether the traditional view of energy efficiency and conservation – that they require government subsidy and regulation to be taken up – will hold in the new markets where the benefits to the customer (lower energy bills, comfort, convenience, 'eco-friendliness') can be 'sold' by competing energy suppliers alongside units of gas and electricity.
- The extent to which energy conservation can be achieved through cost-effective energy efficiency measures is disputed, and there are also disputes over the realizable (as opposed to technical) potential – if energy efficiency reduces the cost of energy to the consumer, it may increase consumption and

some benefits may be taken in increased comfort. Energy efficiency may therefore be detrimental to the achievement of energy conservation.
- Energy conservation involves use of the full range of policy instruments – exhortation, information, regulation, incentives and taxation.

Energy conservation can be seen as rather a conundrum in that its advocates argue that it can be achieved through cost-effective investment in energy efficiency, yet both advocates and sceptics tend to assume that people will not invest in energy saving themselves. It is widely assumed that incentives and/or regulation are required. However, energy saving is different from many other environmental actions (e.g. recycling) in that it can appeal to direct self-interest – people can save money on fuel bills, have a more comfortable home, and so on. Although attempts are made to sell it in this way (notably via the shift in terminology from energy 'conservation' to energy 'efficiency'), the advocates seem to believe that it cannot be sold and therefore lobby for subsidies and regulation. Governments have broadly tended to accept the argument that subsidies are needed, although they have not always been very willing to provide them from taxpayers' money.

Outline of the book

This book is an examination of the development and implementation of energy conservation policy in the context of environmental policy, the role of governments and other institutions, and the nature of policy communities and networks. It considers policies on energy use and conservation in the non-transport sector – i.e. the residential, commercial and industrial sectors.

Chapter one examines relevant policy theories, such as those concerning the differences between procedure-governed and purpose-governed states and the roles of policy communities and policy networks. It outlines the differences between energy conservation and energy efficiency and the nature of the energy market, and it examines theories about the barriers to energy conservation. The chapter also analyses the arguments for government intervention to promote energy conservation and the various motivations that have led to government action – security of supply, social welfare, economic efficiency and environmental considerations. Finally, the chapter outlines the various forms of policy instrument that are used to promote energy efficiency – exhortation, information, regulation, incentives and taxation.

Chapter two gives a brief history of energy policy in the western world mainly since the Second World War and outlines the development of energy policy communities and networks around energy suppliers and government departments, along with the entry of energy conservation interests into these communities since the 1970s. It raises some questions about the extent to which the new environmental agenda of climate change may affect these policy communities and networks. The chapter also focuses on the role of monopoly electricity and gas suppliers in energy conservation and efficiency, and considers what changes privatisation and liberalisation may be making to their role. Factors such as horizontal and vertical integration, the development of least-cost planning and demand-side management and the prospects for a new energy services approach in competitive energy markets are also covered.

Chapter three outlines the role of the European Union and European Commission, which has particular relevance for the case studies of the UK, Denmark and the Netherlands presented in following chapters.

Chapters four, five, six, seven, eight and nine present, respectively, country studies of Denmark, the Netherlands, the UK, the US, Australia and Japan. Each starts with a brief outline of energy policy in the country concerned and then examines the development and implementation of energy conservation policies, and the successes and failures, since 1973. The roles of the relevant policy communities and networks in each country are an intrinsic part of each country study.

Chapter ten looks at the role of energy prices and government action to promote energy saving in terms of their effectiveness in bringing about improvements in energy efficiency and energy conservation in the six countries. It aims to determine whether price is the key factor or whether active energy conservation programmes are more important.

Chapter eleven examines key factors that appear to affect the development and implementation of energy conservation policies and programmes – such as the need for a sense of purpose, the willingness to use intervention, the role of policy communities and networks, and the roles of departments and officials. It concludes by considering whether government intervention might be the problem rather than the solution.

Chapter twelve draws together the main issues and reaches conclusions.

1

Theories and themes

This first chapter examines a number of theories and themes which are central to the book.

- The differences between interventionist and non-interventionist states
- Policy communities and networks (which include government departments) and their influence on policy development and implementation
- The interdependence of policy formation and policy implementation
- Understanding the different terms *energy conservation*, *energy efficiency* and *energy saving*
- Energy pricing
- Why governments are concerned about energy saving and how they intervene to promote it.

Interventionist and non-interventionist states

Types of states and their approaches to economic policy development are often split into the interventionist and non-interventionist. To some extent the distinction is artificial as (except perhaps in early nineteenth-century Britain) the state has played and continues to play a key role in economic development in almost all industrialised societies. However, Wilks and Wright (1987: 277) feel that there is a significant contrast between 'assertive interventionist states and non-interventionist, market dominated states'. Japan and France are examples of the former, the UK and the US being examples of the latter.

These differences stem, according to commentators such as Dyson (1980), from different historical and cultural traditions. Countries like France and Germany (and Japan to some extent), which have experienced much conflict and had to defend their borders and national interests, have, according to Wilks and Wright (1987), developed legal and administrative traditions that stress the need for the state to lead or authorise major economic developments.

The UK and US have had a relatively more peaceful history and a tendency to bloodless political change, which have helped to evolve liberal political traditions and the notion of government acting only in response to popular will. In both countries there is scepticism about the ability or right of government to provide industrial leadership and of the notion of the state as a benevolent public power acting in the common good (Wilks and Wright, 1987).

Another theory is that in countries which industrialised late, such as France and Japan, the state had to have a greater role to enable them to catch up with the earlier, market-led industrialisers like the UK and the US. Dore (1982) describes the concept of developmental intervention, which is designed to promote the competitiveness of the nation in the world economy. The prime example is Japan, where, since the late nineteenth century, the predominant role has sometimes been taken by the state and sometimes by the private sector, but always on the basis of a close relationship between the two. Thus, firms were encouraged to move from activities that might bring high short-term profits into others which would benefit the country in the long term but would produce lower short-term profits.

France is a further example of a developmental state – its postwar planning commission provides a notable contrast to the handsoff approach of the UK at that time (however, one might argue that France had a greater job of reconstruction and hence a greater purpose to will these means). There are also some similarities in Germany and Sweden. In all of these cases, Marquand (1988) would apply the metaphor of the *'economie concertée'* – the state directs and harmonises the efforts of market actors whom it can influence but not command.

These, therefore, are the orthodox views of the strong (Japan and France) and the weak (UK and US) states. For Johnson (1982), the difference between the two is essentially that a regulatory or market rational state concerns itself with the rules of competition (through, for example, anti-trust laws) but does not concern itself with what industries ought to exist. The developmental or plan rational state (e.g. Japan), by contrast, is very involved in shaping the economy and industrial development and in promoting 'national champions'.

However, although these differences are important, all modern governments intervene to promote certain activities or to produce conditions conducive to business. Furthermore, all capitalist societies, to a greater or lesser extent, subscribe to the notion of non-intervention in business, whereas intervention is more accepted in education, law and order, etc. Clearly, this stems from the fact that these other policy areas involve public or merit goods or certain externalities. Thus, even in the more interventionist states like Japan and Germany, intervention has developed through consensus and co-operation between government and business – not coercion of the latter by the former.

The state's relationships with producer groups – unions and employers – can also have a marked effect on the development and delivery of economic policies, including energy policy. In the developmental or neo-corporatist states, according to Marquand (1988), the state shares power with these peak associations and gives them a privileged say in the development of public policy. However, it is not just in the developmental states that these groups have power, as we shall see in the next section.

Policy networks and communities

There are some relationships between the state and producer groups which seem to contradict the strong/weak state thesis. One explanation may be the existence of issue networks, policy networks and policy communities – about which theories have been developed particularly since about 1970, although in the US they can be traced as far back as the 1950s. Particular exponents have been Heclo and Lowie in the 1970s, and Rhodes, Marsh, Wright and Wilks in the 1980s and 1990s.

Wilks and Wright (1987) distinguish between community and network as different phenomena. A policy network may develop around a single policy issue, a set of related issues or a policy process, such as budgeting or planning. Members of a network may be drawn from different policy communities within the same, or even from different, policy areas. Some members of a policy community may be excluded (sometimes as a condition of others' involvement) from a policy network. Wright (1988: 606) defines the policy network as 'the linking process, the outcome of those exchanges, within a policy community or between a number of policy communities'. So, while there is always a policy community for an issue, not all policy communities generate policy networks. 'Relationships between members of a community in general, or in terms of a particular policy issue, may be so inchoate and unstructured that no stable network of resource dependencies is discernible' (Wright, 1988: 606).

What is kept off policy agendas is often as important as what is on them. Key members of a policy network may be able to keep off the agenda issues that would challenge their power. Issues may also remain off the agenda due to fragmentation and lack of organisation among those within a policy community whom one would expect to be advocates for such issues.

These distinctions between policy communities and policy networks may be seen as another set of terminology for the distinction between corporatist and pluralist structures. Corporatist structures are those with 'a limited number of non-competitive organizations, well supported by membership and recognised by government, with representational monopoly' (Appleby and Bessant, 1987: 205). They are thus comparable to policy networks. Pluralist systems are characterised by 'multiple and competitive interest representation, voluntarism ... ' (Appleby and Bessant, 1987: 205). These are more akin to a policy community.

There is a danger that this form of analysis could become swamped by confusing terminology. However, the concept of a continuum from the very closed corporatist to the open pluralistic structure is useful in identifying and analysing how some actors are able to gain considerable power and/or influence while others remain marginalised. It will also be useful in helping to identify the potential for change.

Finally, though, we should not forget Marquand's (1988) thesis that states which retain the market liberal bias (such as the UK) may find difficulty in implementing certain types of intervention – an effective policy network may be able to overcome this, but, as we shall see, such effective policy networks may be easier to establish in the developmental states, thus reinforcing the differences.

The interdependence of policy formation and implementation

Policy choice and formation have tended to be the key focus of social scientists when studying the policy process. Hogwood and Gunn (1984) note that it is only since the early 1970s that social and political scientists have taken an interest in policy implementation. The growing interest in implementation arose with the realisation that many of the policies introduced to tackle major problems such as urban deprivation, industrial restructuring and pollution had brought about little significant change, leading to searches to tackle 'the implementation gap' identified by Dunsire (1978).

Hogwood and Gunn identify several factors affecting policy implementation:

- The availability of adequate time and resources to the programme, both in overall terms and at appropriate points
- Dependence on other bodies for delivery and the degree to which their compliance can be secured
- Understanding of and agreement of objectives by those involved
- Communication and co-ordination
- That circumstances outside the control of those implementing the policy do not impose crippling constraints
- That the policy to be implemented is based on a valid theory of cause and effect and the relationship between cause and effect is direct.

Any or all of the first five points may lead to what Hogwood and Gunn would call 'non-implementation', where policies may fail because they are badly carried out or because other circumstances are unfavourable, such as lack of co-operation from important actors.

Lack of co-ordination is frequently cited as a reason for policy failure. However, any analysis must also take into account the power held by those who need to be co-ordinated. Arguing the need for better co-ordination in policy implementation presupposes that participants have a common purpose but are acting in a contradictory fashion because of ignorance and that, once informed of their role, they will act obediently. Pressman and Wildavsky (1979) suggest that it is more likely that there will be conflict over goals; therefore people can only be 'co-ordinated' by being told what to do – i.e. coerced. This may not be an option, though, for bureaucrats in their relations with other bureaucrats or with other powerful actors, so co-ordination becomes another word for consent and consultation.

These problems of co-ordination or control would seem to lend credence to the notion of an implementation gap, which suggests that implementors are actors with their own agendas who may choose to obstruct or delay policy. Gilliat (1984) accepts that there is a dynamic relationship between the factors that affect implementation – political choice, organisational structure and external environment – but concludes that organisations are ultimately constructed or sustained by political authority. The refusal to tackle fragmented forms of decision-making and implementation thus sustains their power and signals political acceptance of the limits they place on initiatives.

There may be many reasons why politicians accept these limits which are hampering the very policies they are trying to implement. Edelman's work on symbolic politics suggests that politicians may espouse certain policies which they feel they have to be seen to be supporting although they may not intend to do much to ensure their effective implementation. Environmental policies may suffer particularly from this syndrome.

Unsuccessful implementation – 'when a policy is carried out in full and external circumstances are not unfavourable, but none the less the policy fails to produce the intended results' (Hogwood and Gunn, 1984: 197) – is more likely to be caused by the final point in the list proposed by Hogwood and Gunn. However, this reason for failure – that the policy itself was wrong – is, understandably, usually less readily admitted by those responsible for policies.

This key role of political choice is emphasised by Gilliat (1984). Choice may often reflect underlying assumptions on the part of policymakers rather than the political realities of interdependence and difficulties of control. For example, tackling pollution may be approached from the standpoint of how much control can be exerted on industry rather than from wanting to limit pollution as much as is technically possible. Such an approach can impose severe limits on the action that will be considered and taken. Gilliat cites the case of the voluntary promotion of unleaded petrol as an example of policymakers' self-imposition of a constraint that had less to do with organisational dependence than the desire to maintain good relations with the oil companies and car manufacturers. Suggestions that particular policies or programmes would not be feasible may therefore result from a predisposition to respect the autonomy of certain groups, even when governments may be able to challenge it without incurring significant cost or provoking serious resistance (Gilliat, 1984). However, as Gilliat points out, coercion is not ruled out when the state is not sympathetic to the organisation.

Such political choices (e.g. voluntary restraint rather than compulsion) may, of course, be highly effective – although in the example of unleaded petrol it was a financial incentive (a lower tax on unleaded petrol) that boosted take-up rather than voluntary promotion by the industry. But their success will be dependent on whether those involved are committed to action or see the need to comply to avoid legislation in the future. As we shall see, these choices have considerable implications for the energy conservation policies that governments will develop and the means they will use to implement them.

As Barrett and Hill (1984) have emphasised, implementation is an integral part of the policy process and can be affected by the same factors that give rise to compromise in policymaking. The importance of recognising that there can be no sharp divide between formulating and implementing policy is also stressed by Hogwood and Gunn (1984), who suggest that policies are most likely to achieve a successful outcome if thought is given at the design stage to potential problems of implementation. However, it is worth recognising that the expectation of problems in implementation (for example, due to the power of external actors or an unwillingness to confront them, or due to concern that effective delivery mechanisms do not exist) can also constrain policy choice. Central to these considerations of the potential problems of implementation will be the existence of appropriate institutions to take responsibility for implementation, their skills and influence over important actors in the field and their role in influencing political choice.

Political authority and power relationships are, therefore, crucial to the study of policy formation and implementation. A simplistic pluralist perspective, that power is evenly distributed, is clearly inadequate. Even in cases of considerable political consensus over policy goals (almost everyone agrees that global warming needs to be tackled), when discussions start to focus on the methods of achieving them and how much money should be spent, differing interests will soon appear, and some participants will be more likely than others to start from a position of considerable advantage.

Energy efficiency and energy conservation

We move now from general theories of the state and the policy process to clarification of the terms 'energy conservation' and 'energy efficiency'. Although some countries had taken action on energy conservation earlier, it was in the wake of the 1973 oil crisis that most became interested in the scope for reducing energy consumption as a means of lessening dependence on imported oil, temporarily or permanently. The term 'energy conservation' thus came to be used to encompass a wide range of actions, such as restricting electricity supply to consumers at certain times, rationing petrol supplies, encouraging people to insulate buildings, alter thermostats and switch off lights, and setting minimum efficiency standards for appliances.

Until the 1980s the term 'energy conservation' was widely used in most countries when referring to energy-saving measures; however, during the 1980s most of the English-speaking countries (the UK, the US, Canada and Australia) tended to switch to the term 'energy efficiency'. By the late 1980s the European Commission too had switched from energy conservation to energy efficiency as its preferred term. A number of EU countries (e.g. Denmark and the Netherlands) have tended to retain terms whose sense is closer to energy conservation than energy efficiency in their own languages, although they will often use 'energy efficiency' when translating into English. Japan has also retained the term energy conservation.

'Energy efficiency' and 'energy conservation' are, thus, terms that are often used interchangeably but which mean different things, and it is important to distinguish between them, as shown in box 1.1.

Energy saving can be used as a generic term to describe activities or measures directed at achieving either energy conservation or energy efficiency. Energy saving can include physical measures, such as loft insulation or heating controls, or behavioural techniques such as turning down thermostats or turning off lights in unused rooms.

In any one case there may be an energy-efficiency and an energy-conservation effect. For example, by insulating a loft the theoretical reduction in energy use might be 20%. However, some of the benefits may be taken up in warmer room temperatures, and the actual reduction in energy use may be only 10% or even less. Another example is household electrical appliances, whose efficiency has improved significantly since the 1970s. However, people now have

---

1.1 Energy efficiency and energy conservation

- *Energy efficiency* can lead to a range of end results. It can mean using less energy (e.g. electrical power) to achieve the same benefits (e.g. internal temperature, industrial output, etc.), using the same amount of energy but achieving more benefits (e.g. a warmer home, higher output), or using less energy to achieve more benefits. The focus of energy efficiency thus tends to be on the benefit to the end-user or customer.

  Two different types of efficiency may be improved by energy efficiency. The first is *allocative efficiency* – the allocation of resources to particular activities. If fewer resources are spent on wasteful energy use, they can be redirected to other activities. The second is *productive efficiency* – the ways in which resources devoted to particular activities are used. For example, if by investing in energy-efficiency measures a manufacturer can produce 120 units of a product for the same energy input as he previously used to produce 100 units, this will lower his costs and boost his profits, provided that the costs of the energy-saving measures are not so large as to cancel out the value of the increased production.

- *Energy conservation* means using less energy irrespective of whether the benefits increase, decrease, or remain the same. Energy conservation is therefore what has to be achieved to reduce the environmental impact of energy use. If at the same time one wishes to see economic growth, one has to use less energy but also achieve more benefits.

---

more appliances and in some cases efficiency gains have been cancelled out by new appliances being bigger or otherwise more energy-consuming, such as larger refrigerators or freezers as people buy food less often and hence require more cold storage. Improvements in energy efficiency, therefore, may or may not lead to energy conservation.

Energy conservation may not always produce benefits to the consumer (household or business) – it could be achieved by people having lower temperatures in their homes, or by energy-intensive industries ceasing production, for example. At times of crisis (e.g. the oil crisis of the mid-1970s) energy conservation measures in some countries have included power cuts at certain times of the day and petrol rationing. Energy efficiency, on the other hand (which may also lead to energy conservation), should bring real economic

1.2 Energy usage definitions

- *Total final consumption* is the total amount of energy converted from fuels to electricity or other forms such as heat and actually available for specific purposes – another name for TFC is *delivered energy*. TFC is usually recorded by end-use sectors, such as industry, commerce, agriculture, households, etc.
- *Total primary energy supply* includes the losses incurred in producing, converting, transporting and distributing fuels and electricity to final consumers. Some of the main losses occur in the generation of electricity from other fuels (older coal and oil power stations have efficiencies of only around 30%, newer gas-fired ones of around 50%) and in the transmission and distribution of electricity to consumers. The losses from TPES are on average twice the value of TFC in the case of electricity (for every unit delivered to end-consumers two are lost), but only 5–15% of the value of TFC in the case of liquid, gaseous or solid fuels (for every unit delivered to end-consumers 0.05–0.15 units are lost). The substitution of electricity for other fuels for heating leads to a reduction in final energy use (at the point of use electricity is 100% efficient whereas a modern gas boiler will achieve on average around 75% efficiency) but an increase in primary energy use when the losses in production and transportation are taken into account.

benefits to consumers in terms of lower energy costs to maintain or improve their standard of living (for domestic customers) or productivity (business customers) and should therefore also benefit the economy as a whole.

Some other energy terms need to be defined. The energy usage of a country can be assessed in two main ways – total primary energy supply (TPES) or total final consumption (TFC). These terms are explained in box 1.2.

Energy intensity (or *energy ratio*) is the relationship between TPES and gross domestic product (GDP). Energy intensity can be affected by many factors, including climate, industrial structure, the average size and type of buildings, the types of fuel used directly and assumptions about the fuels used for electricity generation. Improvements in a country's energy intensity can result from factors other than improved energy efficiency, including exchange rate fluctuations, fuel switching and the decline of heavy industry.

As the definitions of TPES, TFC and energy intensity imply and as we shall see throughout this book, economic factors and changes in economic structures can have a significant effect on energy demand.

Energy market imperfections and barriers to energy saving

Given its potential benefits, one might assume that opportunities for energy efficiency would be eagerly taken up by consumers and that there would be a thriving market for suppliers of energy-saving products and services and more energy-efficient appliances and other equipment. However, in most countries, it is estimated that between 20 and 40% of the reduction in energy use that could be achieved through the wider application of energy-saving measures has not yet been taken up. Imperfections in the energy market and market barriers are given as the reason why many of these opportunities are not being realised.

There are several problems in applying the perfect competition model to the energy market. First, there are clear examples of market failure. Externalities (factors that are unpriced) mean that the pursuit of profit cannot be guaranteed to serve the public interest. The most obvious externality that is unpriced is pollution from energy generation and supply. Another important consideration is that the heat and light provided by energy, like education, are generally considered to be necessities (or 'merit goods'), which it is undesirable that people should have to go without.

However, even allowing for intervention to remedy such aspects of market failure, there are problems with some of the principal features of the perfect competition model: price-taking; perfect knowledge; and profit maximisation. Looking first at price, although the market mechanism is normally based mainly on short-term profit considerations, the large-scale investments required in energy supply mean that profits can be slow in coming. Yet, while capital investments are large – particularly in electricity generation, transmission and distribution – the marginal costs of supply are low, giving an incentive to sell as many units as possible, for example, by offering low-price off-peak tariffs, which may cover only marginal costs. Customers will have little incentive to change from one fuel to another if they pay only marginal costs.

Energy suppliers have also tended to be mainly powerful monopolies, duopolies or part of an oligopolistic market with no real competition. The energy market can generally be considered to be oligopolistic – consisting of a small number of large producers who are continually trying to second guess one another in terms of prices – rather than the perfect competition model of many small sellers each with an insignificant effect on supply and, hence, unable to influence price. Where energy industries have been nationalised, profit maximisation has not been an overriding consideration.

Market entry has never been easy due to the large-scale investment required in supply capacity. Of course, in many countries only licensed monopolies (state or private) were allowed to supply, and, even with liberalisation, the incumbents can make entry difficult for new suppliers by imposing high charges for the use of transmission and distribution networks.

Even if perfect competition were to be attained, it might not lead to overall allocative efficiency in energy use. The 'energy market' tends to focus on competition between different fuels, yet consumers actually want light, heat or motive power rather than units of gas or electricity. If these needs can be satisfied through buying fewer units of electricity or gas, it is certainly in the interests of the consumer, but it may not be in the interests of the suppliers except where they are competing for market share and improving efficiency makes (say) electric heating more competitive with gas. A good example is the low-energy compact fluorescent light bulb. A 20 W compact fluorescent bulb provides light equal to that provided by an 80–100 W incandescent bulb for one-quarter to one-fifth as much electricity. As gas lighting is not a practical option in the 1990s, electricity companies do not have to worry about losing market share to gas in this area; hence, they have tended to be reluctant to promote low-energy lighting except where they have been encouraged or compelled to do so by regulators.

Energy saving is not viewed as comparable to energy supply, even though it can be an alternative means of meeting needs for heat, light and power. It is therefore unlikely to be offered by existing supply companies or new entrants who seek to compete primarily on price per unit of gas or electricity with their established competitors.

Such features of the energy market, it is argued, have contributed to and, indeed, caused some of the barriers to energy saving. These barriers have been well documented since the late 1970s and include:

- The lack of independent information and advice – for most consumers their only source will be their local gas or electricity showroom, where the advice is neither impartial nor comprehensive.

- For most households and businesses energy costs are relatively insignificant, which does not provide much motivation for action – especially where investment in energy saving could take several years to recoup in terms of lower fuel bills. Low-income households and small businesses that do find energy a significant cost are often unable to afford the capital investment required to reduce their bills.

- Rented property in the domestic and commercial sector poses special problems. Some tenants are not even aware of their energy costs if they pay for heating with their rent. Where tenants do pay bills themselves, they may be unwilling to invest if they do not plan to stay long. For landlords there is little incentive to invest in energy saving if all the benefits are taken up by tenants but their value is not sufficient to command higher rents.

- Energy supply is dominated by a few large companies with an interest in increased sales who often require very low rates of return on investments in supply due to their dominant position in the market for an essential commodity. By comparison, energy-saving measures and services are provided by many small companies that do not have comparable market power; and consumers require a much more rapid rate of return on energy-saving measures than energy companies need from supply investments.

- The price mechanism cannot work as effectively as it does in many other sectors because most purchases of energy-using products are made infrequently. Most people cannot replace a car, house, heating system or large appliance with a more efficient one (or one using a different fuel) the minute that energy prices go up. This is one of the main arguments used in favour of high energy-efficiency standards for energy-using equipment, particularly household appliances which may be replaced only every ten years or even less frequently.

A further barrier is the 'hassle' factor, supplemented by the scepticism factor, although some analysts would say that these are not market barriers at all but, rather, evidence that consumers are making rational choices in not taking up energy-saving opportunities. Many theoretical calculations of the cost-effectiveness of energy-saving measures may underestimate transaction and switching costs, particularly in terms of the time investment required of the consumer. In the case of businesses, small projects may impose large overhead costs (e.g. staff time, other improvements, removing equipment), which give the project a longer payback period than the cost of the measure itself would suggest. For households, difficulties finding contractors who can do all the tasks concerned – and, in many areas, difficulties finding competent installers – exacerbate the hassle factor. The least-cost action might be to keep paying an energy bill by direct debit rather than to spend time researching options for saving energy and then still more time getting the work done, especially if the potential savings are small and/or the investment would take many years to recoup in lower bills.

The problems caused by the hassle factor are exacerbated by the fact that many businesses and householders are sceptical about the savings that are claimed for certain measures. It is certainly true that the same measures can produce widely different energy savings in different circumstances. Some scepticism may therefore be reasonable, and it is not surprising that a rational consumer should be wary of spending money on something whose benefits he or she is uncertain of. Thus, another reason why energy users may choose not to invest in energy saving is because they see greater benefits in competing investments. For businesses, by comparison with investment in new production machinery, energy saving – even if it offers the same rate of return – will not provide the potential benefits of keeping ahead in new technology. Similarly, householders may prefer to spend money on a new bathroom or kitchen or a holiday, which they feel provides them with more benefits than insulating their walls and roof.

Energy pricing

Energy prices are set by the interaction of demand and supply and, where fuels can be easily transported, it is world demand and supply that affect prices. Oil and coal are traded on world markets and their prices also influence the prices charged for fuels that are traded nationally or regionally, such as gas. Since 1973 the world has experienced a number of major changes in energy prices, beginning with substantial rises after the 1973 and 1979 oil crises, followed by a substantial fall in oil prices in the mid-1980s, since when oil prices

Table 1.1   *Crude oil prices, 1972–96, in US dollars (real 1990 prices*)*

1972	1973	1978	1979	1982	1984	1986	1990	1991	1994	1996
$11	$50	$35	$70	$53	$40	$17	$22	$25	$15	$18

*Calculated using GDP deflator at market prices.
Source: Department of Trade and Industry (1997).

have tended to remain at fairly low levels or even to fall further, apart from short-term price increases such as during the Gulf War crisis in 1990–91.

These price changes can be illustrated by comparing the prices for crude oil from 1972 to 1996, as in Table 1.1. As the table shows, the price of crude oil rose dramatically between 1972 and 1973, falling back somewhat by 1978, only to rise still further in 1979. In 1980 the price began to fall and remained around the US$15–17 level from 1986 to 1990/91, when it rose to US$25 a barrel, followed by a further decline to 1994. 1995 and 1996 saw small increases, and the price in 1996 was $US18 a barrel (US$22 a barrel in actual 1996 prices). The introduction of liberalisation of energy markets in the 1990s has also led to further falls in real energy prices in many countries.

Energy prices can be left to the market or governments can intervene to keep them low through subsidies or raise them via taxation. Subsidies have been used in many countries for various reasons, including promoting energy diversity and security, keeping prices low for consumers or protecting indigenous energy industries. For example, many countries have subsidised coal production to enable it to compete in the world or national markets and hence preserve jobs in the industry. Nuclear power has received substantial subsidies over the years in many countries through government investment in research and development, much of it done under defence rather than energy budgets. A number of governments have, since the 1970s or 1980s, provided subsidies for renewable energy sources to enable them to compete for market share with fossil fuels and nuclear power.

The principle of taxing pollution or resource depletion, rather than setting limits or restricting them altogether, dates back to work by Pigou (1920) on welfare economics. The problem with environmental taxes is that they may be difficult to set at the right level.

If set too low, too much pollution will still occur, and this may cause considerable damage which may not be realised for some time. If the tax is set too high it may reduce economic efficiency. In practice, discovering the 'right' level will, of course, be impossible as no one will have perfect information and be able to predict behaviour fully. So taxation will have to be rather rough and ready, which suggests that it may be less suitable for pollution that has clearly identifiable, short-term and/or local effects (e.g. sulphur dioxide and oxides of nitrogen, often known generically as 'acid gases'), but perhaps more suitable for pollutants with longer-term effects and where the effects are less clear cut, such as greenhouse gases. Ironically, however, more governments have introduced taxes on acid-gas emissions in power generation than on greenhouse-gas emissions.

Economic theory suggests that high energy prices should encourage energy saving (through frugality of use, by promoting capital investments in measures which can reduce energy use or by encouraging a switch from energy-intensive to low energy-usage activities). Some analysts feel that pricing is often a more useful tool than other forms of intervention, although others say that it fails to tackle some of the key barriers to energy conservation. The general consensus is that pricing is a useful part of any strategy (if prices are low it is difficult to motivate people to save energy) but that it may have limited effect if not backed up by other measures.

Prices of electricity, gas and district heating supplied to household and, often, small business consumers are, in most countries, regulated in some way by national or state governments. Prices charged to larger consumers are sometimes regulated but in other cases are subject to negotiation between the customer and the energy supplier. A wide range of consumer taxes is applied to energy, usually as a means of raising revenue rather than for environmental or security of supply purposes.

The amounts of tax applied to energy vary enormously from country to country, however. Among International Energy Agency (IEA) member countries (all EU countries, plus Norway, Turkey, the US, Canada, Australia, New Zealand and Japan), Denmark is the only one that has consistently used taxation as a major instrument of its energy policy. Until 1994 the UK was one of the few major countries that did not add a general sales tax (VAT) to energy used by domestic consumers. Australia still does not levy any taxes on electricity use, although some states levy a small tax on gas use.

Since the early 1990s Denmark, Norway, the Netherlands, Finland and Sweden have introduced some form of environmental energy taxation, primarily to reflect the carbon content of fuels and to discourage use of fossil fuels.

Why are governments concerned about energy saving?

Four different motivators have led to government interest in energy efficiency or conservation: security of supply; economic efficiency; help for poor households; and environmental concerns. Without intervention, it is argued, not all of the environmental, social welfare, economic and other benefits of energy saving will be taken into account, particularly because the environmental and health disbenefits of energy supply are not internalised in the prices charged for energy.

Security of supply
Historically, the main reason for governments to promote energy saving was to conserve supplies at times of crisis. For example, the coal shortages experienced in much of Europe and Japan after the Second World War led to efforts by a number of countries to conserve stocks – often reducing supplies to households to ensure that industry could get enough to maintain production. The other obvious example was the 1973 oil crisis, as a result of which many governments introduced a range of short- and long-term measures to promote better use of energy as a means of reducing dependence on imported oil.

During the 1970s concerns were also first raised about the limits to growth and that the world might run out of fossil fuels in the foreseeable future. In the late 1990s few people seriously believe that world reserves of fossil fuels are likely to be exhausted in the foreseeable future. However, as the demand for energy goes up and the most economic reserves of fossil fuels are exhausted, prices could rise dramatically. Fossil fuels are in no imminent danger of being exhausted, but they could, in the decade after 2000, start to become much more expensive.

There are also concerns among many Western countries about threats to security of supply if they have to rely more on fuel supplies from unstable sources. For example, a number of EU countries may have to import gas from Algeria and parts of the Commonwealth of

Independent States (CIS) as North Sea gas reserves are exhausted. Avoiding wasteful use of energy will thus help to preserve accessible, secure and low-cost energy supplies for longer.

Long-term security of supply is not a factor that today's energy customers will take into account. Energy suppliers may consider it to a limited extent, but they may be more concerned about maximising short-term returns on capital. This suggests that security of supply is an externality which is not accurately reflected in the market price for energy. In view of the uncertainties (new reserves of gas or oil may be found, nuclear power and/or renewables may become more competitive), large-scale and costly intervention may not be justified on security of supply grounds alone. However, energy efficiency is being seen by some countries as part of an effective and low-cost insurance policy against future threats to security of supply. The White Paper on Energy, agreed by the European Commission in December 1995, recognises the 'scope for strengthening security of supply by ... enlarging choices with the promotion of energy efficiency' (European Commission, 1995b).

Improving economic efficiency
Throughout the 1980s many of the arguments in many countries for government intervention to promote energy efficiency were based on economic efficiency. It was argued that it was a waste of national resources for so much money to be invested in energy supply when it could be better invested in energy efficiency, and that industry and households could save money that could be used for other purposes. However, the arguments for government intervention on the grounds of efficiency need to be examined carefully.

There are certainly good reasons for governments to try to ensure that households and businesses have adequate information on which to make their decisions. The case for information for businesses is particularly strong on economic grounds as resources wasted on inefficient energy use could often be used more productively else-where in the economy, creating jobs, boosting productivity, boosting exports, etc. Governments have thus tended to be keen to ensure that households and businesses have adequate information on which to base their decisions.

However, the economic arguments for other sorts of intervention – such as regulation, taxation and/or subsidies – are more contro-versial. If, on the basis of adequate information, a householder chooses to continue to pay higher heating bills than he or she needs to (either because of inertia, or because he or she would rather spend money on a holiday than invest it in a condensing boiler), why, in economic terms, should this be of concern to anyone else? In the case of businesses, some might say there is more reason for governments to ensure that inefficient practices are weeded out. But others would say that the competitive process, through which inefficient firms will be forced to improve or be replaced by the more efficient, will tend to do this more effectively than any government intervention.

Concern for low-income households

Yet another concern which has driven government intervention has been social welfare – to enable low-income households (particularly the elderly and disabled) to have warmer homes at lower cost. There are well-established health benefits in terms of fewer respiratory diseases, reduced risk of strokes in the elderly and – at the most extreme level – reduced risk of deaths from cold-related illnesses (Keatinge, 1986). These benefits are felt by health budgets, in terms of fewer people needing treatment for cold-related illnesses, as well as by the people themselves. The benefits are difficult to quantify but have been estimated as worth anywhere between £50 million and £800 million per year in the UK (King, 1992).

Low-income households tend to be less likely to live in an energy-efficient home than the better-off. The differential between poor and better-off households is particularly marked in the US, the UK and Ireland, although it tends to be less of a problem in other EU countries, particularly Scandinavia, Germany and the Netherlands.

The 'energy efficiency' of housing is generally calculated by assessing two variables: the thermal efficiency of the building; and the cost of running the heating system. So homes that are energy-inefficient will tend to have poor insulation and heating systems which are expensive to run. Low-income households spend a greater proportion of their incomes on fuel than better-off households. However, poorer households tend to spend less in absolute terms on fuel than the better-off. This lower spending in absolute terms, coupled with lower energy efficiency, means that those with low incomes often underheat their homes and that therefore they often need to use more heat as well as to use it more efficiently. The term 'fuel poverty' is used to refer to the effects of this interaction of income and housing conditions.

Investment in energy efficiency will enable poor households to achieve a warmer home at a lower cost – 'affordable warmth' (Boardman, 1991) – and will thus lead to a more efficient use of resources than would enabling them to spend more money on energy. However, poor households lack the capital to invest in energy-saving measures and often find it difficult to borrow due to poor credit ratings. The health and welfare benefits to poor households, the benefits to the health service and poor households' lack of capital have, therefore, been considered to justify government intervention. Improving energy efficiency for poorer households has been a particular focus of policy in Australia, the UK and the US; in the latter case there has also been concern about adequate access to cooling in the summer months because of the health risks to elderly people and babies from overheating.

It has also been argued, in studies such as those by the Fraunhofer Institute (1985) and Krier and Goodman (1992), that energy saving can help poor households by creating jobs for the unemployed. Large-scale programmes to insulate housing or develop combined heat and power (CHP – see box 1.3) district-heating schemes, for example, would create many jobs in both manufacturing and installation.

However, as well as the direct creation of jobs, energy-saving programmes can have negative or positive indirect effects on employment. On the positive side there is the re-spending effect – when money that would have been spent on inefficient energy use is released for other purposes. On the negative side, lower energy demand may result in job losses in the traditional energy supply industries – for example, at power stations or in building and maintaining transmission and distribution systems. Krier and Goodman (1992) found that their estimate of 82,460 direct jobs created by investment in energy saving was offset by a loss of 98,000 jobs in energy supply. However, they estimated that the re-spending effect would create a further 91,010 jobs, thus leading to a significant net gain in employment.

Because the net impact on jobs depends on the re-spending effect, it is difficult to prove that investment in energy saving *per se* would be a more effective way of creating jobs than any other investment. However, some programmes (for example, home insulation) can create jobs which are particularly suitable for many of the long-term unemployed.

1.3 CHP/cogeneration

CHP/cogeneration is an alternative means of electricity production from a conventional power station in that the heat that would normally be wasted is used to heat buildings or provide steam for industrial processes. As such it converts fuels to useful energy at efficiencies of 70–85% compared to 30–50% in conventional electricity generation (30–35% for older, conventional coal, oil and nuclear generation; and 45–50% for gas-fired generation developed since 1990, which in 1998 accounted for 22% of electricity generation in the UK).

CHP/cogeneration schemes can be small-scale (to serve a factory, hotel or block of flats) or similar in size to a major power station. The term 'combined heat and power' is used in the UK and some parts of Europe, while 'cogeneration' is used in other parts of Europe and in the US.

Environmental concerns

Since the late 1980s environmental arguments for energy efficiency and energy conservation have once more come to the fore. This time, however, it is not so much the need to conserve resources as the effect of the use of energy (particularly from fossil fuel sources) on the environment that is receiving attention. There is now a widespread scientific consensus on the need to take action to reduce greenhouse-gas emissions, and many countries are also taking action to reduce other emissions, such as sulphur dioxide and oxides of nitrogen, which contribute to acid rain and air pollution

Reduced use of fossil fuels would lead to lower greenhouse-gas emissions and the emissions that contribute to air pollution. However, reducing energy demand may not be the only option. Another alternative is to increase the supply of energy from sources that produce lower emissions – for example, within the fossil fuels, by switching from coal to gas. More radical reductions in emissions can be achieved by switching from fossil fuels to nuclear power and renewable sources such as wind, wave or solar energy.

However, the greenest unit of energy is the one saved rather than the one used, no matter how cleanly it is generated. Gas still produces greenhouse-gas emissions, even though at a much lower level than coal. Nuclear power produces no emissions in use, but the construction of nuclear power stations is as environmentally intrusive as any other power station and further environmental costs may be incurred in dealing with nuclear waste and decommissioning. Even though they do not emit CO_2, renewable energy sources do have environmental impacts, such as the visual intrusiveness of wind-farms. Manufacturing and installing energy-saving materials and equipment will produce environmental impacts at those stages, but, once installed, units of energy can be saved with no further impact.

The environmental benefits of energy efficiency/conservation and the environmental disbenefits of energy supply are not normally included in energy prices – they are thus considered to be classic externalities, which, without government intervention, are unlikely to be taken into account.

How governments intervene to promote energy saving

Since the early 1970s governments have intervened to ensure that energy-saving measures are taken up more widely through regulation, taxation, information, exhortation and incentives.

Exhortation involves publicity and awareness campaigns – for example, television and press advertising aimed at residential and/or business users and posters and leaflets giving advice on energy use in the home, office or factory. Almost all governments use exhortation to some extent.

Information implies more specific targeting of the message than exhortation, for example through energy information centres or telephone advice lines to answer specific questions from householders and businesses. Another option is energy labelling of appliances so that customers can see which are the most energy efficient – this has been undertaken in many countries including the US and the EU. In some countries there have been initiatives to energy-label buildings (e.g. Denmark and the UK).

Regulation usually involves setting minimum standards. Many governments require newly built homes and other buildings to meet minimum standards (overall thermal performance or, for example, to have at least 200 mm of loft insulation). Minimum standards have also been set in some countries (notably the US) for the energy efficiency of appliances such as refrigerators and washing machines and office equipment such as computers.

Taxation of energy use has tended to prove less popular with most governments due to its unpopularity with businesses and households.

However, some countries (notably Denmark and Japan) have used taxation for many years, particularly to reduce dependence on energy imports. Since the early 1990s a number of governments have looked more seriously at energy taxes to reduce energy use and greenhouse-gas emissions. Several European countries now have a carbon tax, and there has been much debate within the EU about an EU-wide tax, which, to date, has foundered due to opposition from industry and a number of member states.

Incentives usually take the form of grants or low- or no-interest loans towards energy-saving measures or individualised energy advice (energy audits). For households, the most common measures assisted are loft insulation, draughtproofing, cavity wall insulation and heating system and controls upgrades. For industrial and commercial users, help is most often provided for energy audits, boiler refits or changes (e.g. from coal to gas) and for on-site CHP/cogeneration.

2

Energy policy and policy communities

The development of energy supply, 1800–Second World War

At the beginning of the nineteenth century the idea of converting coal to gas in a central plant and piping the gas to customers was developed and, in 1812, the Gas, Light and Coke Company became London's first gas company. At the same time gas street lighting was being introduced in cities in the US and in Paris and Brussels. By the 1850s gas was being produced from coal in most parts of the US, Europe and Australia and was being used for lighting buildings as well as for street lighting.

Electricity was also first developed in the first half of the nineteenth century, although initially developments were much slower than for gas. The first uses of electricity were commercial and industrial applications of arc lighting (e.g. in lighthouses, theatres and factories), but in 1882 Thomas Edison and Joseph Swan (who had separately invented the electric light bulb) formed the Edison and Swan United Electric Light Company to provide serious competition to gas lighting. As electricity cannot be stored, some uses for electricity outside peak periods had to be developed to make it commercially viable. These included electric motors in industry and the conversion of horse-drawn trams to electricity, using overhead cables.

It was in the US that oil was first discovered and put to commercial use in the mid-nineteenth century. With the beginnings of the commercial exploitation of natural gas in the 1930s by oil companies in the US and the first use of nuclear power for peaceful purposes to generate electricity in the 1950s, the major players in the energy market of the second half of the twentieth century – coal, oil, gas and nuclear power, and electricity produced from all of these – were firmly established.

Post-Second World War energy policies – pile it high and sell it cheap

In the immediate post-war period most of Europe and Japan needed more coal than their run-down industries could produce. Britain was faced, from January to March 1947, with one of the worst winters ever and power supplies almost collapsed. Over two million people were laid off from work, exports were disrupted and restrictions were placed on the use of electricity for cooking. In late April the use of gas and coal fires was banned until September to conserve supplies for the next winter.

The Minister of Fuel and Power, Hugh Gaitskell, aimed to boost productivity and to cut consumption. By the end of January 1948, demand for direct use of coal was falling but demand for coal to produce electricity continued to increase – consumption of electricity doubled between 1938 and 1948. Gaitskell tried to get the industry to agree to higher tariffs in peak periods to reduce demand, but he faced stiff opposition from the Chairmen of the Area Electricity Boards, of whom he said: 'I was really horrified that so many men, earning so much money, should be so silly. The trouble, of course, is that they are all madly keen to sell electricity and just cannot get used to the idea that at the moment they should stop people from buying it.' (Gaitskell, 1983: 78–9).

The slight price increases that Gaitskell secured made so little difference to demand that they were not worth the adverse political effects and the scheme was abolished in the following winter. Thus, despite initial success in getting individual consumers to cut their coal use, the conservation ethos was short-lived. The failure to get the newly nationalised electricity industry to raise prices backs up Gilliat's theory that the failure to confront power is often the key issue in such cases (Gilliatt, 1984). However, it was probably the undoubted unpopularity among consumers (voters) of price increases that made it politically difficult to tackle the industries and sealed the fate of Gaitskell's plans. This early loss set the scene for future problems with the supply industry.

Like the UK, Japan faced a crisis in coal production after the war, plunging the country into an acute energy crisis. Output fell from 4,000,000 tonnes per month during the war to 554,000 tonnes per month in November 1945 due to the repatriation of many Chinese and Korean miners. In December 1945 the new Coal Agency's first job was to move Japanese miners from metal to coal mining. Initially, the policy did not work very well, and during the autumn of 1946 the economy virtually collapsed due to acute coal shortages.

To tackle these problems, the system of priority production was invented by a small group of advisers working for the prime minister. Priority production was a scheme to concentrate all of the economy's assets in a few strategic sectors, regardless of the effects this might have on civilian consumption or inflation. Coal production was given first priority for loans and subsidies and a new system of distribution was set up to ensure that the steel and other strategic industries got as much coal as they needed. Priority production was successful, which was just as well as it fuelled inflation and caused significant hardship for the Japanese people.

The US also faced problems of shortage immediately after the war, but the problem was with oil, which had become the more important fuel in the US. Oil shortages had been a problem during the war, but the post-war economic recovery exacerbated the situation as sources of supply lagged behind demand due to depleted reserves, inadequate refinery capacity and a tanker shortage. Action by some refiners to ration supplies, and claims by retailers that the large oil companies were creating a shortage to force prices up, created an atmosphere of crisis by late 1947.

The US government made two responses. First, the National Petroleum Council (NPC) (the peacetime equivalent of the Petroleum Industry War Council), whose members were senior executives of the oil and gas industry, was asked by the Secretary of the Interior to come up with a plan to tackle the crisis. Initially, the NPC was not keen to become involved since it feared anti-trust action by the Justice Department and it raised the spectre of government control, to which the industry was strongly opposed. However, in December 1947 the NPC suggested a range of measures that government, the industry and consumers could take to alleviate the impending emergency.

Following passage by Congress of the Anti-Inflation Act in January 1948, which allowed voluntary agreements by industries to allocate goods without driving up prices, and confirmation by the Attorney General that he would grant anti-trust immunity, the NPC eventually agreed to the Secretary of the Interior's (Julius Krug) request that they formulate a voluntary allocation programme (to allocate oil to different sectors of the economy).

The second act was to step up efforts begun during the war to develop synthetic fuels (synfuels – the artificial gas or petroleum substitute produced by heating coal, lignite or oil shale in the presence of water vapour). In January 1948 James Forrestal, President Truman's Secretary of Defence, recommended to Congress a US$8 billion synfuel programme to provide national security of energy supply. Krug supported these proposals, and a bill was introduced into Congress to authorise government help for synfuels. The oil industry, however, opposed the Krug and Forrestal proposals and the bill, seeing a threat to oil's position and the potential for greater government involvement in energy, towards which they were also suspicious and hostile. Although some minor support for synfuels was agreed, the oil industry's opposition, combined with changes in the energy market, effectively scuppered any major investment.

As Vietor (1984) observes, President Truman had scarcely declared an energy emergency in the spring of 1948 before it was over. Within months domestic oil stocks began to rise, natural gas became more widely available, the coal industry began to increase output levels and the US became a net oil importer. The era of cheap and plentiful energy resources had come, making the development of synfuels unnecessary.

After the Second World War the supply of gas, oil and coal in western countries increased and their prices fell, thus encouraging more widespread use. Electricity prices in particular fell with the development of large-scale power stations that could generate electricity more efficiently. Lower energy prices contributed significantly to rising prosperity in most Western countries. A key feature of this increased prosperity has been rising demand for energy-consuming goods and services – made all the more attractive by low energy prices. Abundant cheap supplies of energy have thus proved to be their own stimulus to rising energy demand.

The 1973 oil crisis

The key role of energy in the economies of Europe, North America and Japan meant that they were in for a severe shock when, in 1973, the oil producers introduced both a major price rise and an embargo on oil exports to the US and the Netherlands. The oil-producing countries (largely Middle Eastern and some African countries) had formed OPEC (the Organization of Petroleum Exporting Countries) in 1960 to resist pressure on their prices from their major customers (the large US, European and Japanese oil corporations), but until the early 1970s OPEC had little success. However, by the early 1970s Europe, the US and Japan were heavily dependent on imported oil to meet rising energy demands, which led to a significant shift in the balance of power. When the oil corporations refused, in October 1973, to pay the US$6 a barrel demanded by its members, OPEC announced a unilateral price increase and a total embargo on oil exports to the US and the Netherlands because of these countries' support for Israel in the Arab–Israeli war of October 1973. The immediate effect was severe fuel shortages in the main energy-using countries and emergency measures by their governments to ration use. As oil supplies were restored, but at much higher prices, the impact was felt not only in terms of heating, electricity and transport costs but in most areas of the economy, with rising oil prices contributing significantly to inflation. The second oil crisis in 1979, when the Shah was overthrown in Iran and that country's output all but ceased, reinforced the sense in Europe, the US and Japan that the days of cheap energy might be over for good.

Countries reacted to the oil crises in different ways. In the UK and some Scandinavian countries the 1973 oil price hike gave the impetus to North Sea oil and gas exploration. Other countries began to look more to nuclear power, although it was only in France that a major nuclear power station-building programme was pursued successfully. It was at this time that many countries first launched energy conservation policies and programmes and when many of them first set up energy conservation offices within their energy ministries.

The development of energy policy communities and networks

Gas and electricity supplies were originally developed by private enterprise, but as these energy supply sources became increasingly important and essential to households, businesses and transport, governments felt the need to intervene and regulate or even take over control completely through nationalisation or municipalisation. Governments and government-appointed regulators began to set gas and electricity prices and impose obligations to supply, so suppliers had to make sure that they had sufficient capacity (transmission and distribution networks as well as power stations and gas-manufacturing capacity) to meet all demands for their fuel.

The inevitable consequence of this government involvement in energy supply was the establishment in the lead-up to, during and just after the Second World War of energy ministries or departments to oversee relations with nationalised or regulated energy industries and, hence, the development of policy networks consisting of the ministry and the gas, electricity, nuclear, oil and coal companies. The UK, for example, which had previously handled energy matters within the Board of Trade, set up its Ministry of Fuel, Light and Power in 1942. Japan established its Fuel Bureau as an external agency of the Ministry of Commerce and Industry in 1937. The US was the most notable exception to this trend in that it set up a number of separate institutions and agencies to deal with various energy matters just before and just after the war (for example the Federal Power Commission was set up in 1928 and had its remit extended to include gas in 1938; the NPC was set up in 1947 to continue the wartime work of its predecessor), but it did not set up an energy department until the 1970s.

A further important development of the role of energy ministries – which consolidated the importance of the close working relation-ships within the energy policy networks – was demand forecasting to plan for new energy supply capacity. Officials in energy ministries were obviously highly dependent on the co-operation of and infor-mation from energy companies in developing these demand forecasts as the ministries themselves had very limited knowledge on which to base any forecasts.

The results of this forecasting were to show sharp increases in energy demand in all industrialised countries from the late 1940s on. Rising demand came from a number of sources – new housing built to replace that damaged in the war, new electrical appliances, increasing transport use and new factories. The general picture in the 1950s seemed to be that as living standards or GDP rose, so did energy demand, the two showing very similar percentage increases. In the early days of forecasting there was a tendency to underesti-mate demand growth, but by the mid- to late 1960s the forecasters had begun to err on the side of caution (mindful of the obligation to supply) and to overestimate demand growth. This trend to overesti-mation was exacerbated by the fact that the close correlation between percentage increases in GDP and energy demand started to fall off in the 1960s. In that decade in the UK, for example, GDP growth of just under 3% a year was accompanied by rises in final energy demand of about 1.5% a year, and this was despite the fact that energy prices were stable or even falling in real terms.

The explanation for this change is that a number of factors, including industrial restructuring and fuel switching, led to improvements in the ratio of TPES to GDP (the energy ratio). Innovation (new machinery, appliances, building standards, etc.) plus increasing returns to scale from larger-scale production bring improvements in energy efficiency over time. At times when energy prices are rising faster than general inflation this energy efficiency effect tends to become even more marked as people seek to economise on fuel use in their homes and businesses and substitution occurs – consumption switches to goods and services that require less energy to produce and use, and companies may try to substitute energy-intensive capital, for example, by greater use of labour. Considerable industrial restructuring may take place – for example, out of heavy engineering and into information technology. The increasing use of gas to generate electricity, in power stations which are 50% efficient compared to efficiencies of 30% in older power stations, is one example of how fuel switching can lead to lower energy use per unit of GDP.

Changes in economic structure in Western countries over the three decades from the end of the Second World War thus induced significant changes in energy demand. The initial effect of post-war reconstruction and economic growth from the late 1940s to the early 1960s was huge increases in demand. However, from the mid-1960s technical and structural changes led to a fall-off in demand growth, and this trend was given greater impetus by the fuel price increases of the 1970s.

Yet it was not until the 1980s that the trend for energy demand to rise much less than the growth in GDP began to be recognised by most governments, although, as Patterson (1990) has described, a number of independent analysts such as Amory Lovins in the US and Peter Chapman and Gerald Leach in the UK recognised and highlighted this phenomenon from the early 1970s. These innovative analysts, as Patterson describes them, were based outside the established policy networks of government and energy industries – usually in universities or non-governmental research institutes or environmental organisations. Not in a position, therefore, to implement their ideas or to get them accepted within the established policy networks, they began to build up their own international network over the 1970s and early 1980s at the time when environmental groups were also becoming interested not just in analysing and campaigning on energy issues (e.g against nuclear power) but also in advocating positive alternatives – energy conservation and renewable energy – to nuclear power and dependence on fossil fuels.

A further arrival on the energy policy scene from the late 1970s onwards was the energy conservation industry, which began to develop in many countries as a result of government policy responses to the 1973 oil crisis, which stimulated the demand for insulation materials, heating controls and energy managers in industry. Environmental groups, some consumer organisations, academic researchers and the energy conservation industry, together with newly established energy conservation units or agencies in many energy ministries, thus formed the beginnings of an energy conservation policy community.

Efforts to establish energy conservation programmes

Energy conservation programmes were first established by most governments in industrialised countries after 1973 as a reaction to the oil crisis, primarily as a means of lessening dependence on imported oil and improving security of supply. In some countries (notably the US), a further motivation was problems with nuclear power programmes – cost overruns and delays in construction and commissioning nuclear reactors began to make the nuclear option far less attractive. There were also growing concerns about the environmental impact and safety of nuclear power, leading to considerable delays in obtaining planning permission to build reactors as fewer people wanted to live near to them. This, combined with increasing oil prices, began to make energy conservation an attractive option, and many countries developed initiatives such as grants for home insulation, energy labelling of appliances and information campaigns to communicate a 'save it' message.

By the mid-1980s, however, despite these various initiatives, environmental groups felt that there was still much more scope for energy conservation. A key problem was felt to be the orientation of the private electricity- and gas-supply companies, who had a strong incentive to supply more units of energy and – the environmentalists suspected – a hugely influential role in persuading governments not to pursue vigorous action on energy conservation.

Lucas (1985) studied the influence of institutional structure on energy policy in five West European countries in the early 1980s – France, Denmark, Italy, Sweden and West Germany. He found that organisation for energy supply was much better developed and co-ordinated than for energy use, thus making it difficult to implement energy conservation policies. One of the key problems is that many energy-saving programmes have to affect the decisions and actions of millions of consumers and, to do so, require decentralised delivery mechanisms that can work close to the consumer. By contrast, government experience is mainly in running or regulating a few large-scale industries. Energy conservation had many diffuse, unco-ordinated actors and no efficient professional lobby and so had come to be seen as a high-risk policy by comparison even with nuclear power, which the civil servants knew would eventually result in power stations – even if they were late, over-budget and below expected capacity.

So, despite the wide range of measures that have been tried, many countries have found it difficult to introduce and run effective government programmes to promote energy saving.

Energy saving and the electricity and gas industries

The structures of the electricity and gas industries – covering production, transportation, distribution and supply – are outlined in boxes 2.1 and 2.2. It should be noted that the terms 'supply' and 'suppliers' are often also used to refer to the whole of the gas and electricity industry.

Given the problems which governments have had in developing energy conservation programmes compared to the rather more effective development of energy supply, it is not surprising that governments, regulators and advocates of energy conservation have tried to make or persuade the supply companies to promote energy conservation. On the other hand, the idea of electricity and gas companies promoting energy conservation – which would reduce demand for their product – seems nonsensical. Most governments have set similar priorities for state-controlled or regulated gas and electricity utilities: to meet all demand for their fuels and to minimise the price to customers. Private sector gas and electricity companies usually want to maximise commodity sales to maximise profits. A supply-orientated mentality is, therefore, what is expected and what has been delivered.

2.1 The electricity industry

- *Generation* – the production of electricity from primary fuel sources such as coal, oil, gas, nuclear power, wind, waste materials, etc. Generation is not a natural monopoly and many countries have for some years allowed competition in this area.
- *Transmission* – the high-voltage network of overhead or underground (or undersea) cables used to transport electricity from power stations to the distribution system in the area where it is going to be used. Transmission is considered to be a natural monopoly.
- *Distribution* – the low-voltage network used to transport electricity to final users, usually in a specific area. It is generally considered to be a natural monopoly.
- *Supply* – the sale of electricity to final users. In most countries supply and distribution are not regarded as separate functions as both are undertaken by the same monopoly business. The UK is the main example of a country where supply and distribution are recognised as separate functions. Although distribution is a natural monopoly, many suppliers could have access to a local distribution system to sell electricity to final users.

However, following the oil price shock in 1973, gas and electricity companies in many countries took on the conservation message to some extent so as to be seen to act in the national interest in terms of security of supply. Many companies began to promote *wise* use – not wasting gas, switching off unnecessary lights, etc. The change in terminology from 'energy conservation' to 'energy efficiency' was eagerly embraced by the energy suppliers as this was not so much about using less energy as about using it more wisely, which could more easily fit with their interests. Energy efficiency can also be used by gas or electricity companies to capture market share from one another. For example, electricity companies have supplied insulation with electric heating to make it more competitive with gas.

Where it could not serve the purpose of market-building, however, energy saving has been seen as a marginal, add-on activity for gas and electricity companies. Perhaps a few information leaflets on energy saving for public-relations reasons – to give a 'green tinge', or satisfy a government or regulator – or the provision of charitable help with insulation for the elderly or disadvantaged households.

2.2 The gas industry

- *Transportation* – the pipe network used to transport gas from the place where it is produced (or the place where it is landed – the beachhead – in the case of gas from undersea reserves) to suppliers or final users. Transportation is regarded as a natural monopoly.
- *Storage* – facilities for storing gas until it is required by gas suppliers or customers. Storage is not regarded as a natural monopoly.
- *Distribution* – the pipe network for transportation of gas to final users. In many countries there is no distinction between transportation and distribution in the case of gas. Distribution is regarded as a natural monopoly.
- *Shipping* – the business of moving amounts of gas through the pipeline network.
- *Supply* – the sale of gas to final users. Gas supply is not a natural monopoly. As in the case of electricity, in most countries supply and distribution are not regarded as separate functions as both are undertaken by the same monopoly business. The UK again is the main example of separation, allowing all licensed suppliers access to the transportation system to sell gas to final users.

Regulation has been the main tool used to alter the supply-side bias of monopoly utilities. One longstanding example is Denmark where, since the early 1970s, waste heat from power stations and industry for district heating has been used alongside measures to improve insulation standards in buildings to reduce dependence on imported oil. Since the early 1980s the regulatory commissions in the US have required the gas and electricity utilities to invest in demand-side management as an alternative to more supply. This system has, since the late 1980s, spread to parts of Europe and Australia and has been the subject of a draft EC directive.

Demand-side management, least-cost planning and integrated resource planning

The main action that has led utilities to develop energy efficiency programmes since the 1980s has, thus, been the development of least-cost planning (LCP), demand-side management (DSM) and integrated resource planning (IRP). A lot of confusion arises due to the often

2.3 Definitions

- *Demand-side management* – encompasses various initiatives to alter the demand side of energy use. These include load shifting (e.g. from peak to off-peak), load reduction, or even load retention and building (to make better use of underused supply, transmission or distribution facilities, e.g. at off-peak periods). Thus, DSM measures can be aimed at reducing peak kW demand or reducing total kWh supplied, but they can also be aimed at increasing demand. DSM, therefore, may not necessarily reduce total energy use and can even increase it in some circumstances.
- *Least-cost planning* – involves calculating the comparative costs and benefits of investing in new supply, transmission or distribution equipment as against investment in measures to reduce demand (usually peak kW demand, but sometimes total kWh supplied) and adopting the cheapest option.
- *Integrated resource planning* – builds on the concept of LCP to incorporate environmental resources (LCP does not always take into account externalities such as environmental costs). IRP tends to be more about reducing total kWh supplied than reducing peak kW demand.

interchangeable use of these terms, which are are defined in box 2.3.

The term 'least-cost planning' has tended to be used less and less as greater environmental concern means that the focus has switched to integrated resource planning. Furthermore, the abbreviation 'DSM' is used not only to refer to demand-side *management* but also demand-side *measures*, meaning the actual techniques (insulation, heating system upgrades, efficient appliances and lighting, etc.) used to deliver the demand side of integrated resource planning. DSM will be used in this book as a generic term to refer to all types of DSM, LCP and IRP initiatives.

DSM/LCP/IRP fitted well with the new orientation to energy efficiency from the utilities' perspective, even though many of the environmental groups and academic researchers who advocated these techniques were more interested in energy conservation.

Liberalisation and privatisation

Until the mid-1980s gas, electricity and district heating supply in most countries was undertaken by utility companies that were either

---

2.4 Definitions

- *Corporatisation* – companies remain in the public sector but are given a greater degree of separation from political control and allowed a greater degree of freedom in terms of access to capital markets. This approach has been widely used in the electricity industry in Australia. Corporatisation is sometimes a precursor to privatisation and may be used as a means of preparing companies for eventual privatisation.
- *Privatisation* – the sale of public sector enterprises to the private sector. The sale might be undertaken through share offers (as in the privatisation of utilities in the UK) or by inviting bids for ownership of the whole company (e.g. the sales of the electricity industry in the State of Victoria in Australia).
- *Liberalisation* – the opening up of markets previously closed to competition or where competition was severely restricted. Typically, this involves allowing companies other than an incumbent monopoly (or duopoly or oligopoly) to compete for business – for example, to generate electricity and supply into a national grid system, or to supply electricity directly to final users via the transmission/distribution system.

---

state-owned (as in the UK and most of Europe), municipally owned (as in Denmark and some major cities in other European countries) or privately owned, but which in each case were state regulated with a franchise for a specific area (as in the US). In all cases the companies would have a state-approved supply monopoly in an area – a city, a county, a state or the whole country. Since the mid-1980s, with the UK as pioneer, but with others such as Norway, New Zealand and Chile also in the vanguard, more and more countries have embarked on privatisation of their state monopoly energy industries or liberalisation of their energy markets in some way. This is part and parcel of worldwide moves begun in the 1980s to privatise large parts of the public sector and, in particular, the public utilities of gas, electricity, water and telecommunications. Box 2.4 gives the key definitions.

Liberalisation is, in the late 1990s, the major development in Europe and North America. Liberalisation has been developed in the UK since the privatisation of British Gas in 1986, and the whole market for gas and electricity (including households) will be open by mid-1999. Norway liberalised its entire electricity market in 1991. The European Commission is working on plans to liberalise both the gas and electricity markets throughout the EU, allowing any member state's companies to compete in all the other members' markets. The US began the process of liberalisation, or 'retail wheeling', in 1996.

It is also important to remember that countries start with different types of organisation of their electricity and gas industries. Some have completely vertically integrated companies, from exploration and/or generation right through transportation/transmission through to distribution. Others might separate generating companies from distribution companies, or grid/transportation networks from generation. What they then choose to do when privatising these companies also varies from those who leave the companies largely in their pre-privatisation form to those who attempt wholesale reorganisation prior to sell-off.

Until the 1990s vertical integration has tended to be more common than horizontal integration in most countries. Indeed, in most countries the typical electricity or gas utility structure until the 1980s was a completely vertically integrated monopoly, or some minor variant on this theme – for example, in the case of electricity, a monopoly generation and transmission company plus local monopoly distribution/supply companies, all of which were owned by the state or local government.

Horizontal integration was less common, although in some countries it was a prominent feature. For example, the US has had a number of vertically and horizontally integrated monopoly gas and electricity companies serving some states or major cities (such as Baltimore Gas and Electric, Pacific Gas and Electric). In a number of Scandinavian countries (e.g. Denmark, Sweden) and other European countries (e.g. Austria) local companies (often local government-owned and usually with monopoly franchises for their area) produce, distribute and sell electricity and heat from their combined heat and power/cogeneration plants. Vertical and horizontal integration are defined in box 2.5.

Vertical integration has traditionally been thought to favour energy saving, based on the US demand-side management model. Having one vertically integrated company certainly made it easier to undertake DSM, but it was not so much vertical integration as retail monopoly that facilitated the US DSM model, making it possible to forecast electricity demand inside a utility's area and then make

---

2.5 Definitions

- *Vertical integration* – is the concentration of more than one function (supply, distribution, transmission/transportation, generation) relating to one fuel in one company.
- *Horizontal integration* – is the concentration of at least one function relating to at least two fuels in one company (e.g. the distribution of gas and electricity).

---

comparisons between DSM and different generation options (Bakken, 1995: 390).

There are, however, some concerns about the vertical integration of supply and distribution. If the supply business were to invest in energy saving for its customers, its distribution business would lose revenue due to fewer power units (kWh) being distributed through the system. Although accounting separation can alleviate the problems, it cannot remove them – the company's management and its shareholders are concerned with total profit, and if more is lost from distribution than is gained from supply, energy saving will not be regarded favourably. The integration of competitive elements (supply and generation) and horizontal integration tend to be viewed as more neutral for energy saving or even possibly beneficial as opportunities for fuel switching (e.g. from electricity to gas) or the use of CHP may be more easily developed.

A clear trend that has been brought in by privatisation and liberalisation is the 'unbundling' of previously vertically integrated functions. The need to unbundle is driven by two main requirements: first, to make the cost structures of monopoly companies more transparent – this greatly aids the task for regulators in setting controls on either the prices which companies may charge or in setting controls on rates of return; and, second, where liberalisation is being undertaken, it is necessary to unbundle the natural monopoly parts of the business from those where competition is possible. This then enables regulators to identify those costs which are attributable to the use of monopoly networks (e.g. gas transportation, electricity transmission) and, hence, which it is legitimate for the incumbent monopoly to charge to competitors for use of the network. In some cases unbundling involves merely an accounting separation of the various businesses (supply, transportation, etc.), which remain part of the same company. In others a more radical approach is adopted, with parts of the business separated into completely independent companies.

Changing energy markets and the implications for energy conservation

As outlined earlier, the energy market has tended to be oligopolistic – consisting of a small number of large producers who are continually trying to second guess one another in terms of price – rather than the perfect competition model of many small sellers each with an insignificant effect on supply and, therefore, unable to influence prices.

Change has however, begun to come about due in part to liberalisation and privatisation but due also to technological change. The development since the late 1980s of modern gas turbines has made possible the development of gas-fired power stations that are quicker and cheaper to build than coal-, nuclear or oil-fired stations, can be run with many fewer staff, offer much higher thermal conversion efficiencies (around 50% for combined-cycle gas turbines (CCGT) and up to 85% in the case of CHP, compared to an average of 35% for coal- and oil-fired stations), and which are much more flexible as they can be built on a very large (1,000 MW plus) or a very small scale (down to less than 100 kW for on-site CHP generation in industry, hotels or blocks of flats).

Liberalisation, privatisation and technical change are, thus, changing the dynamics of the energy market, and this raises some interesting questions for energy conservation. Change in energy markets may open up prospects for the provision of energy saving alongside energy supply – what has come to be described as the 'energy services approach'. Energy service companies are defined as those which aim to maximise efficient and cost-effective supply and use of energy for their customers through competitive purchasing of different fuels, end-use efficiency, CHP, consumption monitoring and management, etc. This distinguishes them from energy supply companies – whose main role is supplying units of gas, electricity or heat – and from energy management companies, whose main preoccupation is energy efficiency services.

How far are energy services being offered in markets where energy supply competition has been introduced? So far, there are only two countries – the UK and Norway – where energy supply competition has existed for long enough for this question to have been tested. The UK experience is dealt with in chapter 6. Energy market liberalisation began in Norway in 1991 and small consumers (including households) have been allowed to switch energy supplier since then. However, households and smaller businesses have tended to find it difficult and expensive to move as they need to purchase new metering equipment in most cases. It is mainly larger commercial and industrial customers who have switched supplier, and few have been requesting and few obtaining energy services (Haaland and Wilhite, 1994). A key problem has been uncertainty about prices. Although energy prices in Norway actually rose for a period in the early 1990s, uncertainty about how prices might move in the future has made customers unwilling to sign long-term supply contracts, which would tend to be necessary if energy services are to be offered. Essentially, suppliers and customers in Norway remain focused on the unit price of energy rather than energy services.

The new environmental agenda of climate change

In addition to the changing energy market, the new environmental agenda also offers new opportunities for energy conservation. The potential risk from a build-up of carbon dioxide in the atmosphere was recognised by some scientists in the late 1960s and, indeed, was raised as an important potential threat at the 1972 United Nations Stockholm Conference on the Human Environment – although at that time there was considerable uncertainty about what the effects on the climate might be. By June 1988, however, when experts from 48 countries met in Toronto, the scientific consensus was clear that carbon dioxide and other greenhouse gases were having a noticeable effect on the climate and the conference called on all countries to reduce their carbon dioxide emissions by 20% by 2005.

In June 1992 most major countries signed up to the United Nations Framework Convention on Climate Change (UNFCCC) at the Earth Summit held in Rio de Janeiro, which required them to reduce carbon dioxide emissions. The target agreed was that in the year 2000 carbon dioxide emissions should be no higher than they were in 1990. The conference of the parties to the UNFCCC, held in Berlin in March 1995, failed to agree any specific targets for the years beyond 2000 but did agree to decide by the conference in

Kyoto in December 1997 on the need for further action beyond 2000. However, Earth Summit II, held in New York in June 1997 as a prelude to the meeting in Kyoto, failed to agree on any targets for beyond 2000. While the EU countries were prepared to reduce greenhouse-gas emissions to 15% below 1990 levels by the year 2010, the US and Canada were unwilling to commit themselves to any targets, despite a stirring speech by President Clinton on the final day of the summit acknowledging his country's role in producing more emissions per head of population than any other country – the US produced 19.3 tonnes of CO_2 per person in 1992, double that of the UK.

Between June and December 1997 there seemed to be little change in the position of the main parties and it looked as if no agreement at all would be reached at Kyoto. In the end, the Kyoto Protocol (summarised in box 2.6) was criticised by US business groups for going too far and by environmental groups for not going far enough, although EU ministers generally welcomed it as more than they had hoped for in view of the opposition from the US and other countries such as Japan and Australia to any meaningful targets.

EU environment commissioner Ritt Bjerregaard said that, following frantic last-minute negotiations, 'the EU has managed to pull the USA and Japan up from very low targets … with substantial loopholes, to more credible targets with safeguards to help to ensure that reported reductions in emissions are genuine'. The EU agreed to reduce emissions by 8% by 2010 rather than the 15% negotiating target with which it went to Kyoto. The main criticisms of environmental groups focus on the level of emissions cuts required and 'loopholes' such as the allowance of emissions trading.

There has been a mixed reaction from industry. Many European industry groups criticised the differentiation agreed between industrialised countries and the lack of any requirements for more advanced developing countries as a potential threat to European business. The Global Climate Coalition (the US grouping of oil, car and electricity industry companies which have lobbied hard against any agreement) pledged their continuing opposition and determination to stop the US signing up to the agreement.

Some sectors of industry, however, see the agreement as more of an opportunity than a threat, including the International Chamber of Commerce. Two business associations have said that EU environment ministers should implement a 15% greenhouse-gas reduction

2.6 The Kyoto Protocol

- Industrialised countries have legally binding targets for reducing greenhouse-gas emissions by the average of the five years 2008–12. The aggregate cut required is 5.2%.
- Different targets for different industrialised countries. The EU, Switzerland and some central and eastern European countries must cut emissions by 8%, the USA by 7%, and Canada, Hungary, Japan and Poland by 6%. Russia, New Zealand and Ukraine must stabilise emissions, while Norway can increase them by 1%, Australia by 8% and Iceland by 10%. The EU may achieve its aggregate target through differentiated national emissions reductions.
- Developing countries are not required to reduce greenhouse-gas emissions. There is provision for additional financial resources and technology transfer to assist these countries.
- An international emissions trading system will be established, allowing industrialised countries to buy and sell excess emissions credits.
- Under a 'clean development mechanism' industrialised countries may finance emissions reductions in other industrialised countries and receive credit for doing so.
- The protocol will enter into force when it has been ratified by at least 6 countries accounting for 55% of total 1990 emissions from industrialised countries.

by 2010 despite the outcome of the Kyoto summit. The International Co-generation Alliance and the European Business Council for Sustainable Energy believe that accelerating the development and application of clean, renewable energies, buildings efficiency technologies and cogeneration systems would give Europe a head start in worldwide markets for these technologies as the rest of the world gets round to making substantial climate commitments. They argue that benefits would also come from the removal of subsidies to polluting energy industries and from accelerating tax reform – switching taxation from jobs to pollution.

However, it remains to be seen what will happen to the Kyoto Protocol as in the US the Global Climate Coalition grouping seems to have won the argument and it is very unlikely that President Clinton will be able to get the agreement ratified by Congress. Without the participation of the US – the world's largest producer of emissions – the agreement will have little effect. Hopes now hinge on a further meeting in Buenos Aires in November 1998 and on the provisions of the Kyoto Protocol for emissions trading and joint implementation/technology transfer.

3

The European Union

Introduction

Within the fifteen member states of the European Union the energy policies and programmes that are developed by the European Commission – and particularly those which are adopted by the Council of Ministers – have been becoming increasingly important since the early 1990s.

Prior to the Maastricht Treaty of 1993, the group of member states was referred to as the European Economic Community (EEC). The Maastricht Treaty amended this to the European Community (EC) and created the European Union (EU), which incorporates the policy areas (e.g. energy, trade, environment, etc.) previously undertaken by the EEC and now by the EC, but it also added common foreign and security policy plus home affairs and justice. The European Community is, thus, part of the European Union. However, although the grouping of the 17 member states is now called the European Union, this is not an actual legal body and so it is still the European Community that signs and ratifies treaties and conventions, such as the UNFCCC. In the energy field relevant policies are thus both EC and EU policies. However, further confusion can be caused as the abbreviation EC is often used to mean the European Commission as well as the European Community. This book uses the abbreviation EU for the Community and restricts the use of EC to refer to the Commission.

As box 3.1 illustrates, all three institutions of the EU participate in the legislative process. However, it is only when legislation has been approved by the Council that it can become EU law, and it is not unusual for legislation proposed by the Commission to founder at this stage due to opposition from one or more member states.

Some legislation has to be adopted unanimously, but in other cases it can be adopted by qualified majority voting, which means that some member states might then have to implement obligations to which they are opposed. Under the co-decision procedure Parliament has extra powers to modify or even veto proposals when qualified majority voting rather than unanimous voting is being used. This is intended to give extra legitimacy to legislation that may be opposed by some member states. Before 1993 the Parliament tended to have only a limited influence over legislation, but the Maastricht Treaty increased the number of occasions on which qualified majority voting can be used and, hence, the use of the co-decision procedure. Parliament is thus becoming more important, although the Council remains the more powerful body.

A brief history of EU energy and environmental policy

There has been no overall EC or EU energy policy to date, although there have been policies for nuclear power through the European Atomic Energy Community and for coal through the European Coal and Steel Community (both were established by treaty as formal EC institutions). The publication, by the Commission, of a white paper on energy at the end of 1995 thus broke new ground in attempts to establish an EU-wide energy policy (see below).

EU environmental policy had its formal beginnings in 1973 when the Council adopted the First Action Programme on the Environment even though there was not, at that time, any provision in the Treaty of Rome for environmental policy. Formal provision was not made until 1987, when the Single European Act amended the Treaty. The Single European Act established a number of principles for environmental policy, including: an emphasis on preventative action; environmental damage should be rectified at source; the polluter should pay; and environmental protection should be built into other EU policies. The Maastricht Treaty gave increased emphasis to the importance of the environment, stating that 'environmental protection requirements must be integrated into the definition and implementation of other Community policies', and it also introduced the precautionary principle, which, as Haigh (1996) has pointed out, has considerable significance for EU climate change policy. The Single European Act and the Maastricht Treaty also brought in the subsidiarity principle – that action at EU level should be confined to

3.1 **The main institutions of the European Union**

- *The Commission* – consists of members nominated by each member state. It is the only institution with the right to propose legislation. Each Commissioner works full time, takes responsibility for a specific area of policy (e.g. energy) and is supported by a Commission directorate of officials.
- *The Council* – the forum in which government ministers from each member state meet to consider and adopt legislation proposed by the Commission. The Council is the key decision-making body.
- *The Parliament* – consists of directly elected representatives of each member state. It participates in the legislative process, usually by commenting on draft legislation proposed by the Commission. It can make amendments to draft legislation, which may then be incorporated by the Commission before the proposed legislation is sent to the Council.

matters that cannot be achieved at the member state level and where action at EU level will be more effective.

These various principles are put into effect via specific items of EU legislation or programmes. According to Haigh (1996), EU acid rain legislation provided one of the first opportunities to test whether EU environmental legislation could be effectively implemented. Although a number of member states were reluctant to see legislation in this area (due to the costs that would be incurred by industry), the issue was successfully forced on to the agenda at EU level in the mid-1980s, resulting in a directive that required sulphur dioxide emissions from large combustion plants to be reduced by 58% from their 1980 levels by 2003. Haigh (1996: 160) says that 'this experience gave the Commission the confidence that it could tackle a major environmental issue transcending national frontiers with considerable implications for the cost of energy'. In his view the experience was crucial in enabling the Commission to approach the issue of climate change with the expectation of taking a leading role.

The first agreement to be reached on climate change was in October 1990, when the Council agreed that CO_2 emissions should be returned to 1990 levels by the year 2000 in the EU as a whole. Although this agreement was not legally binding on member states and also depended on other countries taking similar action, it nevertheless paved the way for the EU to seek to take a leadership role in international negotiations on climate change in the coming years. According to Haigh (1996: 162), it was also a significant factor in the achievement of the UNFCCC at Rio de Janeiro in 1992 as 'the political weight of a combined EC put a reluctant United States under pressure'. Although some EU members wanted much tougher targets at Rio than were agreed, the EU as a whole felt it was better to get some agreement with the US on board.

In the lead-up to the Rio summit the Commission proposed a programme for achieving the EU's target to reduce emissions, which consisted of four main elements: a framework directive on energy efficiency within the SAVE programme (discussed in a later section); the ALTENER programme of support for renewable energy; a combined carbon/energy tax; and a monitoring mechanism for CO_2 emissions. While the ALTENER, SAVE and monitoring initiatives were introduced with little problem (although the SAVE directive was weakened, on grounds of subsidiarity), the proposed carbon/energy tax proved much more controversial and has still not been adopted.

The Council formally ratified the UNFCCC in December 1993. Under the monitoring mechanism, which was adopted by the Council in June 1993, the Commission is required to evaluate the national programmes of each member state to assess whether adequate progress is being made to meet the commitments agreed at Rio. The first evaluation was issued by the Commission in March 1994, and this outlined the various targets for each member state, ranging from 25–30% below 1987 levels in the case of Germany (rather a special case due to restructuring in the former East Germany), 3–5% reductions in emissions below 1990 levels in the case of Belgium, Denmark and the Netherlands, stabilisation at 1990 levels in the case of the UK, Italy and Luxembourg, and increases in emissions in Greece, France, Ireland, Spain and Portugal.

Carbon/energy tax

A carbon/energy tax was proposed by the Commission at a time when a number of member states or prospective members had already introduced or were planning carbon taxes of their own – notably the Scandinavian countries and the Netherlands, with Germany also a keen supporter. However, there were strong opponents to the tax –

notably the UK, which opposed it on subsidiarity grounds, and the less-developed states, which feared that it would hinder their development. Strong lobbies against the tax were also developed in industry (particularly major users of energy such as chemicals and steel) and the energy companies. Although France was keen on a pure carbon tax (given the country's extensive use of nuclear power), it did not want an energy tax; however, a pure carbon tax would have been strongly opposed by countries with a heavy dependence on fossil fuels. Because fiscal measures have to be agreed unanimously, there was no chance of securing the carbon/energy tax. It even took the Council until 1994 to agree a statement that while there would be no EU-wide tax, member states were encouraged to develop their own carbon/energy taxes.

However, the Commission and a number of member states (Sweden, Finland, Denmark, the Netherlands and Germany) did not give up and in May 1995 the Commission reissued its proposal for a EU-wide carbon/energy tax. The 1995 proposal would have allowed members to adopt the tax on a voluntary basis from 1996 to 2000, after which it would have been compulsory. The new proposal retained the 50/50 carbon/energy split and a target levy of US$10 per barrel of oil equivalent by the year 2000, but the split and rates would apply only to countries that decided to introduce the tax, as a means of harmonising rates among those which accepted it. Member states introducing such a tax would be encouraged to reduce taxation in other areas – notably taxes on employment, in line with EU policy to promote growth, competitiveness and employment. Despite amending the directive, however, the Commission still faced fierce opposition. The UK said that it would not approve the proposal because to do so would be a tacit acceptance of having a EU-wide uniform tax rate after 2000. France retained its view that the tax should be based solely on carbon content.

Industry stepped up its lobbying effort in this period. UNICE, a trade association representing European industry, expressed 'intense disquiet' at the priority being given to the tax and said that gas and electricity prices in the EU were already 30% higher than in the US. Opposition also came from the European Petroleum Association, the European Chemical Industry Association and the European Cement Industry Association.

Under the Spanish presidency (July–December 1995) a compromise proposal was drawn up which dropped the idea of a transitional period in favour of a framework allowing countries to apply the tax voluntarily, with a possible review of the need for a EU-wide tax at a later date. However, while this was acceptable to the UK, Spain, Portugal and Greece, which had previously blocked progress, it was opposed by Germany, which felt that member states should reach agreement that the ultimate goal was an EU-wide tax. In January 1996 supporters of the tax – which by then included Austria, Belgium, Denmark, Finland, Germany, Luxembourg, the Netherlands and Sweden – met to reopen the debate and urge the Commission to try again, and it looked as if a new compromise might be reached through a new review of overall energy taxation encompassing excise duties on fuels. A new draft directive was presented by the Commission in March 1997. In further discussions in Berlin in September 1997 France also agreed to support the tax, bringing to nine the total number of countries in favour.

The Commission has, thus, not given up the idea of an EU-wide compulsory tax and views the period to January 2000 as one of transition to harmonised carbon/energy taxes. At the end of 1998 it will produce a report on progress and may try to introduce new proposals. The Commission may find that more countries are receptive to the idea – by the end of 1997 the hard-line opponents had been reduced to the UK, Italy, Spain, Portugal, Greece and Ireland. By early 1998 Sweden, Finland and Denmark already had carbon/energy taxes and the Netherlands had proposed to implement one. In the UK, although the Labour government has in the past opposed energy taxes (such as VAT on fuel), it may be brought round to the idea of an energy tax that would enable it to reduce taxes on employment, given its commitment to tackle unemployment.

The carbon tax has foundered to date largely due to concerted lobbying efforts by energy-intensive industry and energy producers, who have been able to convince their national governments to oppose it. It is notable that, even in those countries which have introduced carbon taxes, energy-intensive industry has usually been exempted. Hence, this provides a good example of the power of the policy networks of energy producers, energy-using businesses and national and EU-level trade/industry departments, which have managed to neutralise the efforts of those in the broader energy policy community (in environment departments, energy conservation industries and environmental groups) who support forms of eco-taxation.

The SAVE programme

The EC began to develop policies on energy conservation and energy efficiency in the 1970s in the wake of the oil price rises. However, by the mid-1980s the Commission recognised that these had had limited effect. In 1986 the Council adopted a target of improving the energy efficiency of final energy demand by at least 20% by 1995, and in 1988 the Specific Actions for Vigorous Energy Efficiency (SAVE) programme was adopted. A number of other programmes already developed by the EC during the 1980s were subsumed into SAVE from 1988. Following further assessment in the late 1980s, a revised SAVE programme was agreed by the Council in 1991 as one of the three main EU-wide programmes to promote energy efficiency. In 1993 the SAVE programme was formally approved as a specific part of the EU's CO_2 emission-reduction strategy.

However, establishing the SAVE programme was not a smooth process and it has suffered from further problems each time new programmes or directives have been proposed. Essentially, these problems boil down to tensions between the various EU institutions involved and the added complications due to the development of the subsidiarity principle and the single market. The Commission's SAVE proposal in 1990 (eventually adopted in modified form in 1991), for example, went through considerable debate primarily between the Commission and the European Parliament. The Parliament called for a much-expanded programme and recommended a budget of 105 million ECU (compared to the 35 million ECU that was eventually agreed). However, the Council was not prepared to approve such a level of funding or to expand the programme as the Parliament would have wished. As a result of these disputes, the start of the programme was considerably delayed. Since then tension has continued between the Parliament, which usually wishes to increase both the funding for and legislative scope of SAVE, and the Council, where the majority of member states favour a less extensive and less *dirigiste* approach.

A wide range of initiatives come under the SAVE programme, including: the development and setting of technical standards and specifications; laws and regulations in the energy-efficiency field; support for training and information schemes; and support for practical pilot projects. Essentially, therefore, there are two sides – a budget that supports projects in member states, which can submit proposals each year to the Commission for approval by the Council; and a legislative side, under which the Commission proposes directives or weaker administrative instruments for agreement by member states. In the latter case directives, recommendations or other instruments, once adopted, have to be implemented by every member state, but a considerable degree of discretion may be left to member states on how they implement them. Legislative measures that have been adopted include a directive setting energy-efficiency standards for domestic central heating boilers (1992) and a directive on household appliance labelling (1992).

The SAVE 2 programme runs from January 1996 to December 2000 and, given the problems the Commission experienced with its carbon/energy tax proposals, has become the EC's key strategy for reducing CO_2 emissions to meet targets agreed under the Climate Change Convention. The emphasis has switched from legislation to promotion in recognition of the problems which SAVE 1 faced due to subsidiarity. A key area for action is the extension of SAVE 1 work on labelling and minimum standards for household appliances. There are also some new elements, including a role in monitoring energy-efficiency progress at national and EU level; promoting energy management in industry, commerce and the public sector; encouraging cities and regions to co-ordinate energy-saving actions in their areas; and linking energy efficiency to other EU programmes, such as those concerned with employment.

The EU's role in the climate change negotiations after Rio

The EU has continued to play a leading role since the Rio summit and, in the lead-up to the first Conference of the Parties (CoP1) in Berlin in March 1995, proposed a protocol for setting targets and timetables beyond 2000 and so may 'claim some influence on the modest outcome of the CoP' (Haigh, 1996: 182).

In 1997, during preparations for the third Conference of the Parties in Kyoto in December, the EU was once again at the forefront, setting an EU-wide target of 15% reductions below 1990 levels by 2010 and urging the US, Australia and Japan to support tougher targets. However, the EU's position was made more difficult by the fact that, according to 1997 figures, only two member states – the UK and Germany – look likely to get close to the 1992 Rio Convention target of stabilisation at 1990 levels by the year 2000.

Indeed, only the UK will meet the year 2000 deadline, with Germany likely to achieve the target by 2005. Between 1990 and 1994 the EU was actually reducing its emissions, although this is thought to have been due largely to the economic recession. With the upturn in economies since then, emissions have begun to rise once more in most countries.

The White Paper on Energy

For the first time the European Commission published a white paper on energy at the end of 1995 – this followed a green paper and an extensive consultation process which had taken place during most of 1995. The White Paper on Energy spells out three broad objectives for European Union energy policy: overall competitiveness, security of supply, and environmental protection. The Commission argues that a common energy policy for the EU is required because of the growing dependence on energy imports and the possibility of energy crises that require collective action. The White Paper outlines a five-year work programme involving market integration, managing external dependence, promoting sustainable development and supporting energy research and technology. Achievement of the internal energy market is seen as a key goal because of the lower energy prices it will deliver. The White Paper stopped short of advocating an energy chapter to the Treaty of Rome as a means of implementing a common energy policy as this would be fiercely opposed by most member states, which are reluctant to give further powers to Brussels.

Under the sustainable development part of the work programme, energy efficiency, renewables and measures to internalise environmental costs into energy prices are discussed. However, the Commission is well aware that the main mechanism for internalising environmental costs – a carbon tax – has met with strong political opposition from most member states. Therefore it talks about the possibility of voluntary agreements with industry.

More specifically on energy efficiency, the Commission proposed in 1996 that minimum standards become an essential requirement in new and existing directives on energy-consuming equipment. An energy working group has been set up to examine the scope for further energy efficiency standards. A strategy for promoting CHP was published in 1997, although this has generally been criticised by

CHP advocates and environmental groups for being too weak – the status is a 'communication', which, in effect, does not require member states to take any action. In 1998 the Commission is reviewing taxation policy and energy efficiency (e.g. the role of excise duties, tax reliefs and VAT on energy consumption and energy-saving products).

Liberalisation of gas and electricity markets

The EU directive on electricity market liberalisation was adopted by the Council in January 1997 and aims to introduce more competition into the wholesale power market and allow more electricity trade among EU countries. All EU member states have to enact the necessary laws to comply with the directive by January 1999.

The directive was finally agreed after a long and rather tortuous process of negotiation and was a compromise between the wishes of those countries (mainly the UK, Sweden and Finland) which were in favour of complete liberalisation and those, such as France, which were strongly against any change that might weaken the position of their monopoly electricity companies. Electricity producers should now be able to sell their power more freely but, in some countries, may have to do so via a 'single buyer' to whom they will sell their power supplies, while in other countries they will be able to sell directly to energy supply companies. The largest customers (above 40 GWh a year) were granted the right to choose their suppliers in 1997; this will be extended to those above 20 GWh in the year 2000 and those above 9 GWh in 2003. The Commission will be reviewing whether liberalisation should proceed any further after 2003.

Liberalisation of the gas market is not as far advanced as that of the electricity market. European energy ministers agreed a programme for opening up the gas market in December 1997, and are working on agreeing a directive to be issued by mid-1998. The plans so far are for 20% of the market to be opened when the directive comes in to force, rising to 28% five years later and 33% five years from then. The largest consumers (including power stations) will be able to choose their supplier first, followed by a progressive opening up of the market to other industrial users.

For households and smaller commercial/industrial users the opening-up of the gas and electricity markets will have little direct effect – there are no plans at present at EU level to allow more than the largest 40% or so of users to choose their supplier (some EU members may liberalise their markets at national level, however, as the UK has done already – see chapter 6). However, by opening up the potential for greater competition at the producer level, liberalisation should have a downward impact on electricity generation and gas supply costs, which could feed through into the prices paid by all consumers. The potential provided for smaller-scale and local generators to sell their power to energy suppliers/distributors may lead to some reduction in transmission and distribution costs, which could also feed through into consumer prices.

The Rational Planning Directive

The amended EC Rational Planning Directive (European Commission, 1997), which would require gas and electricity utilities in EU countries to compare the costs of energy saving with investment in new supply capacity, was approved by the Commission in April 1997 following opinions from the European Parliament and the Economic and Social Committee.

The directive has been amended in a number of significant ways from the original draft published in 1995, which was strongly based on the US experience of integrated resource planning and so was readily applicable to similar situations – i.e. countries with monopoly electricity and gas utilities. In the light of the opinions received and lobbying, particularly from electricity and gas companies, the directive was modified to recognise the differences between monopolistic and competitive markets in the light of the changing nature of energy markets in the European Union. Essentially, the directive is now more concerned to encourage gas and electricity companies to offer energy services – energy-saving goods and services as well as energy supply – to their customers.

Despite these amendments and strong support from environmental and energy-efficiency organisations (such as EuroACE and CoGen Europe), the directive is still opposed by most European gas and electricity utilities and their trade associations, Eurogas and Eurelectric. The energy companies and most member states would prefer to see a recommendation rather than a directive. When it eventually goes before the Council of Ministers it thus looks likely that it will be turned into a recommendation, which will leave implementation to the discretion of member states.

Conclusion

The EU has shown itself to be a leader in the development of international climate change policy, but it has faced considerable problems internally in developing energy conservation policies and programmes – particularly since the late 1980s in its efforts to develop the SAVE programme and in plans for a carbon/energy tax. These problems can be seen in the differing achievements of the two periods 1976–85 and 1986–95.

During the ten years from 1976 to 1985 the EU succeeded in improving its energy ratio by 20%, which represented a significant increase in the rate of improvement compared to the previous three decades. Although the Council set a target of improving the EU's energy ratio by 20% from 1986 to 1995, figures obtained by the UK MEP Anita Pollack show that the EU in fact achieved an improvement of only 5.8% over the period, and that this occurred during the late 1980s – since 1990 there has been a decline in the energy ratio in Europe.

The difficulties in developing and implementing EU-wide energy conservation policies and programmes boil down essentially to the differing national circumstances and priorities of its member states and effective lobbying by industrial interests (including energy suppliers) against many of the policies proposed by the Commission. In many areas these industrial interests have been able to operate through effective policy networks consisting of themselves and their national and/or EU-level trade or industry departments. In the case of the Rational Planning Directive, for example, there was a notable difference between the attitudes of national and EU-level environment departments and the trade and industry departments – with the latter tending to echo the views expressed by the energy suppliers, whereas the environment departments tended to view the proposal much more favourably.

4

Denmark

Political and institutional background

The Danish political system has, since the late 1920s, been remarkably stable, with four parties taking around 90% of the vote and
many smaller ones. There has been no majority government since
1909 (due to Denmark's system of proportional representation);
however, the Social Democrats have been in coalition government
for most of the time since 1920, with two periods of fifteen years in
continuous power. These factors have produced a consensual system
in which legislation and policy tend not to change dramatically.

Political stability was coupled, at least until the 1973 oil crisis,
with a steadily rising gross national product (GNP). Danish growth
was much greater than most of Europe's between 1920 and 1973,
although its position relative to others in Europe began to decline
in the 1970s. The oil crisis heralded a period of political instability
characterised by weak minority governments. The effects of these
changes since 1973 have been alternately to paralyse political action
or to produce major shifts in policy (from high taxes and cuts in
public expenditure to reductions in VAT and increased investment to
create jobs). As a result, Denmark's economic performance during the
years from 1973 to 1980 has been much poorer than that of most
other European countries.

Most civil servants are hired straight from university and work in
the service for life. Generalists have a higher status and tend to be
promoted to higher posts than specialists. Departmental autonomy
rather than interdepartmental co-ordination is central to the civil
service in Denmark. Ministers and top civil servants (especially the
latter) attach more importance to co-ordination with relevant external bodies than to interdepartmental co-ordination. This is because

of the support they get from interest groups and public or semi-public bodies when policies are developed through negotiation with them. These outside interests are often allies of departments in the latters' efforts to secure budgets from the Treasury – which is particularly useful if the policy conflicts with other government policies or may be expensive. Together, therefore, the departments and outside interests form effective policy networks.

Local authorities have a substantial role in Denmark – as in most other EU countries, with the notable exception of the UK. In particular, local authority ownership and control of major utilities (e.g. electricity and water) rather than nationalisation has been the preferred approach in Denmark. While local authorities have had sole control of electricity and water utilities (usually several authorities form the board of each utility), regional natural gas companies have been formed as partnerships between local authorities and the private sector. This key role of local authorities introduces a further important actor into the energy policy network.

Planning has been a central feature of government policy in Denmark for many decades and has four key features. First, physical planning is seen as one of the means of achieving social objectives and an economic balance across the country. Second, environmental considerations, especially the avoidance of pollution, are emphasised. Third, there is an explicit commitment to public participation, especially at the municipal level. Fourth, there is a strong sense that the government-defined public interest, as opposed to private individual interests, will prevail where conflicts arise.

To promote the national interest, avoid pollution and co-ordinate development within the framework of economic policy, the National and Regional Planning Act 1973 makes the Minister for the Environment responsible for comprehensive national physical planning. There is no national plan as such, but national policy is expressed in the form of an annual report or statement from the Ministry of the Environment, which is submitted to parliament. The Minister can also issue national planning directives to safeguard areas for specific purposes (e.g. the natural gas pipeline) or to prevent certain forms of development in certain areas. Regional plans must reflect national policy from the Ministry of the Environment and, in turn, provide the framework for the municipal structure plan and local municipal plans.

The counties have responsibility for the regional plans, which are

> **4.1 Key actors in the Danish energy policy community**
>
> *Government departments*
>   Before 1994 – Ministry of Energy, Ministry of the Environment
>   After 1994 – Ministry of the Environment and Energy
>   Department of Trade
>
> *Agencies*
>   Energy Agency
>   Environmental Protection Agency
>
> *Local authorities*
>   District councils
>   County councils
>
> *Electricity industry* – 100 distribution/supply companies owned by local authorities and consumer co-operatives, with monopoly franchises; nine regional generating companies all owned by the distribution/supply companies; two transmission companies (Elkraft and Elsam) owned by the generators.
>
> *Gas industry* – Dansk Olie og Naturgas (DONG), wholly state-owned, purchases gas from North Sea producers and runs the transportation system; five regional distribution/supply companies owned by regional groupings of local authorities.
>
> *District heating* – distributed/supplied by the electricity distribution companies and more than 300 independent companies.

ultimately approved by the Ministry. These plans are wide in scope – covering agriculture, mining, transport, urban renewal, pollution, preservation of the countryside, etc. The municipal authorities are responsible for the municipal structure plan and the local plan, both of which can be adopted locally without any involvement by the Ministry. Local plans are legally binding on owners and occupiers of property in respect of new developments or renovations. Although building regulations are set at national level, local plans can change the requirements and extend the range of aspects over which control can be exercised.

As we shall see, this comprehensive planning system has set the context for much of Denmark's development and implementation of energy conservation policies.

Structure of the energy market

The Danish electricity industry is mainly owned by companies in which the majority shareholders are local authorities (municipalities) and consumer co-operatives, with some involvement by the private sector. The basic structure is that the local authorities and the consumer co-operatives own the distribution/supply companies (of which there are around 100) which have monopoly franchises for specific areas; these distribution companies own the 9 regional generating companies; and the generating companies own the transmission companies. Despite its apparently diffuse and vertically disaggregated nature, and although transmission, generation and trading are not laid down in statute as monopolies, the electricity industry, down to the level of local distribution and supply, operates to most intents and purposes as if it consisted of two vertically integrated companies – Elkraft and Elsam. These are largely responsible for long-term planning of the transmission systems and generating capacity, control the electricity pools and, hence, all trading, and, in effect, co-ordinate the activities of the 9 regional generating companies.

Danish gas reserves are under state control, with licences issued by the Ministry of Energy. At present only one consortium is licensed for oil and gas exploration and production. The wholly state-owned company Dansk Olie og Naturgas (DONG) purchases gas from this consortium. DONG also owns and operates the gas transportation system within Denmark.

When gas was discovered the government decided that the gas industry should not be vertically integrated but that distribution and supply should be undertaken by local companies, which fit better into the planning system. Although DONG makes some direct sales to large customers, it sells gas principally to the five regional distribution/supply companies, each of which has a monopoly franchise for a specific area and which are owned by regional groupings of local authorities.

District heating is widespread in Denmark as in other Scandinavian countries. It involves the provision of heat to a number of buildings (e.g. a tower block, housing estate or a mixed housing and commercial area) from a central boiler. This may be fired by various fuels – coal, gas, oil – or by waste heat from power stations or industry. When waste heat from power stations or industry-based electricity generation is used, the system is called combined heat and power/district heating. CHP is considerably more efficient than traditional electricity generation (typically 70–85% compared to 30–35% from non-CHP electricity generation). District heating is distributed/supplied by most of the electricity distribution companies and by more than 300 independent companies.

In notable contrast to its Scandinavian neighbours Sweden and Norway, there has been a considerable degree of consensus in Denmark over the established structure of the electricity and gas industries. Even non-socialists have supported the strong local authority role and the joint public/private companies. While Denmark has not been among those implacably opposed to the EC plans for a single energy market (unlike France, Belgium and Luxembourg), it is a sceptic about the benefits and has expressed concerns about the potential effects on its system of environmentally driven planning. However, the consensus has begun to break as industrial users recognise that they might be able to gain access to cheaper power through liberalisation. Danish utilities thus face pressure both to liberalise and to continue to meet tough environmental objectives.

Taxes on oil and electricity were introduced in 1977 and on coal in 1982. Renewable energy is exempt from energy taxation, as is the electricity produced by CHP schemes. The service and production sectors in Denmark are exempt from energy taxes and, while all consumers have to pay VAT on fuel, most businesses can reclaim the VAT paid. The effect of taxation thus falls mainly on the domestic sector, where taxes account for 18% of the price of gas, 53% of the price of electricity and 60% of the price of oil.

In May 1992 the carbon tax was introduced for domestic customers and was extended to industrial and commercial customers in January 1993. The rate of the tax is 100 kroner (Dkr) per tonne of notional CO_2 content, so its effect is particularly to increase the price of coal relative to that of gas. It is applied to final energy supplied to customers rather than to primary energy use. VAT at 25% also still applies and, although industrial and commercial customers mainly get VAT refunded in full, most only get a refund of 50% of the carbon tax – apart from some energy-intensive companies, which are eligible for larger refunds. However, the higher refunds to energy-intensive industry are conditional on them reaching monitored agreements to install energy-saving measures (e.g. CHP) with the Danish Energy Agency.

Development of energy policy in Denmark

Lucas (1985) sees the development of agricultural co-operatives – to market produce and buy equipment for mechanisation and the later development of urban co-operatives for urban trades – as key to the development of energy supply and distribution in Denmark. This was the model adopted for most of the electricity utilities that were developed by the municipalities in urban areas and the agricultural co-operatives in rural areas. According to Lucas, the co-operative structure has been particularly important for the development of district heating, which some of the municipal electricity utilities began in the 1920s as a way of earning further income by selling the heat in the cooling water of their power stations.

After the Second World War Denmark, like most European countries, suffered severe energy shortages but was particularly badly affected due to its dependence on imported coal. However, district heating customers were less affected than others and, much of it being CHP using waste heat from power stations, district heating was seen as an efficient way of using scarce resources. The utilities were not keen on CHP, but they were encouraged to develop it by the majority share-holding municipalities. If they had not, the implicit threat was that the municipalities would develope their own facilities and, hence, gain access to the electricity markets. The shortage of fuel also helped the utilities to realise that CHP was a useful way of maximising its use.

By 1972, with 94% of the country's energy needs met by imported oil and coal, Denmark was highly vulnerable to world price fluctuations. The oil crisis thus gave Denmark a strong reason to diversify its fuel sources and increased the pressure for government intervention to plan and regulate the energy market.

In 1976 the Department of Trade published a major policy statement on its aim to reduce dependence on oil by building up energy reserves, developing a multi-source system of supply and reducing the growth of energy consumption. The measures proposed were home insulation, increased use of CHP/district heating, development of natural gas and renewable energy, increased use of coal, and the development of nuclear power.

The Electricity Supply Act of 1976 gave the state considerable powers to oblige the electricity utilities to burn specific fuels and to build power stations in areas where district heating could be used.

Lucas (1985) notes that the most obvious effect of the new powers was to influence the siting of power stations to favour CHP – for example, locating a new power station near Copenhagen rather than near a new coal port.

After the first oil crisis in 1973 the Danes had some success in improving their energy efficiency and fuel switching, but this began to tail off until the second (1979) crisis, when, although there was no shortage of oil, it was very expensive. Speaking to the House of Lords' European Communities Committee in 1991, Hans von Bulow, Deputy Permanent Secretary of the Danish Department of Energy, summed up the position as follows: 'Therefore, it turned from being simply a supply matter and also became an economic matter and the survival of the country. The total bill to satisfy our demand for energy was equal to the total deficit on our balance of payments per year, so that was pretty serious.' (HL 62-I, 1991: 124). This gave the Danes the motivation to invest in an expensive supply and distribution system so that they could use their North Sea gas themselves rather than export it, which would have been a cheaper and more profitable short-term option.

The Ministry of Commerce was responsible for energy policy until the late 1970s. In 1976 the former Atomic Energy Commission, which had been created in 1955, was disbanded and its secretariat formed the basis of the new Energy Agency, constituted as a directorate of the Ministry of Commerce to implement policies and programmes. The Ministry of Energy was established in 1979 in response to the decision to introduce natural gas into the energy supply system from Denmark's North Sea resources. At the same time the Energy Agency was transferred to the new Ministry. The Agency deals with the production, supply and consumption of energy, drafts and administers Danish energy legislation and translates the government's policy principles into actual programmes. The Agency's major role for most of the 1980s was in heat planning, as draft plans from municipalities had to be submitted to it for approval.

By 1986 the Ministry of Energy had not adopted any specific policies on conservation, this being a function that still lay largely within the Ministry of Housing (the Energy Conservation Unit did not move from the Ministry of Housing to the Energy Agency until 1989). The Agency's role in the industrial sector was limited until 1992, when it took on responsibility for implementing a new law on industrial energy conservation during 1992.

In 1994 the Ministries of Energy and Environment were merged to form the Ministry of the Environment and Energy, with responsibilities for environmental protection, energy and planning. The Energy Agency and the Environmental Protection Agency both come under this Ministry.

Government programmes to promote energy conservation

The main government energy conservation programmes run during the 1970s and 1980s concentrated on space heating as this is where the largest proportion (40%) of energy is used. A law was adopted in 1982 for electrical appliance labelling but was never implemented. During the late 1980s Denmark began planning a new labelling scheme, although this was more to put pressure on the European Commission rather than a serious intention to set up a Danish scheme.

In 1981 the Danish parliament passed an Act to reduce energy consumption in buildings, which aimed to bring all buildings built before February 1979 up to the standard of the 1979 building code. Among the measures brought in by the Act were subsidies for energy-saving investment and subsidised energy audits by qualified surveyors.

Subsidy schemes for housing ran from 1976 to 1985, but those considered most successful operated from 1981 to 1985. Owner-occupiers received 30% grants in the early years, falling to 15%, while tenants received 40% in the early years, also decreasing to 15% in later years. The maximum grant payable was around £700, and over the life of the scheme about £300 million was spent, leading to around £1,000 million worth of investment. The funds were used to support insulation measures and heating systems.

Most energy conservation schemes were wound down from 1984 as the new energy minister in the right wing-dominated coalition took less interest.

Energy-audit/heat-survey scheme

The first heat-survey scheme began in 1975. From 1981 to 1984 householders could obtain a grant towards the cost of a survey and the measures installed as a result of an approved consultant's report (see below). These subsidies ended in December 1984 but, from January

1985, sellers had to provide potential purchasers with either a heat-survey report or an energy certificate (granted for homes which meet certain minimum standards).

A survey of home-buyers between January 1985 and April 1986 found that 72% of single-family houses were sold with a heat-survey report or energy certificate (Birch and Krogboe, 1986). Forty-six per cent of owners had had a survey done voluntarily, with the rest persuaded to have one to meet the buyer's request for a report. However, the momentum dropped in the early 1990s according to the Energy Agency, which estimated that more than 50% of vendors did not comply with the requirement to have a survey (there were no sanctions for non-compliance). The reluctance to have a survey carried out stemmed from concerns about quality and accuracy rather than cost. The scheme has also aimed to keep costs down in various ways, which may have contributed to the poor quality. As a result of these problems a new scheme was launched in 1997 to energy-label all buildings so that information will automatically be available to purchasers, rather than leaving it to householders themselves to initiate surveys. Since January 1997 energy labelling has been mandatory for all buildings used for housing, trade or private service and for public buildings. In contrast to the heat-survey scheme, energy labelling also includes electricity used for appliances, water consumption and CO_2 emissions. In addition to the label, which details current energy costs and emissions, there is also an energy plan for the building, detailing ways to conserve energy and water and the likely cost savings.

Heat planning

By far the most significant energy conservation initiative in Denmark has been the heat-planning programme, although it was embarked on primarily to reduce dependence on imported oil by switching to gas and waste heat from power stations and industries rather than to conserve energy *per se*. Broader energy planning began in Denmark in the 1970s as a response to the first oil crisis and was, at first, particularly concerned with securing a role for nuclear power. The second oil crisis reinforced this and led to the plans for natural gas and heat planning – the 1981 Energy Plan conceded a much greater need for government investment, co-ordination and direction than the 1976 plan.

The most important part of the Danish approach to reducing dependence on imported oil was to change the nature of energy use for heating, particularly in the domestic sector. The Heat Supply Act was passed in 1979 and divided the country into three types of region: areas with CHP/district heating; areas receiving natural gas; and areas that must be heated in other ways. The aim was to encourage the use of gas heating and district heating (especially where the latter is based on combined heat and power) and to discourage the use of electricity for space heating. Electric heating can be used in sparsely populated rural areas where it is not feasible to supply district heating or natural gas.

Under the Act, kommunes (district councils), in co-operation with regional public utility companies (typically covering two or three counties), were required to establish present and future energy needs at the local level. The kommunes submitted their proposals to the county council, which prepared a county-wide heat plan for ministerial approval. To enable them to carry out the process, kommunes were given a number of significant new powers, as detailed in box 4.2.

Once the government had decided to exploit North Sea gas a key difficulty was how to sell enough to justify the expensive infrastructure in a country with little energy-intensive industry, particularly as district heating was cheaper for home heating than natural gas. The solution was zoning of areas to prevent competition between district heating and gas.

By the early 1990s much of the heat planning had been completed, with most buildings being connected either to district heating or to natural gas, although in some of the natural gas areas the proportion of buildings using electricity for heating remained high. The share of CHP in district heating supply had also increased substantially, from 29% in 1972 to 55% in 1988. The main task during the 1990s has, therefore, been to increase the use of CHP and to convert coal-fired district heating to gas or renewables, such as woodchip burning or waste incineration, as well as encouraging more people to switch from electricity to gas and district heating.

An amendment to the Heat Supply Act was passed in 1990 to promote the conversion of district heating plants in areas with natural gas to small-scale gas-fired CHP plants. A three-phase development plan was adopted: the largest coal- and gas-fired district heating plants were converted in 1990–94; the remaining coal- and medium-sized gas-fired plants were converted in 1994–96, and the

> ### 4.2 Heat Supply Act, 1979
>
> The Act gave the kommunes powers to:
>
> - Approve projects establishing new district heating plant or major changes in existing plant
> - Require that a district heating plant use a given type of energy
> - Require that existing and new buildings be connected to a district heating system if necessary to make the project viable.

small gas plants are being converted during 1996–98. Small-scale back-up district heating plants (usually coal- or oil-fired) will also have to be connected into the CHP system if they are located in CHP areas – by January 1996 all such plants had to be connected or have plans for connection under way. Supply companies have had to report to local councils once every two years from January 1991 on how these connections are progressing.

To support the changes to the Act a number of measures were introduced in 1991, including government grants of 15–25% for the conversion of coal-fired district heating plants to CHP, and grants for the construction and renovation of district heating networks that are to be supplied by CHP plants. In 1997 the Electricity Saving Trust was created to provide subsidies for the conversion of electric heating in the gas and district heating areas. As from 1998 the Trust is funded through an increase of charges for electricity of Dkr0.006/kWh levied on domestic and public sector consumers.

The achievements of the heat-planning programme have been impressive. In 1975 70% of space heating requirements was met by individual heating (heating for a single household, office or building using gas, oil or electricity), 20% by non-CHP district heating and 10% by CHP district heating. By 1990 the share of individual heating had fallen to 50%, with non-CHP district heating accounting for 22% and CHP district heating 23%. By 2005 the share of individual heating is projected to fall further to 40% and non-CHP district heating to 8%, with CHP district heating providing 52%.

There have been some conflicts between heat planning and the general planning system. During the 1960s there was considerable migration to large towns, but from 1970 industry moved to smaller communities and population densities began to decrease as low-density housing estates and more single-family homes (instead of apartments) were built at the edges of expanding towns.

Whereas regional planning had been encouraging decentralisation of housing, jobs and services to smaller communities, heat planning encouraged centralisation as higher population densities are needed to make district heating schemes feasible. Developments in the energy field thus strengthened the case for centralisation – which had been the subject of debate throughout the regional planning phase of the 1970s. By 1979, to judge by the annual report of the Minister of the Environment, the energy conservation case had been won: 'One of the assumptions for fulfilment of the government's energy policy is that through location of future urban growth, the necessary basis for supply of energy on a collective basis – natural gas and CHP – can be brought about ... future urban growth ought to be located in larger centres and selected local centres' (quoted in Christensen and Jensen-Butler, 1982).

Energy 2000 and Energy 21

In 1990 the Danish Government issued its action plan 'Energy 2000' (Danish Ministry of Energy, 1990), which outlined new targets for an energy policy to meet environmental concerns. Energy 2000 (box 4.3) placed firm emphasis on renewable energy, CHP and energy efficiency, not only for environmental reasons but also because Denmark's oil and gas resources are being rapidly depleted and the country expects to move from being a net exporter to a net importer within 10–15 years. Denmark will have a particularly tough job to meet its CO_2 target as the paper predicts that emissions in the

---

4.3 Energy 2000

Energy 2000 set a target to reduce CO_2 emissions by 20% from 1988 levels by the year 2005, to be achieved through:

- Support for energy-saving programmes
- A carbon tax on fossil fuels
- Conversion of coal- and oil-fired district heating to gas and of heat-only schemes to CHP
- Greater use of gas and CHP-based electricity generation
- Support for renewable energy sources.

year 2005 will be 22% above the 1988 level rather than the planned 20% below.

Energy 2000 has since been followed up by Energy 21, published in April 1996, which outlines the Danish government's key energy policy objectives for the future. Three priorities are the development of renewable energy sources, energy efficiency (including CHP) and the opening up of the electricity market. Energy 21 reiterates the national objective to stabilise CO_2 emissions at the 1990 level by 2000 and to reduce them by 20% from the 1988 level by 2005.

Demand-side management in Denmark

DSM had its real beginnings in 1986 when the government and the Social Democratic party reached an agreement to promote DSM and greater use of CHP. The Ministry of Energy launched a project to identify the scope for electricity savings, which was managed by the Research Institute of Danish Counties and Municipalities. In response to this the distribution companies developed a number of electricity-saving pilot projects, including: promoting the take-up of compact fluorescent lamps (the price of which has fallen by 50% as sales have risen); promoting energy-efficient freezers; and encouraging the use of energy-efficient lighting by commercial/industrial and public sector customers.

In March 1992 the Danish parliament required all generating companies to develop capacity plans consistent with the Energy 2000 target and in February 1994 the 1976 Electricity Supply Act was amended to oblige electricity utilities to adopt integrated resource planning (IRP; see chapter 2). Following consultation with the industry, the government issued guidelines for IRP in October 1994. The distribution companies have to assess the demand for electricity and conservation potential within their areas, setting out how that potential can be realised through energy efficiency. Elsam and Elkraft also have to produce IRP plans, in collaboration with the distribution companies, for the whole of their supply areas. The IRP process has to take account of a range of issues, including: security of supply; the competitiveness of industry; social and utility costs and benefits; and environmental protection, including national targets on emissions.

The utilities are required to submit their plans (and progress reports) to the Energy Agency once every two years. The plans have to include: a plan for the 'programme period' (the next 8–10 years), a plan considering the more distant future, and a plan describing the intended DSM efforts until the next programme period. The first plans were submitted at the end of 1995 and were the subject of discussions between the companies and the Energy Agency in the spring of 1996, as a result of which the Energy Agency circulated updated guidelines in February 1997 to deal with some of the key concerns raised by the first-stage plans. One of these was the need to ensure that the electricity companies produce plans that are consistent with the country's overall environmental targets. Another is that the guidelines now deal specifically with the theme 'environmental regulation and electricity exchange with other countries in a liberalised electricity market'.

It is not yet clear what the Energy Agency will do with the plans once it has received them, how the utilities' progress will be monitored (and what happens if they do not meet the targets), or how recommendations in the plans for legislation or other regulation will be translated into action. Furthermore, liberalisation may make it increasingly difficult to implement the IRP system. Paradoxically, Denmark seems to have begun to introduce mandatory DSM/IRP just as the US has begun to question its role in a world of energy market competition.

Conclusion

During the 1970s and 1980s a fortunate coincidence of several factors helped Denmark to develop and implement its energy conservation policies and programmes. Energy supply interests never developed a predominant position in energy policy as utilities have been small and under the control of municipalities that have seen the value of conservation in the broader community interest. This key role of local authorities has, thus, altered the nature of the energy policy network which, in many other countries, has tended to be made up of pure producer interests (private sector or state-controlled energy industries) and government departments with a production-orientated ethos (more energy production being seen as the key to meeting the country's energy needs). The existence of a well-developed planning system involving regional and local authorities was central to this different approach, giving these key players in the policy network control over an essential element of Denmark's conservation strategy – the heat-planning programme.

Other important factors in Denmark's success were the choice of one area of heavy energy use – buildings – to target in most programmes, plus the fact that the need to reduce dependence on imported oil provided a strong sense of purpose towards conservation.

Many of the programmes successfully used existing systems and networks and were co-ordinated by committees that included the relevant bodies – not just civil servants – and which had technically competent secretariats to oversee quality control. In these areas, therefore, Denmark managed to establish effective policy networks for energy conservation. Those Danish schemes which have experienced more problems in implementation, such as the energy-audits scheme, seem to have suffered from relying on professionals who it was assumed would be competent rather than providing them with specific training. A lack of enforcement also hampered the later stages when subsidies were no longer available to motivate people to take up the audits. Most of the subsidy schemes seem to have worked well.

Since the early 1990s Denmark has faced new challenges: from the need to reduce greenhouse-gas emissions (given the country's still rather heavy reliance on coal); from its rising electricity consumption attributable to household and office appliances; and from EU plans for energy market liberalisation. The Danish energy utilities are particularly worried that under EU third-party access rules, foreign electricity companies could offer lower energy prices unencumbered by Danish environmental requirements and thus squeeze them out of their own market. This is likely to raise the question yet again of whether energy saving can be a viable business opportunity or whether it has to be imposed as a community service obligation.

5

The Netherlands

Political and institutional background

Dutch government is usually coalition government for three main reasons – the existence of cultural minorities, the multi-party system and proportional representation. Coalition government leads to coalition cabinets and means that these tend to be more collegial than prime ministerial. The Dutch prime minister has few formal powers compared to his counterparts in the UK, France or Germany, for example. While there are many parties, there are only five or six main ones and only four have participated in governments since 1980. The main coalitions have tended to be between the Christian Democrats and the Liberals or the Christian Democrats and Social Democrats. However, an influential party that has not been in government is the Green Left.

Below the national level there are twelve provinces, each with its own directly elected legislature and government. However, their influence on policy in most areas is limited except in the case of environmental protection and physical planning. Their main role is to act as an intermediary between local authorities and national government. Municipal government is more important – until the early 1990s there were 700 local councils, but since then a process of amalgamation of smaller councils has been reducing the number significantly. Much decision-making remains at national government level, and local government receives two-thirds of its revenue from the centre.

There is no central civil service – each department recruits its own staff and sets its own standards. Civil servants tend to stay in one department and often in one directorate, which leads to an emphasis on technical specialists rather than managerial generalists. Government departments tend to develop links for recruitment purposes with particular universities and sometimes also recruit people from organised interests, and vice versa.

Decentralisation is mainly to interest groups, advisory boards and individual government departments (or departmental sections) rather than to provincial or municipal government. The nature of the civil service and the strong role of outside interest groups thus contributes to a tendency to neo-corporatism and decentralisation. According to Andeweg (1993: 167), neo-corporatism is a key feature of the Netherlands' policy process, with a 'bewildering variety of advisory boards, tripartite councils and para-statal organisations'. Dutch interest groups include those representing local authorities, major industry and trade unions and are not just external lobbyists but also participate in government working groups and get involved in policy development. Some direct lobbying is undertaken by large firms, but most are also involved in employers' peak organisations.

After the Second World War there was a major move by government, under the public law organisation of economic activity (PBO) initiative, to transfer some responsibilities to independent regulatory commissions made up of employers, trade unions and government appointees. The government bears no responsibility for the regulations issued by these boards, which can cause problems – Andeweg cites the example of complaints from other EU countries to the Minister of Economic Affairs about a Dutch natural gas company offering cheap gas prices to hothouses where the Minister had to explain that he was not involved. Although it is through the advisory councils and PBO boards that interest groups are officially incorporated into Dutch policymaking, there is also an informal network, and the formal meetings may in effect be just the public rubber-stamping of decisions reached in private meetings.

A number of reasons are given for the development of neo-corporatism in the Netherlands, including the small state thesis – that in an open world economy small states need to develop internal co-operation between different interests to enable them to compete with other economies. The view is thus that the Dutch are consensual by nature and that one reflection of this is that employers' organisations and trade unions are viewed as 'social partners' rather than pressure groups. Whatever the reasons, the end result is the formation of closely knit policy networks of government departments and their relevant interest groups.

5.1 Key actors in the Netherlands' energy policy community

Government departments
  Ministry of Economic Affairs

Agencies
  NOVEM – Netherlands Energy and Environmental Development
  Agency

Electricity industry – thirty-one distribution/supply companies (owned by local authorities), which are also responsible for gas and district heating; four generation companies (directly owned by the distributors or local authorities); and SEP (co-ordination of generation and dispatch, owned by the four generating companies).

Gas industry – distribution/supply (see under *Electricity industry*); Gasunie (joint state–private sector company) undertakes transportation and sales of gas to distributors and some large users.

EnergieNed – trade association for the electricity, gas and district heating distribution companies.

Structure of the energy market

The gas, electricity and district heating industries in the Netherlands are owned mainly by local authorities or by partnerships between these and the private sector. Central government control of the industries covers only approval of major investment plans of the electricity generators plus setting maximum tariffs for electricity consumers. The major responsibility for matters such as the siting of power stations and other environmental matters rests with local (municipal and provincial) government.

Until 1988 all the utilities were directly owned by the municipal and provincial authorities and there was a mixture of vertically integrated and unbundled electricity distribution/supply and generating companies. In 1988 generation was unbundled and four separate electricity generating companies were formed. During the 1980s and early 1990s there was considerable reorganisation of the distributors/suppliers through mergers and the horizontal integration of gas, electricity and district heating distribution/supply. In December 1991 the electricity, gas and district heating companies' trade associations

– which co-ordinate their activities and prepared long-term plans – entered into an agreement with the government to consolidate energy distribution and merged to form a single association called EnergieNed. By 1995 there were only 31 distributors, as against 158 in 1986.

The distribution/supply companies are all owned by municipal or provincial authorities. There are four generating companies, two of which are owned by the local distribution companies, the other two being owned directly by municipal and provincial authorities. Electricity generation and dispatching is co-ordinated by the company SEP (owned by the four generators), which also owns the transmission grid. There is also some independent electricity generation – mainly CHP and wind energy – undertaken by the distribution companies and industrial users.

Almost all the gas sold in the Netherlands is marketed by the national gas company Gasunie, which is jointly owned by the state, Esso and Shell. Gasunie owns and operates the gas transportation network and sells gas to the local energy distribution companies, which sell on to final users. Gasunie also sells gas directly to some large industrial consumers.

The increasing integration of electricity, gas and district heating distribution and supply means that 70% of these companies now supply and distribute two or all three of these. Furthermore, the rapid increase in small-scale local generation (particularly CHP), combined with horizontal integration of supply and distribution, should make energy companies in the Netherlands particularly well placed to maximise new opportunities for integrated energy services as energy market liberalisation develops.

In December 1995 the government proposed to privatise 40% of the natural gas market and 35% of the electricity market within 2 to 3 years; up to two-thirds of the energy market should be privatised within 5 years. The plans are for privatisation of energy supply only and not the infrastructure of transmission, distribution and transportation. Electricity generation would, under the government's plan, be concentrated mainly in one large company created by a merger of the four existing generating companies (owned by local authorities), who would continue to hold the shares in the new company.

The energy market is also being liberalised, with independent producers allowed more equal access to the networks and consumers being allowed to choose their energy supplier. So far only larger business users can choose a supplier, but by 2002 many smaller businesses will also be able to shop around, with full liberalisation coming some time after that date.

VAT at 18.5% is charged on coal, oil, electricity and gas; however, as VAT-registered commercial and industrial users can reclaim VAT, the tax is mainly felt by households and some smaller non-VAT-registered users. There are also environmental taxes on oil, gas and coal and excise duties on oil products.

Energy policy and development of energy conservation in the Netherlands

According to the IEA, the Netherlands energy economy is unique among IEA countries due to the pre-eminent role of natural gas – virtually every home, office, farm and factory is connected to the gas system. Gas provides 60% of fuel for electricity generation and satisfies 52% of TPES, the highest proportion in the world.

The Ministry of Economic Affairs has the primary responsibility for energy policy in the Netherlands. Until 1989 there were three separate agencies, reporting to the Ministry, that had responsibilities for various aspects of policy development and programmes in energy conservation and renewables. In 1989 these were merged to form NOVEM, the Netherlands Energy and Environmental Development Agency, which also reports to the Ministry. The Agency initiates, manages and co-ordinates projects, advises the government on energy conservation, provides advice to energy users and often funds projects jointly with industry to facilitate the marketability of technologies. The Ministry is involved in programme development and assessment and integrates NOVEM activities with government energy policies.

Since the oil crisis in 1973 the Ministry of Economic Affairs has produced three general energy policy papers – in 1974, 1979 and 1995. Papers on some energy policy topics are produced in collaboration with other relevant ministries – for example the Ministry of the Environment is involved in all matters with an environmental policy dimension.

Energy conservation first became a policy issue in the wake of the 1973 oil crisis, when the key policy goals of reducing dependence on imported oil and making the Dutch economy less sensitive to fluctuations in energy prices were established. To support this policy the

government introduced a range of subsidies to induce greater investment in energy conservation and stimulate the development of
energy-saving technologies. In the period from 1973 to 1985 energy
efficiency in the Netherlands improved at the rate of 2% a year and,
as in many other countries, there was a shift towards a less energy-
intensive industry. Economic growth, however, meant that by 1985
total energy consumption was about the same as in 1973.

Dutch energy policy objectives were reaffirmed in January 1985
in a government paper contained in the Final Report of the National
Energy Policy Debate. This paper stressed conservation, diversifica-
tion of energy sources, maintenance of indigenous production and
reduction of electricity supply costs. It also stated that priority was
to be given to the development of renewables and CHP. The energy
conservation budget was increased in 1985 but was then reduced
by 17% in 1986 due a drop in the budget for the home insulation
programme (which had by then reached 60% of targeted buildings)
and the ending of subsidies for conservation in the horticulture
sector. Although the conservation budget was restored to the 1985
level in 1987, it was cut by 75% in 1988 as subsidies were redirected
to support for CHP.

By 1988 most grants for energy-saving measures (apart from CHP)
had been ended – in the case of housing, grants were only provided
if the whole property was being renovated; in industry from 1987
grants were only being made for surveys. These changes coincided
with sharp falls in energy prices after 1985. However, a new programme to promote low-energy appliances and lighting to help
counter the growth in electricity consumption was launched in 1988.
Work also continued in the late 1980s on building standards,
with tougher energy efficiency standards from 1987 and still more
stringent requirements in 1989. Despite this, the annual rate of
improvement in energy efficiency from 1985 to 1990 was only half
what it had been between 1973 and 1985.

The National Environmental Policy Plan

Concerns about climate change began to feature in energy policy
debates in the Netherlands from 1988, leading the government to
propose a National Environmental Policy Plan (NEPP), based on
sustainable development, in May 1989. Parliament approved the
NEPP in 1990. The NEPP proposed that reductions in emissions

5.2 Targets set by NEPP and MAP

NEPP 1 (1990) – stabilise CO_2 emissions at the 1990 level by 1994–95, with a 3–5% reduction by 2000

MAP I (1991) – reduce CO_2 emissions by 9 million tonnes by 2000

NEPP 2 (1994) – 3% reduction in CO_2 emissions by 2000

MAP II (1994) – reduce CO_2 emissions by 17 million tonnes by 2000.

---

would come from three sectors of the economy: recycling and waste management (10%); transport (15%); and energy (75%). The energy sector was thus expected to contribute the lion's share, with two-thirds of the energy sector's savings coming from improvements in energy efficiency and the remainder from reduced coal consumption – to be achieved by using more gas for electricity generation and district heating.

The NEPP also introduced a levy on energy consumers (up to 2% on the unit price of gas and electricity) to fund energy-saving subsidies, and it challenged the energy distribution sector to devise plans to achieve its CO_2 emission reductions using the levy. The energy distribution companies published their first action plan in response to NEPP – MAP I – in spring 1991.

Parliament approved a second National Environmental Policy Plan in spring 1994. NEPP 2's Memorandum on Energy Conservation set out additional measures required to achieve a 3% reduction in CO_2 emissions by the year 2000. In response the energy distribution companies published MAP II in March 1994, in which they committed themselves to almost double their emissions reduction target. The NEPP targets and MAP responses are summarised in box 5.2

The MAP initiative is a good example of Dutch neo-corporatism in action, with each of the plans based on formal written agreements signed by the Minister of Economic Affairs and the directors of EnergieNed. The agreements set out the specific targets in terms of reductions in CO_2 emissions and energy consumption that EnergieNed members have said they can achieve, the types of measures that will be encouraged to achieve the targets, how the measures will be funded (including the levy) and monitoring arrangements.

The environmental action plan of the energy distribution sector

The first plan, MAP I, which ran from 1991 to 1994, involved the companies in a range of projects to promote and install energy-saving measures. A mix of subsidies, marketing and information was used to promote the adoption of energy-saving and emission-reducing measures, including: compact fluorescent lamps; high-efficiency boilers; efficient electrical appliances in, for example, refrigeration; CHP; and insulation.

The greatest success in the period 1991–94 was in the space-heating market (with the introduction of CHP and heat distribution) and energy saving in the household sector. High-efficiency boilers (500,000 units), water-saving showerheads (750,000 units) and low-energy light bulbs (5 million units) were the measures most likely to be implemented in the household sector. As a result of measures taken by the end of 1996, it is estimated that CO_2 emissions in the year 2000 will be 7.2 million tonnes less than they would otherwise have been and that the energy saving will be 27 petajoules (27×10^{15} joules).

MAP II outlined a package of measures to be implemented from 1994 to 2000. For this period the companies have made a clear distinction between user-side measures and production-side measures, emphasising that both will be required to meet the emissions reduction target. As in MAP I, the programme is funded by a mixture of a levy on consumers (Fls310 million a year), the companies' own resources (Fls60 million) and the government (Fls150 million). The consumer levy is limited to a maximum charge of 2.5% on bills – the average will be 1.8% over the whole period.

The bulk of the consumer levy is being used for consumer subsidies (towards insulation, high-efficiency boilers, lighting in non-residential buildings) and to fund marketing, information and promotional campaigns, while the government money is mainly being used for subsidies for CHP/heat distribution and renewable energy (wind, biomass, solar and small-scale hydro). In general, however, there is less use of subsidies than in MAP I and more effort is being made to stimulate the market for energy-saving products and foster lasting changes in consumer behaviour. This is intended to make the whole programme more consistent with the plans for liberalising the energy market. A number of companies are running pilot projects in which intelligent metering is being tried to see if better information encourages consumers to change their behaviour in order to save energy. However, EnergieNed has echoed the views of energy suppliers in many countries in expressing some scepticism about whether energy conservation can become a commercial proposition for suppliers, particularly those competing for domestic customers.

The role of combined heat and power

A number of initiatives were taken during the 1980s to promote CHP, which meant that by 1987 there was 1,400 MW of CHP capacity and 14% of the country's electricity came from this source. The new stimulation programme (detailed in box 5.3), launched in 1987, aimed to increase the amount of CHP capacity by 700–1,000 MW by 1995.

In the late 1980s and early 1990s a significant number of customers in the industrial, commercial, public and residential sector (apartments, nursing homes, swimming pools, hospitals) installed CHP systems to reduce their energy costs, spurred on partly by the government programmes to promote CHP but also, from 1990, by very favourable gas prices for CHP offered by Gasunie to secure a higher share for gas in the electricity supply market. A further incentive for industrial users to adopt CHP was that, from 1990 onwards, many industry sectors agreed energy conservation covenants with the Ministry of Economic Affairs as their contribution to the country's CO_2 targets, and CHP was seen as cost-effective way of delivering their commitments.

5.3 CHP initiatives in the Netherlands

CHP stimulation programme
- Grants of 25–40% for various sectors
- Electricity utilities to pay CHP operators for electricity on an avoided-cost basis, enabling CHP plant to be built on the basis of heat requirements rather than the smaller electricity demand
- Joint ventures between CHP operators and utilities to enable CHP to benefit from the utilities' lower cost of capital.

MAP CHP targets
- MAP I – 3,300 MW by 2000
- MAP II – 5,900 MW by 2000.

For the energy distributors/suppliers there was also an incentive to develop CHP. With their generating assets removed and controls placed on their development of large-scale generating plant – together with the fact that their largest (and often most profitable) customers could, from 1989, buy electricity directly from generators, build their own CHP systems (with the distributors having to buy the surplus electricity at favourable rates) or even import electricity – one solution to the potential threat to their revenue was to start offering CHP to customers, providing financing where necessary. From 1987, after a fairly slow start, the number of CHP units installed by many of the distributors grew dramatically, particularly under the subsidies provided through the MAP initiatives, which resulted in the installation of an extra 2,300 MW of CHP between 1991 and 1994.

By 1995 the Netherlands had over 4,500 MW of CHP capacity, around 75% of it in industry. For the central generators and SEP (the electricity generating and dispatching company) and some distributors who had less success in developing CHP, this meant a loss of base-load electricity sales and potential problems of rising costs to meet peak demand. Indeed, the more customers who took up the CHP option, the worse the companies' position became as their fixed costs had to be spread over fewer kilowatt-hours sold, hence raising the price per kilowatt-hour and further increasing the incentive for on-site CHP for industrial users. There was also the prospect of significant overcapacity in electricity generation. This led, in 1994, to a moratorium on CHP development agreed between the generators, SEP and the distributors whereby SEP agreed to pay industrial customers not to install CHP.

As Slingerland (1997) describes, by 1994 the distributors had in general become very keen on CHP (having increased their 1990 MAP target from 3,300 MW by the year 2000 to 5,900 MW by 2000 in the 1994 MAP plan). However, SEP and the four generating companies persuaded them to agree to the moratorium by offering them a role in central power planning, with an emphasis on larger central plants rather than the smaller, decentralised ones. Given that SEP is owned by the four generators, it is perhaps not surprising that it should have been keener on central capacity. Its role as the transmission and planning organisation would also account for its preference for a more controlled system over increased growth in decentralised capacity. It is perhaps also not surprising that, despite the attractions of decentralised CHP to the distributors, they agreed to support the moratorium proposed by SEP and the generators as they are the owners of the generators and, hence, the ultimate owners of SEP.

What is interesting, however, is that despite the fact that industrial users were strongly opposed to the moratorium, the government did not get involved but left the initiative to the electricity industry, merely expressing support once the settlement with industrial users had been reached. This is consistent with the Netherlands tradition, outlined earlier in the chapter, of devolving power to industry sectors. However, the moratorium did raise questions about the ability of the country to meet its CO_2 target, in which CHP (particularly small-scale decentralised CHP) was intended to play a key part. Yet, given that the Ministry of Economic Affairs had also allowed the energy industry to set its own plan for delivering its share of the target, it could also be seen as consistent to allow the industry to work out how it will do this if reduced CHP development poses a threat. One option may be to undertake further development of larger-scale, centralised CHP (under the control of the main generators rather than energy users).

National Environmental Policy Plan 3

The NEPP3 was published in February 1998. It reviewed Dutch environmental developments since NEPP2 and presented an overall plan for policies to 2003. Increased energy taxation is the most important new initiative in NEPP3. Taxes on energy and on fossil fuels, excluding motor fuels, are to be increased by Fls3.4 billion (Ecu6 billion), effectively doubling energy taxes on households and small businesses. Most of the revenue is to be returned to the economy through reduced income taxes, lower taxes on corporate profits and increased social benefits. The remainder is intended to support energy-saving measures. The government forecasts that the increased taxes will achieve a 7–10 million tonne cut in carbon dioxide emissions – up to 5% of the national total.

Dutch industry greeted the proposal with dismay, saying that it cut across voluntary agreements to reduce carbon dioxide emissions, but environmental groups criticised it for not going far enough. The debate on energy taxes has continued following the general election in May 1998.

Conclusion

The Netherlands presents a particularly interesting case of co-operation between central government and the energy industry to achieve targets to reduce greenhouse-gas emissions. Why did the energy distribution companies develop a plan to help the government meet its CO_2 target? They could have decided to let the government find commercial energy service providers (contract energy management companies) to run the programme. However, the danger for the distributors would have been that the energy services companies would pick the most lucrative sectors (e.g. CHP for large industrial users), thereby cutting the distributors' revenue from traditional supply while giving them none of the revenue from selling energy services. Furthermore, to enable the government to meet its targets, the distributors might have been required to take on the less profitable sectors of the energy services market (small domestic users, for example).

Another important factor is that the energy companies were probably keen to co-operate with the government to avoid further action (such as a tough carbon tax), which the government might otherwise have felt it needed to take to meet its CO_2 target. It is therefore hardly surprising that they reacted angrily to the proposals in NEPP3 for an energy tax. The companies were also provided with the important 'carrot' of the levy on consumers to fund many of the energy-saving measures. This initiative thus fits well into the Netherlands' tradition of neo-corporatism in which the energy utilities are viewed as the social partners of NOVEM and the Ministry of Economic Affairs in delivering the government's climate change programme. The fact that the energy utilities have traditionally been owned by local authorities or by partnerships between local authorities and the private sector has helped to reinforce this perception of them as social partners and, hence, a tendency to collaboration with government.

The utilities, the Ministry of Economic Affairs and NOVEM have therefore formed a cohesive policy network. As in Denmark, the role of local authorities in the utilities has helped to avoid an exclusively production ethos and produced a consensus sympathetic to the need to tackle climate change, although the utilities' reaction to the energy tax proposals suggests that the production ethos has not entirely disappeared.

However, one of the main effects of the NEPP has been to develop an increasing focus on customers by the energy distribution companies. In practical terms this has meant developing commercial and marketing departments to sell energy-saving products and provide advice on energy use. Previously, the main company focus was on engineering to increase their networks and guarantee the safety and reliability of supply. Market liberalisation – particularly the growth of on-site CHP use by industrial customers – has put increasing pressure on the companies' traditional source of revenue (energy supply and distribution) and also seems to be accelerating this trend to the provision of energy services for industrial and commercial users. However, whether the energy services approach can be developed in the household sector remains to be seen.

6

The United Kingdom

Political and institutional background

The United Kingdom's political system has a number of features that to many other countries can seem unusual. First, there is the lack of a written constitution and the role of the monarch, who 'invites' the leader of the party which gains the most seats in a general election to form a government. The parliament consists of two chambers – the House of Commons, in which sit the elected MPs, and the House of Lords, consisting of both those who are there by accident of birth (the hereditary peers) and those who have been ennobled in recognition of their public service or specifically to work on behalf of one of the political parties.

The 'first past the post' electoral system has ensured that coalition government is virtually unknown in the UK. Since the Second World War governments have alternated between the two main political parties – Labour and the Conservatives – although the latter have been in government for longer periods, including most recently from 1979 to 1997, when Labour returned to power. Government tends towards the prime ministerial rather than the collegial (this was particularly so under Margaret Thatcher from 1979 to 1990, and Tony Blair seems to be showing similar tendencies), with the prime minister selecting the cabinet and other ministers and thus having firm control over who is appointed and who stays appointed.

Below the level of national government there is local government, with larger towns and cities generally having unitary authorities responsible for all local administration, whereas in smaller towns and rural areas the responsibilities are divided between district and county councils. Local government in the UK is among the least autonomous in Europe, with no general power of competence – local

councils are allowed to do only those things which are expressly permitted by legislation, whereas in most of Europe councils can do
anything that is not prohibited by legislation. Local government
in the UK is also dependent on central government for most of its
revenue, although about one-third is raised through local property
taxation.

The civil service is admired by many for its traditions of impartiality and high quality, although it is also criticised for being selected
from too narrow an elite, for being too generalist – and thus lacking
specialist skills – and for being too passive, particularly in the area
of economic policy (compared to the Japanese for example). The
civil service mirrors the UK system of an unwritten constitution in
having largely unwritten rules.

Compared to countries like Japan and France, the UK could not
be described as a corporatist state. However, in the development of
its nationalised industries (coal, electricity, gas, railways, steel) from
the 1940s until the privatisation programme of the 1980s it was
possible to see elements of corporatism in the close relationships
between the relevant government departments and these industries,
which together formed close-knit policy networks.

Although the role of special interests and lobbying is not as developed as in the United States, it has become increasingly important
since the 1970s and particularly during the 1980s and 1990s, with
many such interests represented on government advisory bodies and
working parties in addition to the more informal and private system
of meetings and briefings between them and ministers and MPs.

Structure of the energy market

British Gas was privatised as a single company in 1986 and in 1993
was required to separate its transportation business into a company
(TransCo) separate from its supply business (British Gas Supply),
both of which were still wholly owned by British Gas plc until the
company decided to de-merge in February 1997, forming a separate
supply business (Centrica) and transportation/distribution business
(TransCo). Initially, only customers using more than 25,000 therms
per annum were able to buy from suppliers other than British Gas,
but in 1992 the market was opened up for anyone using more than
2,500 therms, bringing in most industrial and many commercial
users and even some large household customers. Since 1996 the

---

6.1 Key actors in the UK energy policy community

Government departments

Department of Energy (DEn), Department of the Environment (DoE) (pre-1992)

Department of the Environment (DoE), Department of Trade and Industry (DTI) (1992–97)

Department of the Environment, Transport and the Regions (DETR), Department of Trade and Industry (post-1997)

Energy Efficiency Office/Energy Environment and Waste Directorate (part of DEn until 1992, then of DoE/DETR)

Agencies

Energy Saving Trust

Electricity industry (see box 6.2)

Gas industry (see box 6.2)

Energy conservation industry and energy conservation NGOs

Association for the Conservation of Energy

Buildings Energy Efficiency Federation

Combined Heat and Power Association

National Energy Action

---

remainder of the gas market has begun to be opened up in stages, and it has been completely open since June 1998.

In England and Wales the Central Electricity Generating Board which, before privatisation, owned all the power generation and the high-voltage transmission system, was split, on privatisation, into three separate and competing generating companies (National Power, Power Gen, Nuclear Electric) and a separate company to run the transmission system (National Grid). The regional electricity boards became regional distribution/supply companies, with a franchise monopoly for all customers in their region with a demand of less than 100 kW (until 1994 the franchise limit was 1 MW). During 1998–99 the remainder of the electricity market is being opened up to competition, including that for household customers.

In Scotland two integrated supply, distribution, transmission and generation companies were created on privatisation – Scottish Power and Scottish Hydro Electric – with Scottish Nuclear formed to take

---

6.2 Energy industries before and after privatisation

Pre-privatisation

Electricity Central Electricity Generating Board (generation and transmission), regional electricity boards (distribution and supply)

Gas British Gas – fully integrated, transportation, distribution/supply

Post-privatisation

Electricity National Grid (transmission), National Power, Power Gen and Nuclear Electric (generation), regional electricity companies (distribution and supply, as well as able to develop generation)

Gas British Gas as pre-privatisation (until 1997); TransCo (transportation) and Centrica (supply) (post 1997); new-entrant gas companies

Energy industry regulators

Office of Gas Supply (OFGAS) (established 1986)

Office of Electricity Regulation (OFFER) (established 1989)

---

on the nuclear power stations. The two Scottish companies have had the same regional monopolies and have been subject to the same rules of competition and timetables as the English and Welsh companies.

Privatisation in Northern Ireland did not take place until 1992. Northern Ireland Electricity (NIE) is the single integrated supply, distribution and transmission company, but the power stations were sold to separate private sector companies. Although NIE does not have a monopoly supply franchise, only a few larger customers buy electricity from other suppliers as they are required to have sophisticated metering to do so. This situation is under review by the regulator.

In England, Wales and Scotland competition in gas and electricity supply has developed to a significant extent, with many gas companies (many of which are subsidiaries of regional electricity companies or owned by major oil companies) operating as competitors to British Gas and all of the regional electricity companies and Scottish companies competing for customers in each others' areas. As a result, commercial and industrial users have enjoyed major reductions in gas and electricity prices (15–20% on average and more in some cases), and in those areas where household users have been able to shop around for gas, price cuts of around 15% have been achieved.

The electricity and gas industries are showing a considerable capacity for reorganising themselves both through new entrants and through the restructuring of incumbents where this is allowed by regulatory authorities. So, for example, most of the regional electricity distribution companies in England and Wales have developed some of their own power generation, while both Power Gen and National Power have been supplying electricity directly to large customers since they were privatised. Horizontal integration is also developing in the UK as all the regional electricity companies have established subsidiary gas companies to enable them to supply gas and electricity to business customers. There have also been a number of mergers and takeovers of electricity companies by UK and US companies.

When British Gas and the electricity industry were privatised the government established independent industry regulators – the Office of Gas Supply (OFGAS) and the Office of Electricity Regulation (OFFER). A key intention was that, although appointed by the government, the regulators would be independent and concerned solely with economic regulation – primarily to be achieved by setting price controls at periodic intervals. As far as energy conservation and the environment are concerned, both regulators were given limited duties and powers.

There has been no deliberate effort to increase fuel prices or to maintain them at a high level – although various levies or taxes have been imposed from time to time for different purposes (e.g. the fossil fuel levy to support nuclear power and renewable energy). The UK did not charge VAT on fuel supplied to domestic consumers until April 1994. Introduced at the rate of 8%, it was due to rise to 17.5% in April 1995, but this was blocked by parliamentary opposition. The new Labour government came to power in May 1997 on a manifesto commitment to cut the rate to 5%. Although VAT is charged (at 17.5%) on fuel supplied to all businesses, most can reclaim this and so are, in effect, exempt. Thus, while real fuel prices increased dramatically in the mid- and late 1970s and the early 1980s, they have generally been in decline since the mid-1980s.

Energy policy from the Second World War to 1973

The history of a strategic governmental role in determining UK energy policy begins essentially with the critical role of energy supply during the Second World War, which led to the creation of the first UK energy ministry – the Ministry of Fuel, Light and Power – in 1942. This was absorbed into the Department of Technology in 1969, only to be recreated, in the wake of the 1973 oil crisis, as the Department of Energy in 1974.

In the immediate post-war period (late 1940s) the need to conserve energy was high on the political agenda, and some progress was made during the fuel crisis of 1947. But the electricity industry could not contemplate any option other than increasing production to meet demand (unsurprising given that one of their statutory duties was to supply all demands for electricity) and, despite his power to compel the industry to act as he wanted, Energy Minister Hugh Gaitskell preferred to carry the industry with him, ending up with a much watered-down scheme that could not work.

Psychologically, this would have been a difficult time to introduce a new austerity measure. The promise of an end to the deprivations of the 1930s and the hardships of wartime had helped to bring Labour to power in 1945. By 1948 the country was looking forward to the benefits of a new age – with electrical appliances and heaters replacing dirty, time-consuming coal fires. It is therefore unsurprising that the politicians did not pursue the conservation option, particularly as building new power stations would also create jobs.

The 'pile it high, sell it cheap' mentality persisted in the 1950s and 1960s as the key strand of UK energy policy. One factor leading to the government commitment to nuclear power in 1955 was the likelihood of coal shortages. It is easy to see how problems with the coal industry and seemingly inexorable rises in demand for energy made the politicians and officials all too willing to believe the lobbyists for nuclear power, who suggested, in the late 1950s, that nuclear power would make electricity so cheap that it wouldn't be worth metering!

As a result, the Ministry of Fuel and Power never co-ordinated the work of the fuel industry as its statute demanded. The statutes of the utilities, which encouraged them to maximise production, and the ethos of the 1940s, 1950s and 1960s clearly would have made this an uphill struggle. And, as the former chairman of the National Coal Board, Lord Robens (1972), has pointed out, the internal organisation of the Ministry exacerbated the problem – the divisions for coal, oil, gas, electricity and nuclear merely becoming 'the mouthpieces of each of the industries'.

British energy policy has thus, since 1945, seen one or two fuel sources as the saviours – at various times coal, oil, nuclear power and gas. Robens considers that the problem was due to Ministers seeking short-term advantages, combined with their reliance on 'talented amateurs' in the civil service. However, his implicit suggestion that the 'amateurs' and ministers should have listened to the industry experts more does not altogether square with reality. Indeed, the industry experts were perhaps listened to far too much by the 'amateur' civil servants, who did not have enough technical knowledge to question what they were being told.

Energy policy and energy conservation since 1973

Several key factors influenced energy policy in the UK in the mid- and late 1970s. The discovery and exploitation of North Sea oil and gas lessened the impact of the 1973 and 1979 oil price shocks. The use of gas for central heating accelerated rapidly in the 1970s and 1980s. The decline in the use of coal continued and the bitter miners' strike of 1974 led to the downfall of a Conservative government.

The Labour government of 1974–79 was the first to introduce a national energy conservation programme with the launch of the 'Save It' campaign in January 1975, which encouraged people to save energy at home, at work and on the roads. Energy-saving loans and grants for industry were introduced in 1974 and 1978. The first subsidies for households were introduced in 1978, administered by the Department of the Environment. In July 1976 the government appointed the first Minister with specific responsibility for energy conservation, while an Energy Conservation Division (ECD) had been set up within the Department of Energy in mid-1975. Also established in the late 1970s were two government agencies to undertake detailed technical work on energy conservation – the Energy Technology Support Unit (ETSU) for the industrial and commercial sector and the Building Research Energy Conservation Support Unit (BRECSU) for work on buildings.

By the early 1980s there were concerns that energy conservation effort was not being effectively co-ordinated. The Select Committee on Energy in 1982 (HC 401-I, 1982) recommended that responsibility be concentrated in one department or separate institution (at the time at least three departments were involved). The Rayner efficiency scrutiny (Finer, 1982) concluded that the ECD was not taken seriously by other divisions in the Department 'since it does not deal with the main unifying themes of the Department – the North Sea and the nationalised industries/electricity supply – and is not perceived as pursuing policies having political priority' (Finer, 1992: 7).

The scrutiny's main recommendation was for an Energy Efficiency Office (EEO), within the Department of Energy, to replace the ECD. For Peter Walker (Secretary of State for Energy 1985–87), the need for the Energy Efficiency Office was due to the UK's poor performance compared to that of many other countries, notably Japan. Walker's approach, as outlined to the Select Committee on Energy (HC 87, 1985) represented a significant shift in emphasis – the Rayner scrutiny's modest aims of a more co-ordinated government approach to energy conservation had been replaced by a new 'national crusade to save energy and cash'. From then began what most commentators would describe as the golden age of the EEO, culminating in Energy Efficiency Year in 1986, with high-profile national advertising campaigns and the 'breakfast briefings' for business leaders hosted by the Secretary of State.

As oil supplies became plentiful again in the 1980s, so the price began to fall – and this was reflected in the prices of other fuels. The 'Save It' mentality was, therefore, no longer considered appropriate. The predominant theme of the 1980s in government was 'efficiency'; hence the renaming of the Energy Conservation Division as the Energy Efficiency Office. The emphasis thus changed from reducing energy use to using energy more efficiently – which, as we saw in the first chapter, can encompass the use of more energy. This change was particularly helpful for the gas and electricity industries, which could now market 'efficient' use of their fuels as a means of capturing market share from each other and, hence, of selling more electricity or gas.

The major change in energy policy in the 1980s was, of course, the privatisation of the gas and electricity industries, in 1986 and 1989, respectively. Privatisation of electricity has been the most significant in several ways. First, it exposed the costs of nuclear power and made the future of the nuclear industry very uncertain. A moratorium on nuclear power development was introduced as a result. The Non Fossil Fuel Obligation (a levy on fossil fuel-generated electricity), introduced primarily to subsidise the nuclear industry, has also given a significant boost to the development of renewable energy as this too receives some subsidy under it.

Second, it has opened up competition in electricity generation and supply. This has helped the development of CHP schemes to serve industrial and many commercial users. Unlike in many other northern European countries, CHP and district heating have never been very significant in the UK. This can be seen to be due to a lack of government financial or regulatory encouragement and/or local authority involvement in energy supply (both factors that have led to CHP/district heating development in Scandinavia and some major cities in Germany, Austria and France) and a lack of interest on the part of the electricity industry which, before privatisation, was committed to the development of centralised, 'out-of-town', large-scale generation, whereas CHP tends to be decentralised and either small-scale or in town (the latter to provide district heating). Privatisation enabled industrial and commercial energy users to choose new suppliers and made it easier for them to generate their own electricity, encouraging many to examine the benefits of CHP and persuading electricity suppliers to offer to install CHP for them to retain them as customers. Privatisation also coincided with the reorganisation (in 1988) of the Combined Heat and Power Association (CHPA) to take on a much more active role of promoting the industry and lobbying government on its behalf, which has resulted in a number of changes to the regulation of the industry (including securing an amendment in the Electricity Act requiring OFFER to monitor CHP development) that have benefited CHP.

Third, this competitive market has, for a variety of reasons, encouraged many developers of new power stations to opt for gas rather than coal – in 1990 coal accounted for 65% of the fuel used for electricity generation, but by 1996 this had fallen to 44%, with gas coming from a negligible proportion in 1990 to account for 21% in 1996. This preference for gas has caused serious problems for the coal industry.

Another important factor has been the establishment of independent regulators with a clear brief to promote competition and to protect the interests of consumers. Although the industries were theoretically 'regulated' when they were nationalised, in practice ministerial intervention was patchy and *ad hoc*. Intervention was most frequently made for non-energy-related reasons (protecting jobs, for example), and ministers of both parties regularly dismissed calls for action on consumer-related issues as 'matters for the industries to decide'.

Since the late 1980s a new issue has been setting the agenda for energy policy – concern about greenhouse-gas emissions, especially carbon dioxide. The UK government signed the 1992 Rio Convention, which commits it to a target of stabilising emissions of carbon dioxide at 1990 levels by the year 2000.

The energy conservation lobby and policy community

Until 1982, it was environmental and consumer groups who took most interest in energy conservation policy. Friends of the Earth had set up projects to insulate the homes of pensioners and, during the mid-1970s, successfully lobbied the Labour government to establish insulation grants. The National Consumer Council (NCC) undertook the first independent review of the grants scheme in 1980 (National Consumer Council, 1980), and one of their key recommendations – higher grants for pensioners and disabled people – was taken on board by the Conservative government in 1981. However, such external lobbying by environmental and consumer groups was in marked contrast to the close-knit policy network of energy supply industries and the Department of Energy that had developed since the Second World War.

The energy conservation industry (manufacturers and installers of insulation materials, heating controls and so on) was represented by a number of small trade associations and was not particularly well organised or influential, and, as Dawkins (1986) has noted, William Doughty, the managing director of Cape Industries (a major insulation manufacturer at that time), proposed a new organisation to represent the industry. The Association for the Conservation of Energy (ACE) was established in autumn 1981 and by the mid-1980s had become the major lobbyist for energy conservation in the UK. This was achieved in two ways: first, by developing a close relationship with the Energy Select Committee (the official cross-party committee of the House of Commons, which itself became a part of the energy conservation lobby and produced many reports critical of the government's performance on energy conservation (Burch, 1989)); and, second, by obtaining substantial amounts of press coverage for the issue.

Dawkins (1986) acknowledged that, although ACE was successful in keeping energy conservation on the political agenda, it did not alter the basic thrust of government policy. He attributed this primarily to the power of the energy supply interests, which had much to lose if demand reduction rather than supply expansion became predominant.

There is certainly much in the vested interests argument. However, part of the problem was also ACE's failure to achieve the sort of 'insider' role that one might have expected for an industry-based body as opposed to an environmental or consumer group. The reasons for this are exactly those which made ACE the recognised leader of the energy conservation lobby – its relationship with the Energy Committee and its success in gaining widespread media attention, both of which tended to publish criticisms more than praise of the EEO. What ACE effectively did during that period was to become an outsider lobby organisation rather than an insider industry peak association.

In 1984 the various trade associations (including ACE) collaborated with the Energy Efficiency Office to establish a new 'trade associations' association' called the Buildings Energy Efficiency Confederation (BEEC). BEEC (renamed the British Energy Efficiency Federation (BEEF) in 1995) met regularly with the EEO (renamed the Energy, Environment and Waste Directorate (EEWD) in 1997, when it took on a broader environmental role in the new Department of the Environment, Transport and the Regions), though its effectiveness was, until the mid-1990s, limited. Although the trade associations felt that the meetings provided a useful dialogue with the EEO, they also expressed frustration with changes of emphasis as government priorities changed during the 1980s and early 1990s. So, while some collaboration between ACE and BEEC and the EEO developed during the 1980s and early 1990s through seminars, publications and other promotional initiatives, its limited nature meant that there was no effective policy network for energy conservation.

A new entrant to the energy conservation lobby in 1988 was, as noted earlier, the CHPA, reorganised to lobby for CHP and which took advantage of the new opportunities created by electricity privatisation. From 1988 on the CHPA developed a close and collaborative working relationship with the Department of Energy and the Department of the Environment, thus forming an effective policy network for CHP which helped to secure a limited number of beneficial changes to electricity regulation.

When the EEO was moved to the Department of the Environment after the 1992 election, ACE began to develop a closer relationship with it. The reorganisation of BEEC into BEEF also had an important effect, partly because it brought in some other trade associations (including the CHPA) who had good working relationships with the EEO/EEWD. The involvement of the Energy Saving Trust – a body which is close to the EEWD – in BEEF is helping to increase the sense of the industry working more closely with the Department and making the change from a looser policy community to a more closely knit policy network. Three policy changes in particular may owe much to this greater cohesion of the energy conservation policy community to form an effective policy network: the establishment of the Energy Saving Trust itself and the passage of the Home Energy Conservation Act 1995 (both of which are considered in detail in sections later in the chapter); and the closer liaison between the Department and members of BEEF over the advertising campaign 'Energy Efficiency', which has been run by the Energy Saving Trust since the campaign's inception in autumn 1996.

Government programmes to promote energy saving

Successive governments have, since the 1970s, run a range of information and advertising campaigns, starting with 'Save It' in the late 1970s, through to 'Monergy' in the mid-1980s and the Energy Efficiency campaign of the late 1990s. These campaigns involve television, press and point-of-sale advertising to encourage people to insulate their homes, fit low-energy light bulbs, etc. Campaigns have also targeted businesses – such as 'Making a Corporate Commitment', which encourages businesses to commit themselves to energy-saving targets. This scheme, however, has been heavily criticised for neither setting nor monitoring actual targets, in contrast to similar initiatives that have been developed in other countries.

So far as setting standards is concerned, there have been minimum insulation standards for new homes and commercial buildings in the Building Regulations since 1965, and these were raised most recently in 1996. In 1992 the government developed the Standard Assessment Procedure (SAP) for home energy rating, showing the energy efficiency of a house on a scale of 1–100. All new homes have to have a SAP energy label, but the use of energy labels for the existing housing stock has, so far, been very limited. Since the late 1980s efforts have been made through private members' bills to make the provision of energy ratings compulsory on all homes offered for sale or rent. Until 1997 this was opposed by mortgage lenders and was rejected by the last (Conservative) government as unwarranted regulation. A new private member's bill on the subject introduced in early 1998 met with more support from mortgage lenders and the new government, although so far it has failed to be adopted as law due to lack of parliamentary time.

After many years of failed attempts to introduce a national scheme, the UK has signed up to EU directives on energy labelling for household appliances. Refrigerators were the first appliances to be labelled, in January 1995; and washing machines have carried labels since April 1996. As a result of lobbying over several years by ACE and two attempts via private members' bills, the Home Energy Conservation Act was eventually passed in 1995.

Another 1990s initiative has been the Best Practice Programme, which is designed to promote case studies of energy-saving initiatives in industry, offices, schools, social housing, hospitals, etc. An important component of the programme is the promotion of CHP towards the government target of achieving 5,000 MW of CHP in the UK by 2000 (compared to 3,000 MW in 1995). A new target of 10,000 MW by 2010 was proposed by the new Labour government in 1997.

Most of these initiatives are concerned with exhortation, information and advice and, to some extent, regulation. However, several other initiatives have provided more direct incentives to save energy. In 1978 the then Labour government introduced the Home Insulation Scheme which, until 1990, provided grants for loft insulation to any household with little or no such insulation. The 1970s Labour government also provided resources to local authorities to fund insulation work in council housing, but this funding was terminated in 1980. Between 1991 and 1994 the last Conservative government ran the Green House Demonstration Programme, which funded heating and insulation improvements and CHP schemes for local authority housing.

Some help with the cost of energy-saving measures has been provided to low-income households since the late 1970s, the current scheme being the Home Energy Efficiency Scheme (HEES), introduced in January 1991 and providing grants for loft and cavity-wall insulation, draughtproofing and heating controls for people who are over 60 or in receipt of the main welfare benefits.

The grants available for loft insulation since the late 1970s seem to have had a significant effect on take-up. In 1977 only 56% of homes had any loft insulation and only 22% had 80 mm or more. By 1996, 91% of homes had some loft insulation and 64% had 80 mm or more. By comparison, cavity-wall insulation – for which there have been no grants, except under HEES since 1997 – had been installed in only 25% of homes by 1996. Double-glazing, for which there have also been no grants, but which has been heavily marketed by private sector firms, was installed in 61% of homes by 1996.

We will now look in more detail at some specific initiatives on energy conservation of the 1980s and 1990s.

National Energy Action

In the mid-1970s a few local Friends of the Earth groups set up volunteer projects to insulate the homes of pensioners using donated or reduced-price loft insulation materials and social security grants. These groups formed part of the lobby pressing for government grants for loft insulation, which were agreed in 1978. These grants, combined with the new Job Creation Programme (started in 1976), encouraged other voluntary groups and local authorities to set up insulation schemes. However, in late 1979 the instigator of one of the original Friends of the Earth projects and leader of the lobby for insulation grants, together with a local colleague and a senior staff member of the National Council for Voluntary Organisations (NCVO – a major UK non-governmental organisation), persuaded the NCVO to set up a national initiative to develop these schemes.

The NCVO secured support at first from two charitable trusts and Fibreglass Ltd (the major insulation manufacturer). After a further nine months of negotiation the Manpower Services Commission and the Department of Energy agreed to provide some support, and Neighbourhood Energy Action (NEA – renamed National Energy Action in the early 1990s) was launched in May 1981. Successive job creation schemes enabled groups to take on unemployed people to do the work and also covered running costs. Low-income clients could claim social security grants to pay for draughtproofing materials, while some of the costs of loft insulation materials could be covered by grants under the Department of the Environment's Homes Insulation Scheme.

The programme has had considerable success, and by 1997 more than two million homes had been insulated. Research conducted for the Department of Energy (Hutton *et al.*, 1985) found that about two-thirds of the benefit was taken up in improved comfort (fewer draughts and higher temperatures) as most low-income households were underheating their homes due to lack of money to afford adequate heat. In terms of energy conservation, therefore, the savings were modest, although in terms of energy efficiency (the priority of the 1980s) the benefits were much more substantial.

This example illustrates a number of themes relevant to this book. First, that the co-ordinating group (NCVO/NEA) can be regarded as a peak association for several hundred local groups around the country that is working closely with the EEO. As the government gradually withdrew most other financial incentives for energy conservation during the 1980s, this was the one area of growth (useful in response to parliamentary questions and select committee inquiries!) – and, from an ideological viewpoint, it was justifiable as market barriers could clearly be seen to be preventing low-income households from insulating their homes.

The second point is how far the lack of government co-ordination might have hindered the initiative. After all, four different government departments were involved. But, if the scheme had started off with all its funding from one department, it seems very likely that it would never – in the climate of the 1980s – have secured the level of funds (around £50 million per annum by 1988) that it did by diverting existing funds to this rather than other schemes. Once it had made itself indispensable to the government, it was much easier to secure substantial permanent funding from one source. As Heclo and Wildavsky (1981) found in their study of the Treasury, officials always try to avoid funding programmes that are small but have the potential to become large by departmental design or lack of foresight. If the Department of Energy had known or suspected that this would turn out to be such a major programme, it would have felt almost duty bound to be more cautious about supporting it.

The third point is that this is one area in which the change of emphasis from energy conservation to energy efficiency was probably beneficial. Most low-income households take up most of the benefit of insulation measures in terms of comfort rather than through any marked reduction in energy consumption. A government with a strong energy conservation objective might therefore feel that resources would be better targeted at those sectors (better-off households and businesses, for example) which would be able to save most energy.

That this network had managed to build itself up into a powerful lobby is illustrated by the fact that grants for draughtproofing were the only social security 'single payments' to be replaced by a grant when the system was changed in 1988 (single payments for other items, such as furniture, were replaced by loans). And, when the programme seemed even more threatened by changes in the job creation schemes and the abolition of loft insulation grants, pressure from NEA supported by a large number of backbench MPs of all parties led to the eventual introduction of a new system – the Home Energy Efficiency Scheme – in 1990. HEES, for the first time, brought together funding for all costs into one system.

The NEA initiative illustrates the value of having an organisation with skills not generally found in the civil service – the enthusiasm and motivation that do not sit easily with the civil service ethos of impartiality; a strongly proactive rather than a more detached analytical approach; and detailed knowledge of the subject. NEA also managed to develop a network of organisations around the country by linking up with many varied groups, something of which most civil servants have no experience.

Finally, the NEA experience shows that in the UK energy conservation has often required outside initiative to get government departments to act. It was voluntary-sector initiative (particularly in the form of a small group of highly motivated individuals) that persuaded Ministers to support the idea and brought together separate programmes run by four government departments – Energy, Environment, Employment and Health and Social Security. The NEA programme is one which almost certainly would never have been developed if left to government initiative alone. It required the active involvement of an external organisation working closely with the relevant government departments and bringing in different skills, thus forming for one area of energy conservation the type of effective policy network that had long existed for energy supply.

Efficiency of electrical appliances

Work to examine the potential for energy labelling of domestic electrical appliances was begun in the late 1970s by the Labour government. At that time the EC also did some work on energy labelling of appliances, but it was unable to reconcile the various interests. By 1987 a pilot scheme had been launched by one area electricity board and other boards were considering doing something. Secretary of State Peter Walker wanted to see the scheme extended to involve all retailers but had not had much success in persuading them. The issue received further attention from 1988 with talk of an EU-wide labelling scheme.

In 1990 the EEO commissioned some research on electrical appliances which found that efficiency could be improved by around 40% if all appliances met the standards of the best commercially available on the world market (Department of Energy, 1990). Based on experience in a number of countries, the study concluded that labelling had little influence on consumers' decisions about which appliances to buy but that, when combined with financial incentives, more efficient models became the favoured products so that retailers stopped selling less efficient models. Mandatory minimum standards would, however, achieve the most substantial change – the Californian Energy Commission estimated that minimum standards in California reduced state-wide peak demand by 4.5% (1750 MW) between 1980 and 1990.

Following publication of its report and further consultations with appliance manufacturers and consumer and environmental groups, the EEO proposed a voluntary labelling scheme under which the most efficient appliances would be awarded a label. John Wakeham, Secretary of State for Energy, said: 'we believe that a voluntary system would be more flexible and could be implemented faster' (HC 91-III, 1991: 152). Yet the Department had already spent fourteen years trying to set up a voluntary scheme!

British manufacturers have opposed the setting up of a scheme ever since those early days – publicly professing support 'in principle' but giving all sorts of reasons why it would not work in practice. Essentially, their concerns boiled down to the lower standards of many UK appliances and their fears that they would lose out to more efficient foreign models.

The voluntary scheme was launched in November 1991. Due to continued opposition from manufacturers, the EEO decided to set up the scheme with retailers instead. However, at the launch only the regional electricity companies agreed to participate in labelling all refrigerators and freezers on sale in their shops. Despite continued efforts, the EEO was unable to persuade other retailers to join the scheme or to secure the labelling of more appliances.

The EU's mandatory labelling scheme started in 1994, with the first labels appearing on fridges and freezers. Yet, if the British government had been prepared to adopt a more robust approach to the industry, the UK could have had a labelling scheme many years earlier and, in all probability, much more efficient domestically manufactured appliances. And, despite their opposition to the idea of labelling or standards, manufacturers may eventually be happier with compulsion. In evidence to the Select Committee on Energy a representative of the Consumers' Association said that, in the case of banning CFCs in aerosols, the trade associations had moved 'very quickly from arguing that it is all impossible ... to everybody trying to advertise their products not containing CFCs ... . It is very often the case that manufacturers are prepared to make these steps when they see it is a level playing field, it affects everyone equally; I think no one is prepared to make the first move because it can place them at a commercial disadvantage' (HC 91-III, 1991: 94).

The Energy Saving Trust

The prices charged by the privatised utilities for gas and electricity are controlled by the RPI-X formula set by OFGAS and OFFER. One type of cost was not initially subject to RPI-X – the purchase of gas (from the North Sea) or electricity (from power stations). These costs could be passed through to the consumer in their entirety and could therefore increase at or above the rate of RPI inflation. Energy conservation advocates said that this created a disincentive to investment in energy efficiency. The Association for the Conservation of Energy argued for a system similar to that used by the regulatory commissions in the US to encourage least-cost planning (see next chapter). In 1990 a report by ACE commissioned by OFGAS concluded that the price formula was 'an active disincentive operating on British Gas to undertake gas conservation and efficiency investments which could provide the least cost gas services to consumers' (Brown, 1990).

In autumn 1991 Sir James McKinnon, the director general of OFGAS, announced a new gas price control to operate from 1992 that would include an 'E factor' allowing 100% of the costs of approved energy efficiency projects to be passed on to gas customers. As a result of discussions between the Department of Energy (where the EEO was then based), British Gas and the regional electricity companies, the Conservative manifesto for the 1992 general election

---

6.3 Energy Saving Trust – initial schemes

- E factor condensing-boiler scheme – 10,000 rebates of £200 each.
- 20 residential CHP schemes (in social housing and nursing homes, etc.), also under the E factor.
- Autumn 1993 promotion to boost sales of low-energy light bulbs (CFLs), cutting the price by one-third with a subsidy of around £5 per lamp. 750,000 CFLs were sold during the promotion.
- Network of local energy advice centres (LEACs), funded by the DoE.

---

contained the pledge that 'Together with British Gas and some of the Regional Electricity Companies, we will establish an independent Energy Savings Trust to promote energy efficiency' (Conservative Party, 1992: 11).

In the Second Year Report on the Environment White Paper (Cm 2068, 1992), the government set out in more detail the role envisaged for the Trust, with the emphasis on the need for financial incentives to consumers. However, public expenditure constraints meant that the money would not come from the taxpayer. Instead, the government viewed the energy utilities as 'well placed to deliver such incentives'.

In June 1992 the Prime Minister signed up to the UNFCCC, which committed the UK to stabilise carbon dioxide emissions at 1990 levels by the year 2000. Based on government projections, this meant that the UK would have to achieve savings of 10 MtC (Department of Trade and Industry, 1992). In December 1992 the Secretary of State for the Environment published a discussion document (Department of the Environment, 1992) on the UK's programme for limiting emissions, which suggested that the Energy Saving Trust could deliver savings of 2–3.5 MtC funded by a levy of around 3% on household energy bills.

Sir James McKinnon had issued guidelines on the E factor in June 1992 (OFGAS, 1992), which included details of the three pilot projects approved in principle: grants for gas condensing boilers; grants to low-income owner-occupiers for efficient gas fires and water heaters; and grants to landlords (e.g. local authorities and housing associations) for residential CHP schemes. The Trust commenced work in April 1993 and four projects were launched in the first year of its existence, as detailed in box 6.3.

In November 1993 a new gas regulator, Clare Spottiswoode, was appointed and expressed concern about the level of funding required. Yet only a few weeks later the Prime Minister launched the UK's climate change strategy, which assumed that the Trust's major programmes were going to proceed: 'The Trust ... has set itself a target of achieving savings of at least 2.5 MtC by 2000 ... . The energy saving measures that will be promoted will include insulation, heating controls and cavity wall filling. These schemes ... will be launched in 1994' (Cm 2427, 1994: 21).

Spottiswoode made her concerns about the E factor public in an appearance before the Trade and Industry Select Committee, where she said that 'The E factor was introduced ... to encourage British Gas to look at saving energy where it was economic to do so, so it was looking at demand side systems, it was going to be cheaper than ... developing a new North Sea gas field ... it was not introduced in order to deal with the Government's CO_2 remit ... and yet it is being hijacked into that, in my opinion' (HC 185, 1995: 93).

At the Environment Select Committee session on 30 March 1994 Spottiswoode accused her predecessor, Sir James McKinnon, of acting illegally in authorising expenditure under the E factor that, in her view, amounted to taxation (HC 328, 1994). She had decided that the grants for gas condensing boilers would end that month and that the residential CHP scheme would finish at the end of the pilot phase in April 1995. None of the other schemes proposed by the Energy Saving Trust would be approved, but she would consider new proposals if they were consistent with her views on the purpose of the E factor. In July 1994 the Trust and British Gas submitted formal proposals to OFGAS for seven new schemes, which were all eventually rejected by OFGAS apart from one which British Gas decided not to pursue.

Spottiswoode later provided the Committee with Counsel's opinion (HC 328, 1994) which confirmed that the E factor was not a tax and, accordingly, withdrew her allegations that her predecessor had acted illegally. However, Counsel's opinion also confirmed that she had the discretion to decide that a scheme which would raise the price of gas (by however small an amount) would have an adverse effect on customers and should not proceed whatever the energy efficiency improvements it might deliver. Department of the Environment and Department of Trade and Industry officials confirmed (HC 328, 1994) that it was within the discretion of the director general not to allow expenditure. The government had no way of compelling her to act differently and so would have to fund the Trust itself or introduce new primary legislation.

Professor Stephen Littlechild, director general of OFFER, approved £100 million (£1 per customer per year) under the supply price control Standards of Performance (SoP) scheme for energy efficiency projects from 1994 to 1998 and a further £50 million in 1998–2000. He too, however, has been less willing to provide funding than Ministers had hoped. Littlechild announced the results of his review of the distribution price control in August 1994: 'if the required level of expenditure were to be substantially greater [than that allowed for under supply] ... it would raise issues more appropriately dealt with through general fiscal policy rather than through price control mechanisms proposed by a regulator. I have concluded therefore that it would not be appropriate for me to propose any further allowance for specific expenditure on energy efficiency projects ... ' (OFFER, 1994: 33).

Following the Select Committee sessions with Spottiswoode in early 1994, the Trust and others in the energy conservation lobby put pressure on the government either to require OFGAS to implement a levy for energy efficiency or to provide funds itself. A key focus for lobbying was the Gas Bill, which was introduced in the 1994–95 session of parliament to open up competition in gas supply to all customers. However, when the Gas Bill was published in March 1995 it contained no reference to a levy or to the Energy Saving Trust.

Early in 1995 the Trust told the Environment Select Committee that, on current financial projections, it would be unlikely to deliver emission cuts of more than 0.3 MtC, as opposed to the 2.5 MtC originally envisaged (HC 229, 1995). However, government projections of CO_2 emissions published in March 1995 confirmed that even without action by the Trust emissions in 2000 would be below the 1990 level of 160 MtC because of greater use of gas and nuclear power for electricity generation than had been envisaged when the last projections were published in 1992. Thus, the last Conservative government no longer felt that it needed the Trust to the extent that it did back in 1992. The Rio target would be comfortably met without the Trust and there was no pressure to look beyond the year 2000 – particularly as many countries, unlike the UK, would not even meet the 2000 stabilisation target.

> **6.4 Energy Saving Trust – targets and spending**
>
> - Original target: 2.5–3 MtC reduction in emissions by 2000
> - Original spending envisaged for 1993–2000: £1.5 billion
> - Likely target (1998 estimate): 1 MtC reduction in emissions by 2000
> - Likely spending in 1993–2000: £300 million.

Some comfort for the Trust came in May 1995 when the government announced that it would provide it with £25 million in 1996–97, £15 million in 1997–98 and £10 million in 1998–99. The funding for 1997–98 and 1998–99 was subsequently increased to £19 million. However, this was well below the original expectations of the Trust, as box 6.4 shows.

The Trust still has an important, albeit very different, role from that originally envisaged and has managed to run a wide range of programmes since 1995. A key role has been running the major national advertising and promotional campaign 'Energy Efficiency' for the government – a new departure for the government, which has previously run such initiatives (e.g. Save It and Monergy) itself. Energy Efficiency was launched in late 1996 and continues under the new Labour government. Another area of activity for the Trust has included promoting the development of energy services companies (ESCOs), which package energy efficiency and energy supply to customers. Other activities are detailed in box 6.5.

The history of the Energy Saving Trust raises some important issues about the role of the regulators and the government. It shows how government action can be frustrated if it has to rely on the co-operation of key actors whom it cannot control. This lack of control was, of course, something which the government deliberately created when the utility regulators were established, with great stress being put on their independence.

It is worth noting, however, that the government does control who is appointed as a regulator. When Spottiswoode was interviewed for the job the issues of gas competition were discussed in detail and it is inconceivable that someone who was not sympathetic to the government approach would have been appointed. Energy conservation, the environment and the Energy Saving Trust were not discussed, but, clearly, if the government felt strongly about them

---

6.5 Energy Saving Trust – activities since 1995

Programmes continuing or launched since 1995 include:

- Local energy advice centres
- The E factor residential CHP scheme made further grants during 1995–97
- Electricity SoP schemes – subsidies for low-energy light bulbs, storage heaters for low-income pensioners and other energy efficiency projects in homes, schools and small businesses
- Supporting local authorities in the implementation of the Home Energy Conservation Act 1995
- Promotion of efficient domestic appliances and office equipment.

---

it could have appointed a director general of OFGAS who was sympathetic to an approach similar to McKinnon's.

The government even passed by an opportunity to partially remedy the problem during the passage of the Gas Act 1995. The Earl of Cranbrook (a Conservative and then Chairman of a countryside quango, English Nature) proposed that the Act empower the Minister to give guidance on sustainable development to the OFGAS director general, but the government rejected this suggestion. Furthermore, the Gas Act 1995 makes a sharp contrast between the duty concerning competition and those relating to energy saving and the environment. The duty concerning efficient use of gas is secondary to the primary duties and requires the director general only to 'promote' it. Competition was made one of the primary duties, and the director general is required to 'secure' effective competition rather than to promote it or take it into account.

One of the government's reasons for privatising the industries and putting them under the supervision of regulators was to remove the temptations to Ministers to use them to realise other policies (social, employment, etc.), but the ambitions of the government for the Energy Saving Trust appeared to the regulators like attempts to use the industries to raise levies for environmental purposes, as opposed to raising the money through taxation. In the end, though, the issue was not so much about the principle of who should impose a levy as about the politics of taxes on energy consumers. For the government, the attraction of E factor-type levies was that they were not taxation and would not count as public spending. The furore over the introduction of VAT on domestic fuel meant that the idea of the government legislating for a specific levy on fuel bills to fund a CO_2-reduction programme was a non-starter, as too was any thought that either of the two main opposition parties would seriously advocate such a proposal.

The Home Energy Conservation Act 1995

The passage of the Home Energy Conservation Act illustrates the successes that can be achieved by an effective lobby in a climate which does not initially look very hopeful. The Act requires local authorities to prepare reports to the Secretary of State on the energy efficiency of all housing in their area, identify how significant energy savings could be made and estimate the reductions in CO_2 emissions that would result. The Act also requires the Secretary of State to set a timetable for implementation.

The Act had its origins in a ten-minute rule bill on energy conservation introduced in the 1992–93 parliamentary session. The bill failed due to lack of parliamentary time, but it attracted widespread support among MPs and from the Association for the Conservation of Energy, which began a campaign to persuade consumer and environmental organisations and local authorities to support it. The Liberal Democrat MP Alan Beith adopted the Energy Conservation Bill as a private member's bill in the 1993–94 session. Meanwhile, ACE secured support from organisations including the Gas Consumers Council, Friends of the Earth, Age Concern and many other environmental and consumer groups. All three local authority associations and 150 individual local authorities gave their support – which was crucial because it was on local authorities that the responsibility for implementation would fall.

In February 1994 the bill completed its committee stage without opposition. However, at the report stage the government proposed 216 amendments and 7 new clauses, effectively sabotaging it by making it run out of parliamentary time. The reason why the government was so opposed to the bill was never made clear, although there were a number of theories. One was that the government was concerned that, if effective, the bill would hit the revenues of the privatised electricity companies – and this was of particular concern in view of the government's intention to sell its remaining 40% share in National Power and Power Gen in March 1995. Another was the concern that local authorities would use the bill to lobby for extra resources to implement the energy-saving plans.

In November 1994 the Liberal Democrats devoted an opposition day debate to the bill. On this occasion the government tabled an amendment to the Liberal Democrat motion stating that the House 'deplores the proposals in the Energy Conservation Bill which would impose unnecessary burdens on public expenditure as well as on central and local government' (HC Debates, 1.11.94, col. 1362). The government's motion suggested an even tougher stance by Ministers, who had, until then, at least expressed support for the bill's aims. The occasion was particularly difficult for the Parliamentary Under Secretary of State for the Environment, Robert Jones, who, while chairman of the Environment Select Committee, had been one of the bill's sponsors. Jones had to respond to the later stages of the debate and support the government line that compulsion was unnecessary and undesirable.

The government's majority in the House of Commons meant that its amendment was carried. However, Liberal Democrat MP Diana Maddock introduced a slightly amended version in December 1994. Once again, the bill had cross-party support, with five Conservatives among its twelve sponsors. This time the bill's supporters were to meet with much more success. Despite the fact that he had had to take the government line in the November 1994 debate, junior Environment Minister Robert Jones proved to be helpful and supportive and, in June 1995, the bill passed through its third reading and an implementation date of April 1996 was agreed.

Why did this bill eventually succeed? Success was due in no small part to the enormous range of support, both within and outside the House of Commons, that ACE's lobbying efforts had managed to build up. ACE's increasingly positive relationships with the EEO since 1992 also helped. Officials in the Department of the Environment regarded the bill as a positive initiative and so were supportive of Robert Jones, the relevant Minister, who had been a sponsor of the earlier bill. Also crucial, however, was the fact that it was never very clear why the government was opposing the bill in the first place as it was a relatively modest measure with no immediate significant public expenditure implications. Concerns for local authority independence did not, as Alan Beith put it, sit very well with government moves since 1979 to increase central government control over local authorities. Some within the government would no doubt have disliked it as one more interventionist measure when the government was committed to deregulation. In the Treasury there was almost certainly concern that the reports produced would reveal poor levels of energy efficiency that would provide useful ammunition to those lobbying for more resources. However, in the end it was probably the case that those against the bill within the government were not so strongly opposed, whereas its supporters were strongly in favour and thus had a good opportunity to wear down the opposition by promising to keep putting the bill forward at every session until it was adopted.

Will the market deliver energy efficiency ?

The approach of the government, Spottiswoode and Littlechild, from 1994 on was to emphasise the opportunities for energy efficiency when the energy markets are fully liberalised in 1998. In mid-1994 the Energy Saving Trust commissioned research into the extent to which suppliers were offering and customers requesting energy efficiency packages in those markets already open to competition – industrial and commercial users. The survey (Owen, 1994) found that few suppliers offered such energy services and that few customers asked for them. Most customers were looking for, and most suppliers were offering, reductions in the unit price of gas and electricity. Further research (Owen and King, 1997) found little change on the customer side but that suppliers were more likely to offer a range of services to customers (even when asked only about supply) than they were in 1994. The main development has been electricity companies offering CHP to retain valuable industrial/commercial customers who would otherwise switch to other suppliers that do offer CHP. Many of the suppliers interviewed felt that competing solely on price was not a sensible long-term commercial strategy as margins were now being squeezed tighter and tighter.

However, the 1997 report concluded that energy services competition is still a tiny part of the energy market and that it remains fragile owing to low energy prices and continuing expectations by customers that energy prices will fall further. In the household sector the outlook is not at all encouraging as by autumn 1998 no suppliers had developed energy services packages even though a number have talked of doing so.

Conclusion

Although limited attempts have been made to conserve energy at times of crisis (e.g. the coal shortages of the late 1940s and the oil crisis of 1973), the main emphasis of government policy in the United Kingdom – whichever party is in power – has been to increase supply and to keep fuel prices as low as possible.

During the late 1970s, as fuel prices increased, governments introduced some initiatives to promote energy conservation. However, in the 1980s fuel prices fell in real terms as North Sea oil came on stream, and the emphasis shifted to energy efficiency rather than energy conservation. The emphasis of energy efficiency on benefits to the individual household or business (lower bills, a warmer home, greater productivity for each pound spent on fuel) chimed much more with the ideology of economic agents acting in their own interest than did energy conservation (using less fuel) in the national or public interest. This change in terminology was more than semantic and was symptomatic of a firmly non-interventionist approach.

In 1983, for example, in evidence to the Commons Energy Committee, a Department of Energy official said: 'if the state were to decide to subsidise energy conservation investment ... the extent to which investment would occur which otherwise would not have taken place would be difficult to measure' (HC 310, 1983). In 1990 the message was much the same: 'Energy efficiency measures are by definition in the economic interests of energy consumers ... . The Government therefore starts from the proposition that consumers do not need subsidy, regulation or financial incentive or penalty ... as long as the market is working properly' (HC 91-I, 1990).

Intervention was thus seen as a last resort, although grants for loft insulation introduced by the Labour government in 1978 were retained until 1988 for all households and until 1990 for low-income households. The Conservative government introduced the Home Energy Efficiency Scheme in 1990 to enable low-income households to continue to receive help with loft insulation and draughtproofing. Subsidies therefore came increasingly to be seen as necessary only for low-income households.

In the early 1990s there seemed to be a change of view with the publication of the Environment White Paper (Cm 1200, 1990) and the subsequent annual progress reports. 'In the past, the Government has concentrated on providing information ... ; but it is unlikely that information programmes by themselves will realise the full scope for savings. ... financial incentives to consumers to improve their energy efficiency provide the way forward' (Cm 2068, 1992). This quote is in sharp contrast to the statement made to the Energy Select Committee only two years earlier. Nor did it seem that these concerns were limited to a 'ghetto' of an environmental report. In the first Annual Energy Report, published as a follow-up to a commitment given in the 1993 Coal Review White Paper (Cm 2235, 1993), it was stated that 'The Government's energy policies are founded on the underlying policy concerns of improving UK competitiveness and achieving sustainable development' (Department of Trade and Industry, 1994). Yet the Energy Saving Trust and Gas Act episodes suggest that government policy in 1992–96 did not really take on the environmental imperative and that, where a choice had to be made between the environment and competition, the latter was considered more important.

When the Department of Energy was abolished after the 1992 general election, energy efficiency and conservation (including CHP) became the responsibility of the Department of the Environment, but the rest of the DoE's remit was transferred to the Department of Trade and Industry. Energy conservation had always been the Cinderella of the Energy Department against the much larger divisions devoted to each of the energy supply options – coal, gas, oil, electricity – which formed effective policy networks with their relevant industries. Ironically, once these industries had been largely privatised and their departmental divisions shrunk in size, energy conservation stood its best chance ever of becoming a more important and central part of the Department's focus, with probably much more potential for developing a close-knit policy network between the Department and conservation interests. The difficulty after 1992 for energy conservation is that since then the DTI has been largely responsible for energy policy – for example, although CHP is a responsibility of the Department of the Environment, Transport and the Regions, much of the action required to promote CHP development tends to be in the area of gas and electricity regulation, which come under the DTI and the energy regulators. OFGAS and OFFER receive their funding from and mainly relate to the DTI – creating the opportunity for the development of a new energy supply- and competition-orientated policy network. An indication that such a network has indeed formed is the low priority given to energy efficiency and conservation in the appointment of a new OFGAS director general in 1993 and in the Gas Act 1995.

In the lead-up to the Kyoto conference in December 1997 the new Labour government committed itself to a more demanding target to reduce CO_2 emissions to 20% below 1990 levels by the year 2010 and promised more action to promote energy efficiency. The fact that the new Department of the Environment, Transport and the Regions is headed by the Deputy Prime Minister may also be a positive omen. However, in autumn 1998 it remained to be seen whether the rhetoric would be translated into significantly more action.

7

The United States

Political and institutional background

There are two key features of the US political system that funda-
mentally affect the policy process. The first is its federal nature,
whereby responsibilities are shared between the federal government
and the fifty state governments, both of which can legislate their own
policies and programmes. This means that there can be considerable
differences between states in terms of the policies adopted on social,
economic, environmental and many other matters.

Second, at both the federal and state level there is a separation of
powers between the executive/administration (President/Governor)
and legislative (Congress) arms of government. The Administration
may propose policies and programmes, but these will have to be
approved by the Congress where changes in the law are required or
if there is a need to set or renew a budget appropriation. Congress
may also initiate policies itself, but these can be vetoed by the
President.

As a result of the separation of powers at federal level it is often
very difficult to initiate new policies due to the failure to get agreement between the President and Congress. Such policy stalemates
happen particularly when there is Republican President but a
Democrat-dominated Congress or vice versa. The autonomy of the
states also means that policies may differ significantly between them,
and this – combined with differing economies and resources – can
make for very different interests between the States, which helps to
feed the stalemate in Congress.

Another important feature of the US system, which probably
derives in large extent from the existence of a diffuse decision-
making system, is the importance of lobbying by a wide range of

special or state interests and the importance of opinion polls in influencing policymaking. It is also worth noting that it can be easier (or at least seem easier) for ordinary citizens to influence the policy process than in many other countries – because of this diffuse decision-making process Congress members may be more susceptible to pressure than many MPs in the UK, for example. The greater openness of many processes (e.g. regulatory commissions hold utility rate-setting hearings in public and utilities are required to put virtually all information in the public domain) also means that there are many more opportunities to influence decision-making than in countries such as the UK where such processes take place largely in private between regulators and the industries they regulate.

Unlike in many European countries (particularly the UK) and Japan, the permanent civil service in the US is of lesser importance in the development of policy owing to the widespread system of political appointments of senior staff in government departments who remain only while their party is in power. The permanent civil service is, in general, of a lower status and tends to be more concerned with implementation, whereas the political appointees have the key roles in policy development. This, therefore, tends to increase the opportunities for interest groups to lobby the Executive – and indeed to influence who is appointed to some of the key positions.

Structure of the energy market

Most of the energy industries are in the private sector although the federal government owns a substantial proportion of the nation's oil and gas resources.

Gas production is carried out by the major private sector oil and gas companies and 10,000 smaller producers. Private sector companies own and operate 23 major interstate pipelines. Local distribution/supply is on the basis of monopoly franchises for over 1,000 municipal companies and 100 private sector companies, but the latter cover all the major urban areas and account for 95% of gas sold.

The electricity industry consists primarily of vertically integrated private sector (investor-owned utilities – IOUs) companies which own generation, transmission and distribution/supply facilities. To date (1998) these have largely operated on the basis of service territories or monopoly franchises for specific areas, although there has

7.1 Key actors in the US energy policy community

Government departments
Department of Energy

Regulatory bodies
Federal Energy Regulatory Commission (FERC)
Environmental Protection Agency (EPA)

State governments
Public utility commissions
California Public Utility Commission

Gas industry – private sector oil and gas companies produce gas and operate interstate gas pipelines; distribution/supply by monopoly franchises, 95% of which are private sector companies, remainder are run by local authorities.

Electricity industry – mainly vertically integrated generation, transmission, distribution/supply by private sector monopoly franchises. Some competition in generation. Supply being opened to competition late 1990s/2000s.

Industry lobby group
Global Climate Coalition

Environmental lobby group
Rocky Mountain Institute

been some inter-utility and interstate trade in generation. The IOUs own almost three-quarters of the US's installed capacity and produce more than three-quarters of the electricity sold to retail customers. The remainder of the electricity supply is owned and operated by the federal government, local authorities or a few rural co-operatives.

The regulatory commissions, which regulate energy, water and transport utilities, have been in existence for several decades. The California Public Utilities Commission (CPUC), for example, traces its history back to the Railroad Commission established by an amendment to the state constitution in 1911. It became the CPUC and embraced other utilities in 1946. The commissions see their duty as balancing the interests of consumers of monopoly services with those of the shareholders in the utilities. The commissions set the prices that the utilities are allowed to charge customers and the rate of return they are allowed to earn, regulate service standards and monitor safety.

The first attempts to introduce competition into the energy market were made under the Public Utility Regulatory Policies Act, 1978 (PURPA). Non-utilities were permitted to enter the wholesale generation market without being subject to the rate regulation applied to utilities provide that they used either cogeneration or small-scale generation, including renewables. Utilities were obliged to purchase the output from such facilities located within their franchise areas, usually at the avoided cost of the most competitive alternative source of supply. As a result of PURPA, the number of non-utility generators grew rapidly during the 1980s and early 1990s, although by 1994 they still accounted for only 7% of installed capacity. By the early 1990s this development had begun to slow down and it was recognised that further action would be required to encourage greater competition in the energy market.

The Energy Policy Act, which became law in October 1992, was designed to provide such a stimulus to competition. First, it lifts remaining ownership restrictions on power generation, thus giving affiliates of utilities new powers to develop generation (a similar concession to that offered to non-utilities under PURPA), provided that they do not sell electricity to a corporate utility affiliate without prior approval of the relevant public utilities commissions (PUCs). Second, it increases the power of the Federal Energy Regulatory Commission (FERC) to require utilities to provide third-party access (retail wheeling) for other generators to their grid system, even where this would mean that the grid had to be expanded.

At federal level, it is only on oil for domestic use that any tax is applied outside the transport fuels sector – and this only represents 5% of the final price of oil to consumers. There is no VAT or general consumption tax in the US, although general sales taxes of between 2 and 6% are applied to gas and electricity prices in some states. Furthermore, there have been and continue to exist a number of energy-related tax credits and exemptions for energy production and production-related investment, which help to encourage the energy supply side and keep prices down.

Prices of gas and electricity sold to consumers are regulated by the state PUCs on a rate-of-return basis. However, in their use of incentives for DSM (see below) many of the PUCs have attempted to tip the balance in favour of energy conservation investment.

US energy policy since the Second World War

The federal government has had a role in some aspects of energy policy since the First World War and the 1920s – in minerals leasing, taxation, anti-trust law and foreign oil policy. However, it was the Second World War that led to more substantial government intervention (in particular, to secure oil supplies to industry and the war effort) and which paved the way for post-war energy policy.

Although a Coal Commission had been set up just before the war to regulate the industry, its authority was allowed to lapse during the war as the coal industry was felt to be settling down following years of problems and decline. The Federal Power Commission (FPC) was formed in 1928 to regulate electricity transmission, and in 1938 the Natural Gas Act extended its remit to include interstate trade and transportation of gas, but not pricing for local distribution and supply.

In 1947 the National Petroleum Council became the successor to the Petroleum Industry War Council to provide data and make policy recommendations to the Secretary of the Interior. The Council was a forum for oil industry leaders to meet and discuss public policy issues among themselves and with key officials of the federal departments involved in matters likely to affect the industry. As Vietor (1984: 38) notes: 'the Council's quarterly meetings in Washington, and those of its committees, provided opportunities for consensus building, within the industry and between business and government'. The Council's power derived largely from its control of information on which the Interior Department was dependent – according to Vietor, this was the only source of expert analysis that Congress and the government had for making decisions about post-war energy policy. The existence of the Council thus obviated the need for an energy department – the oil and gas division of the Interior Department remained small, its staff were usually recommended by the Council and it had no power other than that it derived from the Council.

By the 1950s the US had large established private sector coal, oil and gas industries and a developing private sector nuclear industry. All were and continue to be regulated to some extent by federal and state governments (the latter via regulatory commissions) and all have developed and maintained relationships with relevant government departments and regulators. However, there was no strong sense of an overall energy policy – more of relevant government bodies having policies relating to the fuels with which they were concerned.

From the late 1940s until the early 1970s energy demand grew far more rapidly in the United States than in most other industrialised countries. Between 1946 and 1968 the population increased by 43% and gross national product by 59%, but the production of electrical appliances increased by 1,040% and of air conditioner units by 2,850% (Rosenbaum, 1981). By the mid-1970s the US consumed one-third of the world's total energy production but had only 6% of the world's population.

Prior to the 1973 oil crisis, the US had no central energy department and no effective means of co-ordinating the work of the plethora of agencies and departments involved in energy policy. Energy policy had, in effect, been developed by small, fuel-specific policy networks of government departments, agencies and the energy industries, with the industries (as we saw earlier in this chapter) often taking the lead role in the running and staffing of key agencies. By the early 1970s responsibility for energy policy was split between about sixty departments and agencies, including the Interior Department, the FPC, the National Petroleum Council, the Federal Energy Administration, the Atomic Energy Commission and the Environmental Protection Agency. In 1973 President Nixon proposed a Department of Energy and Natural Resources; however, there was considerable dispute between the government, Congress, business and the growing environmental lobby over the form that reorganisation should take, so reform was limited to establishing the Energy Research and Development Administration (ERDA).

When Carter came to power in 1976 he had already proposed a Department of Energy, and frustration with the inability of the existing structures to develop effective energy policies had grown to such an extent that Congress passed the Act required to set up the Department in August 1977. The new Department of Energy combined most of the Interior Department's energy development responsibilities with those of the ERDA, the Federal Energy Administration and the FPC. The Department was also given a responsibility for energy conservation which, from the start, included the idea of using energy more efficiently as well as reducing its use. Two quasi-independent agencies were brought under the Department's umbrella: the Energy Information Administration, to provide energy data from independent sources so that government would no longer have to rely

exclusively on industry; and the Economic Regulatory Administration to control gas imports and enforce oil price regulations.
The FPC was renamed the Federal Energy Regulatory Commission
(FERC) and was constituted as a near-autonomous agency under the
umbrella of the Department.

Apart from during the Second World War and in the couple of
years immediately after, the US had no experience of energy shortages prior to 1973. The post-war problems of oil shortages were
short-lived, and by the middle of 1948 oil, coal and gas were becoming plentiful and cheap. A range of initiatives were introduced by the
Nixon, Ford and Carter administrations in the 1970s to reduce
dependence on oil, with varying degrees of effectiveness. Nixon
introduced some rules on energy saving in federal offices and banned
large power plants from burning natural gas or oil if they had the
capacity to use coal instead – although in fact no such conversions
were achieved. Ford attempted to impose various taxes on energy
and to deregulate prices (which would have led to increases) to
reduce demand, but both of these moves were rejected by Congress
as a potential burden on consumers, particularly the poor. During
both the Nixon and Ford administrations some tax credits and other
subsides for energy conservation measures, such as home insulation,
were also introduced.

Oil imports had begun to increase as early as the 1950s, with
domestic production unable to meet demand. By the time of the
1973 oil crisis the US was using oil for nearly 45% of its total energy
needs, and about one-third of the oil used was imported. Prior to
1973 energy prices in the US, particularly of electricity, were low by
international standards. The utilities were relatively unconstrained in
the development of new capacity and in moves to increase sales of
electricity. So neither consumers nor utilities had any interest in
energy conservation.

When Carter came to power oil and gas prices were still low and
consumption was rising in all sectors. Carter's television addresses to
the people exhorting them to save energy, describing energy conservation as the 'moral equivalent of war', were initially very successful
largely because so much energy was being wasted through behaviour
that could be changed with no serious effect on lifestyles and the fact
that there was a sense of national crisis due particularly to petrol
shortages and huge price rises in a country that is so dependent on
the car. At that stage the emphasis was on reducing unnecessary

7.2 Carter's National Energy Plan

Proposals included:

- incentives for insulation and solar heating, such as tax credits for the better off and grants for the poor
- regulatory exemptions and tax credits for CHP
- a mandatory coal-conversion programme
- reform of the utilities – with the aims of diversifying the nation's energy supplies, developing the use of indigenous renewable energy sources, encouraging competition in the electricity market and promoting energy conservation.

wastage, for example by turning lights off in empty rooms and offices, turning down thermostats and switching off outdoor lighting.

However, Carter's National Energy Plan met with a rather more mixed reception. Many of the proposals outlined in box 7.2 were accepted by Congress (albeit on a more modest level than proposed), but it refused to support Carter's proposals for various tax penalties. One key part of the plan that was adopted was the utility reform proposals, which became the 1978 Public Utilities Regulatory Policy Act referred to earlier.

In the late 1990s the main responsibility for energy policy in the federal government is vested in the Secretary of State for Energy and the Department of Energy (DOE), which runs federal energy efficiency programmes. The Federal Energy Regulatory Commission (FERC) is a DOE agency responsible for certain regulatory functions in relation to electricity, natural gas and oil. Several other departments have a role in energy policy. These include the Department of State, which leads on international energy matters; the Department of Justice, which is responsible for anti-trust laws; and the Environmental Protection Agency, which sets environmental standards for the energy industries.

Energy conservation programmes from the mid-1970s to the mid-1980s

Energy labelling of appliances and minimum standards began in a number of US states in the mid-1970s in response to the 1973 oil crisis. Mandatory energy labelling was introduced nationwide in

1975, and the first state to set minimum standards for appliances was California which, in 1978 introduced them for refrigerators. California subsequently introduced further minimum standards for other appliances and a number of other states followed suit during the late 1970s and early 1980s. National standards were introduced following the National Appliance Conservation Act 1987 (see below).

As a result, the efficiency of domestic appliances in the US has increased significantly since the early 1970s. By 1985 new refrigerators, for example, used on average half the energy of those available in 1975 – average annual consumption being 1726 kWh in 1975 and 930 kWh in 1985 – despite being, on average, larger in capacity. This reversed a trend from 1947 to 1972 for the electricity consumption of refrigerators to increase due to growth in capacity and new features such as automatic defrost. However, the number of refrigerators sold in the US also grew by 33% over the same period (Rosenfeld and Price, 1992).

During the late 1970s and throughout most of the 1980s there was a range of programmes to support energy conservation. These included the Residential Conservation Service, in which a mixture of federal, state, oil-overcharge and utility funds were used to help subsidise energy conservation investments by householders and the Weatherization Assistance Program for Low Income Households. The history of the oil-overcharge funds is that, in response to the Arab oil embargo, the US government imposed price controls on crude oil and petroleum products from 1973 to 1981. In the early 1980s a number of successful law suits were filed against Exxon, Amoco and other oil companies for overcharging during that era. These suits yielded large refunds, which were distributed to state governments for use in ways that would return benefits to consumers who had paid higher energy costs during those years. Of the total $5.7 billion received by 1986, $3.2 billion went to the states for energy conservation programmes.

In the industrial sector programmes included grants and loans and advice provided under the Waste Energy Recovery Program, the Co-generation Program and the Improved Energy Productivity Program for energy-intensive industries.

Support for energy conservation by the Administration declined from 1980 onwards despite a tendency for Congress to boost funding. State and local governments, the utilities and private sector firms were contributing larger and larger proportions of funding – a trend which the Administration supported in line with its policy of relying largely on the operation of the market to bring about gains in efficiency. The new approach symbolised the shift from energy conservation (appropriate in an era of high prices and concerns about energy security) to energy efficiency (with lower energy prices and few worries about energy supply, the emphasis was on economic and other benefits to the consumer).

A number of decisions taken by the Administration in 1985 and 1986 highlighted this new approach. First, at the end of 1985 the tax-credit programmes for residential energy conservation investment were ended. Second, an internal Administration decision in October 1986 increased the allowable level of heating and lowered the allowable level of cooling in federal buildings. Finally, in November 1986 the President refused to sign and, hence, vetoed a bill to set nationwide standards for domestic appliances on the grounds that this would deny consumers the choice of the cheapest appliances. As in the UK, this veto owed much to lobbying from appliance manufacturers, who were afraid of losing sales or having to alter production capacity to meet the new standards.

However, the National Appliance Conservation Act was eventually passed in 1987 after gaining all-party and industry support. It provided for minimum efficiency standards to be set and updated for a range of appliances and followed on from the energy labelling of appliances that has been required since the late 1970s. The 1987 Act required the government to review energy conservation standards for twelve types of household appliance, including refrigerators, freezers, washing machines, dishwashers, air-conditioners, ovens, dryers and heat pumps. The first actual standards were set in 1989. In May 1991 the DOE set stricter standards for dishwashers, washing machines and dryers, and further strengthening of these and other standards has taken place since 1992 under the Energy Policy Act. As a result, US appliances tend to equal or better the best European standards in unit energy consumption terms, although most US homes still use far more energy on appliances than those in Europe due to lifestyle factors (more and bigger appliances). Most notably, US fridges are, on average, twice the size of those in European homes.

In the early 1990s efficiency standards for light bulbs and light fittings were introduced. The Department of Energy also sets energy efficiency standards for new residential and commercial buildings, which are mandatory for federally owned buildings and provide a basis for state and local governments to incorporate energy require-ments into their own building codes. Every state has some such provision in its codes.

The development of demand-side management

The oil price rises and the Arab oil embargo led to significant increases in electricity prices after many years of low and stable prices. Furthermore, since the late 1970s many electricity utilities in the US had been faced with the prospect of capacity shortfalls and the need to construct new power stations. However, public hostility to new power stations (particularly nuclear) had grown, making it increasingly difficult to build them and putting up the costs. A number of regulatory commissions, spurred on by lobbying from environmental activists, began to suggest that utilities might find it cheaper to invest in measures to cut demand for electricity rather than build new power stations.

These factors motivated states such as California and Massa-chusetts, which were particularly dependent on imported oil for electricity generation, to examine energy conservation methods. The environmental movement was thus on fertile ground in arguing that large power stations were costly and environmentally undesirable. While the states and the federal government introduced various measures to promote energy conservation, many state regulatory commissions, particularly in California, realised that they would have to change the nature of energy utilities to bring about substan-tial changes in energy use.

In the mid-1970s California set up the California Energy Com-mission (CEC), which worked with the California Public Utilities Commission to set spending targets for energy conservation and load management for the state's four investor-owned utilities. By imposing penalties for not meeting the targets, the CPUC and CEC were able to induce substantial activity by the four utilities, whose expenditure on energy conservation peaked at around $160 million per annum in 1984.

However, as oil prices fell in the early 1980s and the easy energy savings had been achieved, and with a change to a federal adminis-tration that was less enthusiastic about environmental matters than the Carter Administration, enthusiasm for California-type initiatives waned. Yet, within the regulatory bodies and among environmentalists interest was maintained and the concerns about costs and planning restrictions on new capacity remained. The leading environmental campaigner was Amory Lovins, who had set up a research group called the Rocky Mountain Institute, based in Colorado, to propound the concept of the 'negawatt' – which translated the value of energy conservation measures into the equivalent of megawatts not consumed. From small beginnings in the early 1980s, Lovins' message became more and more widely accepted – although, as Sioshansi (1996) has observed, few people could understand the economics of his calculations, which purported to show that it was cheaper to save a negawatt than to generate a megawatt and even, as his theory developed, that negawatts were 'not just a free lunch, but one you are paid to eat'.

Lovins and other environmental groups gained increasing influence with the regulatory bodies, who were looking for ways to encourage the utilities to continue their 1970s energy conservation efforts – particularly to help avoid the need for new power stations. However, the regulators were up against a formidable problem in that the electricity utilities said that energy conservation (despite Lovins' negawatt concept) was not an economic option for them.

California still led the way and the CEC began to explore whether DSM could be made attractive for utilities through changes to the incentives and disincentives set by regulators. The main problems were that the utilities would lose income if they sold fewer kilowatt-hours and they would have to spend money on planning and running DSM programmes that offered risk but no reward for shareholders as such investment would not be added to the asset base on which the regulators calculated allowed rates of return. A key factor in getting the regulators to recognise the problem was the development of collaboration between environmental and public interest groups and the utilities to make the case both for the removal of disincentives and for the provision of rewards to utilities that engaged in DSM activity.

The solution identified by CEC and CPUC was to make utility profits less dependent on the numbers of units sold and to enable the utilities to earn profits on DSM activity. A further spur to activity is that many states have required utilities to carry out integrated resource planning – to produce resource plans comparing supply-

---

7.3 DSM facts and figures

- In 1993, 439 utilities spent $2.8 billion on DSM measures aimed at promoting energy saving, while customers spent an additional $1 billion (Hadley and Hirst, 1995). Average expenditure was around 1.5% of utility operating revenue, but some utilities spent as much as 12%.
- In 1993, 44,000 GWh was saved and peak demand was cut by 40,000 MW (Boyle, 1995a).
- By early 1994, 18.6 million residential customers, 730,000 commercial and 144,000 industrial customers had been involved in DSM programmes (Hirst *et al*. 1995).
- By 1994, 26 states had introduced some form of incentive or had removed disincentives for utilities to undertake DSM activities and a further 11 states were considering such action.

---

and demand-side options – and a number of states have been looking seriously at how to internalise external environmental costs of electricity generation and transmission. Where states had not already adopted IRP, the 1992 Energy Policy Act required the public utilities commissions to consider introducing it.

DSM has thus been seen as a triumph for the cause of energy efficiency and the environment, enabling hundreds of millions of dollars to be spent on insulation, upgrading heating systems, subsidising the costs of low-energy lighting and efficient appliances, etc., leading to significant savings in power consumption or in peak demand where demand has been shifted from peak to off-peak, and hence enabling investment in new capacity to be postponed or cancelled. Many (particularly the more recent) US schemes have achieved significant verified energy savings and/or reductions in peak demand. There are environmental benefits to the energy savings achieved and gains in social welfare from schemes targeted at low-income customers. However, questions have been raised since the early 1990s about the practice and effects of DSM by the utilities. Among these are:

- That the claims for energy savings, particularly in the early schemes, were often exaggerated, poorly monitored and rarely verified (Joskow and Marron, 1992 and 1993). This problem tended to decrease over time as the regulatory commissions required more evidence of the benefits (Boyle, 1995a).

- That insufficient attention was given to the 'free-rider effect' (people who would have made the investment without the subsidy), which may have been substantial in many programmes.
- That as DSM measures were often given away (or very large subsidies used), they were often taken up by households which had limited potential to make energy savings (London Economics, 1994). Again, this problem tended to diminish over time as the regulators required greater justification for the use of subsidies (Boyle, 1995a).
- That many of the programmes run by the utilities were costly and inefficient. Indeed, the utilities had every incentive to make the schemes as costly as possible given that they were allowed to add the costs to their capital base and earn a return on it. This is, of course, a problem which applies to all forms of capital investment made by regulated utilities and, in that sense, energy saving was being exposed to the same inefficiencies that affect supply-side investments (such as power stations and transmission networks) in regulated utilities.
- That the PUCs were overgenerous to the utilities in terms of the incentives provided at the expense of customers and that the projected long-term benefits of reduced investment in supply-side capacity are not being transferred to customers.
- That the cost to customers was not fully accounted for in the assessment of cost-effectiveness – in particular, transaction costs and the 'hassle' factor were not included in most cases.
- That where DSM did help to defer supply investment it preserved older and inefficient generating plant and inhibited the development of newer, more efficient plant (HC 648-I, 1993).
- That DSM has not really transformed the US utilities from the supply ethos – energy saving has been viewed as an add-on, regulator-mandated programme peripheral to their main activities and, hence, dispensable if conditions change. With the development of competition in supply, many utilities want to drop their customer-funded DSM programmes so that they can lower their rates to compete for customers.

DSM schemes that reduce peak demand should, by definition, meet the standard economic 'no-losers' test – no ratepayer should have to pay higher unit charges because expenditure on DSM measures should directly displace expenditure on supply-side investments. DSM schemes which reduce total demand may be more problematic as these would reduce the utility's revenues without necessarily reducing the need for expenditure on the supply side. However, while it would appear that most DSM programmes were directed to reducing peak rather than total demand, few have been subjected to this test. So, although participating customers certainly gained from DSM and the utilities themselves did not lose, the majority of customers (who did not receive subsidies) paid higher rates for their gas and electricity than they would have done if the schemes had not gone ahead.

One of the most influential criticisms of DSM programmes and Lovins' negawatt concept came in an article by two economists at the Massachusetts Institute of Technology (Joskow and Marron, 1992). They concluded that no one could say with any precision what a negawatt cost but that the real costs were likely to be substantially higher than those quoted by people such as Lovins, owing to: inaccurate measurement of energy savings (which could affect costs by about 50%); failure to account fully for administrative costs (increasing costs by 10–20%); and failure to take account of free riders (a further 25–50% increase in costs).

However, the main criticism that can be levied against the DSM movement is not so much against DSM itself – which, despite the various reservations outlined above, did deliver environmental and other public benefits – but against the system of funding and its impact on the future of energy-saving initiatives in a liberalised energy market. The key question is: did the utilities actually need the financial incentives that they were given to undertake DSM? To answer this we need to examine some of the history.

The 1970 National Environmental Policy Act (NEPA) required all federal agencies to consider the significant environmental effects of proposed major federal actions. One of the first important test cases was in 1971 when the District of Columbia Circuit Court of Appeals held that the Atomic Energy Commission must comply with NEPA in considering applications for construction permits and operating licences for nuclear power plants. Compliance in such cases involves preparing an environmental impact statement, which can take months or even years. According to Fogleman (1994), this enabled opponents of projects to delay them, often for many years, by challenging the agency's compliance with NEPA requirements. Securing approval for nuclear plants became particularly problematic in the wake of the explosion at the Chernobyl nuclear reactor.

Also significant were the Clean Air Act Amendments of 1970, which require the licensing and regulation of facilities that emit pollutants and provide for civil and criminal penalties for non-compliance, as well as authorised 'citizen suits' enabling private persons or groups such as environmental organisations to sue a regulated facility for non-compliance if the EPA has not acted. Environmental organisations became very active in such lawsuits in an attempt to get polluting facilities closed down and force industries (including energy companies) to invest in newer and cleaner technology.

Finally, the form of tariff regulation undertaken by the regulatory commissions in the US was making it very difficult for the utilities to obtain an adequate return on capital investment as recovery only commences when plants become 'used and useful' – which effectively prohibits recovery during what can prove to be lengthy construction phases. Furthermore, in the 1980s there was an increasing incidence of cost recovery on new plant being wholly or partially disallowed by the regulatory commissions on the grounds that the investment, or the way in which it had been carried out, was imprudent.

As a result of these factors, utilities began, from the early 1980s, to move away from building large new plants to look at options for balancing supply and demand that involved less commercial risk. These included extending the economic life of existing power plants, power transfers between regions, electricity imports from Canada, better load management and ways of encouraging efficient use of energy by their customers. Thus it seems likely that the utilities would have been forced anyway to undertake more DSM (particularly to reduce peak demand), and the necessity for additional incentives, particularly on the scale provided, looks at best questionable.

This view gains even more credibility when one sees that the main outcome of DSM activity has been to reduce demand growth – energy demand is still increasing but at a slower rate. Pacific Gas and Electric in California (regarded as one of the leaders of the DSM movement), for example, expects to meet 75% of annual customer demand growth from 1990 to 2000 through DSM – instead of adding nearly 3,500 MW of capacity, it expects to add 2,500 MW (Weinberg, 1994).

Plans to open up the US electricity market to retail competition have been a great blow to the DSM movement as the utilities are concerned that their large and valuable industrial customers can now develop their own power generation or move to independent producers who are not required to run DSM programmes and who will therefore be able to offer cheaper rates. Since about 1994, therefore, many of the regulated utilities have been asking the public utilities commissions to end DSM requirements. This situation is rather ironic when it seems that some forms of DSM might have been an economic option for the utilities anyway given the constraints on developing new capacity outlined above. However, the received wisdom has become that DSM is a costly exercise and therefore utilities faced with competition from suppliers not required to undertake it want the 'burden' removed.

The 1992 Energy Policy Act

The Energy Policy Act 1992 (box 7.4) was the most significant piece of US energy legislation in more than a decade and set the goal of raising overall US energy efficiency by 30% over 1988 levels by 2010. Various small-scale subsidies and tax credits were established for residential and business consumers. Within the industrial sector it set standards for electric motors and some other categories of industrial equipment. The Act also made provision for guidelines for industrial insulation and energy-efficiency audits and for a study of the effectiveness of voluntary industrial efficiency targets combined with mandatory reporting of efficiency indicators.

In the domestic and commercial sector the Act extended the range of appliances covered by mandatory minimum efficiency standards and required the strengthening of many existing standards. It also

---

7.4 Energy Policy Act 1992

Main features included:
- liberalisation of the electricity market
- promotion of IRP by the utilities
- promotion of energy efficiency
- tax incentives for renewables and alternative fuels
- tax incentives for independent gas and oil producers
- mandatory conversion of federal and state vehicle fleets to alternative fuels
- reform of the nuclear licensing process to encourage nuclear power plant construction.

established voluntary or mandatory labelling programmes for new categories of equipment, such as windows, and strengthened state and local efforts to tighten and enforce building codes. Finally, a key feature was that public utilities commissions that had not already done so were required to consider IRP for energy utilities and apply rate-making systems which ensure that investments by utilities in conservation and energy efficiency improvement can compete with supply options.

The Act was passed by Congress in October 1992 at the end of a three-year process that had begun with the Bush Administration's proposal for a National Energy Strategy (NES) in 1989. The development of this by Energy Secretary James Watkins involved a series of public hearings to establish a public consensus, the outcome of which was to place great stress on energy efficiency and environmental issues. However, according to Eikeland (1993) this did not find favour with Chief of Staff John Sununu, the Office of Public Management, the Treasury or the Council of Economic Advisors. In the absence of a strong lead from the President, Sununu and these three departments, Eikeland reports, managed to sideline the climate-change issue and to cut the Environmental Protection Agency out of the process, so that when the NES was released in February 1991 it was much more supply-orientated and sceptical about climate change.

The NES also rejected the idea of energy taxes as a means of constraining demand and, instead, made proposals for new oil exploration and production in Alaska and the continental shelf to meet demand, for measures to promote the development of clean coal technology and renewable energy and to streamline the planning process for nuclear plants. Environmental groups reacted with hostility to the proposed NES, while the energy supply industries tended to be generally satisfied.

In the meantime both the House of Representatives and the Senate Energy Committees had been working on their own versions of an energy strategy and bills. Both of these gave a greater emphasis to energy saving than the NES, although a number of compromises had to be reached with the Bush Administration – specifically over any attempt to introduce energy taxes or tough climate-change targets. In an April 1992 letter to House Speaker Tom Foley, President Bush said that he would not accept provisions that would 'limit economic growth by mandating targets and timetables for future greenhouse-gas emission levels, either generally or with specific references to carbon dioxide' (quoted by Eikeland, 1993).

In the end the energy supply interests fared – as might have been predicted – rather well in the Act itself. The controversial NES proposals on major oil production in Alaska and the continental shelf were removed, but tax relief for smaller oil producers was left in. Proposals to encourage alternative fuels for transport and to streamline the planning process for nuclear plants also survived. The Energy Policy Act made a number of minor provisions for energy saving. However, some of the its main provisions related to opening up the wholesale electricity market to competition (see below), which was always likely to have a severe effect on one of the Acts' key measures to promote energy saving – the requirement on public utilities commissions to consider an IRP approach to utility capacity or resource planning where they had not already done so.

As Eikeland notes, the global climate issue was not well integrated into the Act, although it did require the Energy Secretary to establish a national inventory of greenhouse gases and mandated him to appoint a Director of Climate Protection to take part in international discussions and monitor domestic and international policies for their impact on greenhouse-gas emissions.

The Clinton Administration raises and dashes the hopes of the environmental lobby

At the time the Act was passed it was considered by many environmental groups to represent something of a step forward for energy saving in that some of the overtly fossil fuel supply measures in the NES were rejected, that there was recognition of IRP and even that the beginnings of a positive approach on climate change were discernible. The election of the Clinton government in November 1992 was seen as the promise of further progress in view of positive statements made by both Clinton and his vice presidential nominee Al Gore in the run-up to the election. Indeed, Gore had even published a book on the importance of policies to protect the environment, including tackling global warming (Gore, 1992). The fact that when Clinton came to power in January 1993 there was a Democrat President and a Democrat Congress was also seen as a sign of hope that environmental policies would actually be implemented and not be subject to the gridlock and action of the fossil fuel and nuclear lobbying interests.

One of the first steps was the new Administration's decision to add 'reducing greenhouse gas emissions' to the list of key policy goals that had been identified by the Bush Administration. Proposals in April 1993 for the federal year 1994 budget included an energy tax, much greater expenditure on R&D for energy efficiency and renewables and cuts in the nuclear R&D budget, although fossil fuel and nuclear energy supply programmes still accounted for 45% of the budget, as opposed to 20% for energy saving. However, it was signalled that a shift in budget priorities towards energy efficiency, renewables, alternative fuels and natural gas was planned for 1995–98.

In October 1993 the Climate Change Action Plan was announced, following the President's commitment the previous April to return US emissions of greenhouse gases to their 1990 levels by 2000. The plan contained fifty new or expanded initiatives with an emphasis on voluntary agreements or partnerships (see box 7.5).

As part of his plan to reduce the budget deficit, President Clinton proposed, in February 1993, a tax on the energy content of most fuels. The House of Representatives approved a revised form of the tax in May 1993, but the Senate rejected it a few weeks later. Further congressional negotiations resulted in a compromise tax on transportation fuels, which came into effect in October 1993.

The defeat for the President over his energy tax proposal also deflated much of the optimism felt up till then by the environmental movement. Energy taxes have, since 1993, been effectively abandoned because of fierce opposition from the coal and oil industries. With the election of a Republican-dominated Congress in 1995, Clinton found that many of his environmental policies were going to be much harder to implement, particularly given the lobbying power of the traditional energy industries. In spring 1995 a concerted campaign to slash a range of federal budgets called not only for budget cuts but also for abolition of the Department of Energy itself.

This campaign was based both in ideology and populist politics. At the ideological level much of the new 1995 Republican intake was strongly committed to the concept of minimal government, the practical expression of which was to advocate the abolition of government departments, laboratories, research institutes, etc. The leader of the Republican task force on energy (which proposed the cuts), the 1995 new entrant Sam Brownback, is quoted as having said that 'there is no more reason for a Department of Energy than

---

7.5 Climate Change Action Plan

Some of the main features were:

- Climate Challenge – electricity utilities to enter voluntary agreements with the DOE to reduce or limit their greenhouse-gas emissions in the most cost-effective way – e.g. DSM, switching to lower-carbon fuels, methane capture and forestry schemes.
- The Energy Star Buildings programme to promote efficient heating, cooling and air-conditioning systems.
- The EPA's Green Lights programme (agreements with commercial companies to upgrade lighting systems) was to be expanded to include new partnerships with utilities.
- The DOE and EPA were to form new Golden Carrot partnerships with utilities and manufacturers to accelerate the commercialisation of high-efficiency residential and commercial appliances.
- National marketing of home energy-rating systems and encouraging mortgage lenders to provide loans to home-buyers to finance energy efficiency improvements.

---

a Department of Automobiles' (Boyle, 1995b: 2). Energy saving and renewables, which had been so strongly advocated by Clinton and Gore, came in for special attention because this Democrat support meant that they were seen as inherently left-wing issues. Reinforcing this ideological split was work by right-wing think-tanks, which viewed minimum efficiency standards as a denial of consumer choice.

The practical political dimension was the desire to cut the federal budget and, hence, taxes, which meant that those budget areas which did not fit in with the ideology were the prime targets. Support for energy saving and renewables was viewed as unwarranted corporate welfare, serving the interests of the energy conservation and environmental lobby and constituting a burden on taxpayers.

One casualty was efforts to increase appliance and lighting energy efficiency standards. Although new appliance standards were pushed through in 1995, the compromise was to drop new lighting standards in the wake of hard lobbying from major companies in the lighting industry, who were concerned that much of their existing lighting manufacturing capacity would not meet the new standards and would become obsolete. Overall, the energy efficiency budget for 1996 was cut by 25%, down from $750 million in 1995. The insulation programme for low-income households was particularly hard hit, with its budget cut by around 45%. Similar substantial cuts were made the following year in the budgets for 1997.

The US position in the lead-up to Kyoto

Perhaps one of the most effective examples of the continuing power of the energy supply policy networks in the US was the effect on its position in the negotiations leading up to the Kyoto climate change conference in December 1997. Ever since the Rio conference the industries that considered they had the most to lose from action to curb emissions – the oil, electricity and car industries – have mounted a fierce, well-funded lobbying effort, targeted particularly at Republican members of Congress, who, given their views on energy saving and environmental concerns as left-wing preoccupations, were likely to be sympathetic to the campaign and who, of course, could effectively block any action agreed by the President.

The industry not only has used direct lobbying but has also made use of dissident scientists who question the reality or causes of climate change and have formed themselves into a series of lobbying associations, frequently also involving many energy-intensive industries. The most high-profile of these associations has been the Global Climate Coalition (GCC), whose members include all the major oil companies, many of the large US electricity utilities, the leading car manufacturers and energy-intensive industries including, chemicals, paper, steel and aluminium.

During 1997 the GCC was engaged not only in much direct lobbying of Congress members and international climate change negotiators but also in mounting a high-profile television and press advertising campaign in the autumn to convince both Congress and the American public that the Global Climate Agreement would be bad for America, particularly because developing countries would not be required to reduce their emissions. The text of one advertisement read: 'the UN global climate agreement would force American families to restrict our use of the oil, gasoline and electricity that heats and cools our homes and schools, gets us to our jobs and runs our factories and businesses. We'd have to pay more for energy and in turn, prices for goods and services would rise'. Another focused on the effect on jobs 'because it will be cheaper to make things like cars, steel, cement and chemicals overseas, that's where American jobs will go' (both quoted in Greenpeace, 1997a).

Despite the efforts of the GCC, however, an agreement was reached at Kyoto that industrialised countries will have legally binding targets for reducing emissions of greenhouse gases by 2012. The US target of 7% is lower than that for the EU, Switzerland and some central and eastern European countries, which must cut by 8%, although it is higher than for other countries – notably Australia, which is allowed to increase its emissions by 8%. However, the GCC did not admit defeat. William O'Keefe, Chairman of the Global Climate Coalition, said: 'This agreement represents unilateral economic disarmament. It is a terrible deal and the President should not sign it. If he does, business, labour and agriculture will campaign hard and will defeat it' (Greenpeace, 1997b). Even if the President does sign, it seems unlikely that he will be able to get the agreement ratified by Congress.

Energy market liberalisation

California's public utilities commission (CPUC), having been in the lead in establishing DSM, also led the way in responding to the Energy Policy Act by proposing, in April 1994, to restructure the state's electricity industry, allowing competition for all customers by 2002. This started a debate on the future of DSM in a liberalised market. The CPUC went through a protracted consultation and lobbying process leading up to an announcement in December 1995 of its plans for market liberalisation. During that period much effort was made by environmental groups to preserve DSM activity, while the incumbent utilities argued against having to undertake any activity that would raise their rates and make them uncompetitive with new entrants.

The CPUC's plans allow customers three main options. First, to stay with their local utility and continue to buy at regulated prices. Second, to contract to buy from a power broker at predetermined prices – the brokers take the risks and gain the benefits of buying on a range of contracts and pool price fluctuations. Third, enter into direct-access agreements with generators or suppliers of their choice, who will have the right to use the transmission/distribution system to deliver power to them.

To preserve some investment in energy efficiency and DSM (along with other activities deemed in the public interest, including renewables and assistance for low-income consumers), the CPUC decided that a Public Goods Charge (PGC) should be established – in effect a non-bypassable levy on retail rates charged by all suppliers. The minimum surcharge has been set at 3.1% of customers' distribution charges – utilities can raise more, but most are expected to raise the minimum when the surcharge begins in 2002. In the interim, from 1998 to 2001, the CPUC has set minimum annual amounts that can be raised to fund energy efficiency schemes, ranging from \$32 million to \$106 million depending on the size of the utility.

However, the CPUC has said that all customer-specific energy efficiency projects (e.g. customer incentives to buy CFLs, insulation, etc.) should be undertaken as commercial activities rather than being funded by the PGC. The PGC is intended only to be used for market transformation and stimulation activities, including the provision of information to consumers.

In the meantime a number of other state PUCs and energy commissions have also produced plans for market liberalisation, including New York, Wisconsin, Massachusetts, Rhode Island, Maine, New Jersey, North Carolina and Iowa. The PGC or public service charge (PSC) appears to be one of the main routes being considered to maintain funding for energy saving. PSCs also cover other public obligations that may be placed on suppliers – for example fuel bill assistance to low-income households or some forms of research. Another important development is that many PUCs have decided that the money collected should be handed over to an independent body under regulatory supervision and control rather than being administered directly by the utilities. The CPUC, for example, has appointed a nine-member independent board to take over the administration of public funding for energy saving. Furthermore, in many states the utilities will not retain their position as sole delivery agent – other groups will be able to bid to the independent agencies for funds to run energy-saving programmes.

The prospects for energy services

In some sectors the prospects for energy saving being provided on a market basis rather than through a PGC look encouraging. Industrial consumers have started to develop their own on-site electricity generation, often CHP, as a means of reducing their energy costs. Utilities are naturally extremely worried about such moves, which could leave them with 'stranded investments' of energy supply capacity on which they cannot generate enough sales. The response of some, therefore, has been to offer to build and operate on-site CHP units for their consumers, thus giving the consumer the benefits of efficient generation while preserving revenue for the utility.

Some utilities are also offering a range of energy services, alongside energy supply, as a means of winning or keeping market share. Energy services like DSM can help utilities where customers can shift their demand to off-peak periods, thus avoiding the need to build new capacity that might only be required to service peak demand and so would not provide a sufficiently high return on investment. The need to avoid the construction of potentially under-utilised peak capacity is likely to increase with the introduction of competition in electricity supply, which means that utilities will no longer have captive customers to finance their investments. Another motivation to develop energy services is that they are unregulated – unlike the core utility service of electricity or gas supply to franchise customers. There is thus greater scope for profit with, of course, also greater risk.

However, so far, as in the UK, these developments are restricted to the industrial and commercial sector and it remains to be seen whether similar initiatives will be aimed at households. Some utilities have started to develop market transformation activities, such as the Power Smart programme developed in Canada by BC Hydro, which has now spread throughout Canada and to many US utilities. Power Smart is, effectively, a product-endorsement programme, designed to increase customer confidence in energy-saving products, combined with some product discounts – all intended to boost sales of the products concerned. The aim of these programmes, however, is not just to boost sales on a one-off basis but to lead to a lasting transformation by getting the products more widely taken up and accepted and, through volume sales, helping to reduce prices. This sort of initiative may help to boost the marketability of energy saving for households.

Conclusion

Many analysts have criticised the inability of the US to develop a comprehensive energy policy (e.g. Lindberg, 1977; Uslaner, 1987).

Every President since Richard Nixon has proposed a national energy policy, but none has succeeded in achieving much of what they originally wished to have included in such a policy. President Carter tried, in the wake of the 1973–74 oil crisis, to impose energy taxes, but these proposals met with fierce resistance and the eventual result was some minor incentives for energy conservation and a small tax on energy-inefficient cars.

Faced with the hostility of the powerful coal industry lobby, President Clinton had to considerably water down plans for an energy tax designed to help meet CO_2 and SO_2 targets. The US's position in the climate change negotiations during 1997, when it opposed the tougher targets proposed by the EU, was also due to the lobbying by the energy and automobile industries – particularly the Global Climate Coalition. Energy suppliers and energy-intensive industries are well linked into government departments and agencies via policy networks that have grown up over many years. This, combined with effective lobbying of Congress members (who are very susceptible to arguments about potential effects on state economies and jobs) and a political system in which power is split between legislature and executive, creates the conditions for well-organised lobby groups such as the GCC to have a powerful influence on policy formation.

There are various explanations for why the US has difficulty in developing national energy conservation policies. One is that bills which attempt to tackle energy policy affect so many other policy areas (environment, industry, health, etc.) that they end up being referred to many different Congressional committees, and any bill that is sent to more than one committee is less likely to succeed. Another is that the US system, with its division between the executive (President) and the legislature (Congress), makes it very difficult to enact any policy that is not supported by both.

Some of these difficulties may help to explain why in the US the main initiative since the 1980s has been DSM by the energy utilities, developed at the level of individual states rather than at federal level. The utilities relate to the regulatory commissions, which are appointed by the state governor but are one step removed from and independent of the state governments. Also, DSM may have considerable voter appeal in offering utility customers subsidies for energy-saving measures designed to save them further money on their fuel bills.

Although the regulatory commissions would deny that they have suffered from 'regulatory capture', they do rely on the utilities for information and therefore could be said to form policy networks with them. The success of DSM owes much to the fact that environmental groups managed to get their message through not just to the commissions but also to the utilities, thus effectively becoming a part of the policy network rather than having to work from the outside.

By their nature, those policies which would perhaps achieve the greatest energy conservation effect involve measures, such as tight regulation or energy taxes, that are likely to be highly unpopular with both influential lobby groups (such as industry) and/or voters in general. According to Uslaner (1987), members of Congress tend to enact distributive policies that provide benefits to their constituents (often referred to as the US 'pork barrel'), but many energy conservation policies (taxes or regulation) would not provide such benefits and, indeed, may impose costs or restrictions on activity or choice. This, then, would help to explain why those policies which have been passed have tended to involve the provision of subsidies (e.g. for energy-saving measures, synthetic fuels or renewable energy). The US looks unlikely, for the foreseeable future, to change this.

8

Australia

Political and institutional background

Australia has, like the United States, a true federal system in which powers are split between the Federal (or Commonwealth) Government and state governments. As in the US, this means, in practice, that there are significant areas of policy over which the states have control rather than the national (Federal/Commonwealth) government.

The Australian Commonwealth Parliament consist of two houses. The lower house, the House of Representatives, is directly elected and the more populous states have greater representation. In the upper house, the Senate, every state has the same number of representatives, making it not only a check on the powers of the lower house but also a means of ensuring that the smaller states (in terms of population) are not dominated by the more populous ones.

The Australian Labor Party formed the Commonwealth Government for thirteen years from 1983 to 1996. Throughout much of the 1980s the Labor Party was in power in many of the states, but by the early 1990s the Liberal (Conservative) Party had gained control in most, and, in 1996, it formed a national government. However, Labor had one win in 1995 when it regained control of New South Wales. The 1983–96 Labor Commonwealth government pursued many policies that had much in common with those of Conservative governments in the UK, including the privatisation of state-owned industries, liberalisation of markets and an efficiency drive in government operations.

Responsibility for energy policy is divided between the Commonwealth and state governments. The Commonwealth Government is responsible for taxation, trade, foreign investment, overseas borowing and offshore energy resources, the key department being the

Department of Primary Industries and Energy. Environmental policy matters are dealt with by the Department of the Environment, Sport and Territories (DEST), which also has two executive agencies – the Environmental Protection Agency (EPA) and Environment Australia.

The state governments have responsibility for the energy companies within their states, including pricing, the development of energy resources and projects onshore, environmental assessment and standards. In Victoria (see box 8.2 on p. 148) energy responsibilities are split between two departments – the Department of Natural Resources and Environment (DNRE) and its executive agencies, the Environmental Protection Agency and Energy Efficiency Victoria, deal with most technical and environmental issues. Energy Efficiency Victoria (called Energy Victoria until April 1998) evolved from the Victorian Solar Energy Council in the late 1980s – its annual budget had declined by almost half in real terms to less than $2.5 million by 1998. The energy policy branch of the DNRE was moved to the Department of Treasury and Finance in 1995 to deal with restructuring of the energy sector. Victoria has not had an energy department since 1986, apart from a brief period of reinstatement in 1992–95. New South Wales has had a Department of Energy since the 1970s.

Co-ordination of the energy policies of the states and the national government is undertaken through the Australian and New Zealand Minerals and Energy Council (ANZMEC), which is composed of the relevant ministers from each state, the Commonwealth Government and New Zealand.

Structure of the energy market

Historically, the electricity transmission systems have been owned by the state-owned utilities. The size of Australia and the distances involved mean that to date no national grid has been established. However, the states of Victoria, South Australia and New South Wales and the Australian Capital Territory are interconnected. Most generation, distribution and supply has been undertaken by state monopolies, with some involvement (in Victoria, New South Wales and Queensland) of local government in distribution and supply. There are some independent power producers in some states – largely industrial or agricultural users with on-site generation. Some of the local government-owned distributors have some small-scale generation capacity.

8.1 Key actors in the Australian energy policy community at national level

Commonwealth Government
Department of Primary Industries and Energy
Department of the Environment, Sport and Territories (DEST)
Australian and New Zealand Minerals and Energy Council
(ANZMEC)

Environmental and consumer groups
Australian Consumers Association
Nature Conservation Council

Coal is the main fuel used for electricity generation and its proportion has actually been increasing in recent years – from 66% in 1990 to 70% in 1995. Hydro at 20% and natural gas at 9% account for most of the remaining electricity generation. Oil still accounts for about 1% but has been in decline for many years. There is no nuclear generation due to a policy presumption against it.

The Australian electricity industry has been undergoing reorganisation and restructuring – starting with corporatisation and now moving to privatisation and the introduction of competition – since 1990, particularly in New South Wales and Victoria. The election of a Liberal/National Party federal government in March 1996 and the fact that the Liberal Party is in power in all the states apart from New South Wales, where the Labor Party has a one-seat majority, has intensified liberalisation trends in Australia. However, even under the Labor Commonwealth government and a Labor state government in New South Wales, liberalisation has been very much the trend.

The first stage was the establishment in November 1990 of the National Grid Management Council (NGMC) by the Commonwealth and state heads of government. The NGMC was charged with investigating the feasibility of a national electricity grid, overseeing major restructuring of the industry and opening up generation and supply to competition, including interstate trading. A National Electricity Code was agreed in 1997 to allow for trade between interconnected states – Victoria and New South Wales will take part in the first stage of an interstate market. In some states separate businesses are being established to carry out the four functions – supply,

8.2 Key actors in the energy policy community of Victoria

Government departments
Department of Natural Resources and Energy
Department of Treasury and Finance

Agencies
Energy Efficiency Victoria

Electricity industry
Pre-1995 – State Electricity Commission (state-owned), responsible for transmission, generation, distribution, supply; plus some local authority-owned distribution/supply companies.
Post-1995 – a transmission company, five generating companies, five distribution/supply companies (incorporating the former municipal companies), all in the private sector.
Brunswick Electricity (until 1995) – municipal electricity company.

The Regulator General (since 1994)

Gas industry
Transportation, distribution and supply – state-owned.

generation, transmission and distribution. In others the functions are being unbundled and ring-fenced.

In Victoria the State Electricity Commission (SECV) and the municipal electricity distribution/supply companies were reorganised during 1995 into a separate transmission business, five generating companies and five distribution/supply companies. The five electricity distribution companies were all sold in the same year, mainly to US electricity companies. All Victorian power stations except the two gas-fired power stations (which in 1998 remained of low value due to the excess of low-priced coal-fired capacity) were sold to a number of Australian and international buyers during 1996–97 and the transmission grid was sold in 1997.

In New South Wales (box 8.3) Pacific Power (formerly the State Electricity Commission) was transformed into separate generation, distribution and transmission companies, which were 'corporatised' but remained under state government-ownership in 1998 – despite the Premier and Treasurer being keen to privatise the industry, the

---

8.3 Key actors in the energy policy community of New South Wales

Government departments
Department of Energy

Agencies
Environmental Protection Authority (EPA)
Sustainable Energy Development Authority (SEDA)

Electricity industry
Pre-1995 – State Electricity Commission (state-owned), responsible for transmission, generation, distribution, supply; plus twenty-five local authority-owned distribution/supply companies
Post-1995 – corporatised and disaggregated (but still state-owned) transmission, generation and distribution/supply companies; six municipal distributors/suppliers (created by mergers)
Pacific Power

Gas industry
AGL, a privately owned transportation, distribution/supply company, plus some smaller private sector companies

Environmental and consumer groups
Australian Consumers Association
Greenpeace
Nature Conservation Council

New South Wales Labor Party remained opposed. The other (mainly municipal) distribution/supply companies were reduced in number from twenty-five to six, but remained in public ownership in 1998.

Queensland, South Australia, Western Australia and Tasmania are also separating the distribution/supply, generation and transmission functions, corporatising the businesses and facilitating private investment in new plant and infrastructure. In early 1998 South Australia announced its intention to sell off its electricity assets.

Gas production is a private sector activity. Gas transportation pipelines are owned by state governments – only the states of Victoria and New South Wales have any interconnection. Several major gas distributors/suppliers have always been privately owned, notably AGL in New South Wales. The rest are owned by state governments through statutory bodies or companies. Regulatory and structural reforms began to be undertaken in 1997 to remove barriers to trade in gas – these include the drafting of a national third-party access code. However, in the absence of pipelines connecting the separate state markets it will be some time before such competition can be developed.

There is no VAT or general consumption tax in Australia – although the Liberal Commonwealth government was re-elected in October 1998 on a manifesto pledge to introduce a goods and services tax. There are excise duties on oil products, including heating oil, and on coal production. Some states impose taxes on gas sales – for example, Victoria has a levy on large gas users, but there are no taxes on electricity consumption. There are also two types of price and tax intervention that tend to encourage supply. First, there are price concessions for pensioners, some large energy users and rural electricity consumers. Second, there are tax credits and exemptions for mining activities, including energy production.

Development of energy conservation policy

Australia differs from many other IEA countries in that industry and transport tend to account for higher than average proportions of energy use while the residential and commercial sectors account for less. For example, in 1988 transport accounted for 39% of TFC (the IEA average was 30%), whereas residential and commercial accounted for 18% (IEA average: 32%). In the 1970s, because of its low-cost energy (coal and oil), Australia developed a lot of energy-intensive industry such as cement and aluminium smelting. However, since the late 1980s the fastest growth in energy use has been in the residential and commercial sectors as the use of appliances, heating and air conditioning began to increase.

Various initiatives were taken in Australia during the late 1970s and early 1980s to promote energy conservation in the wake of the oil price increases. However, in 1986 the IEA concluded that Australia had achieved only modest progress in energy efficiency improvement compared to most other member countries. By 1992 energy intensity in Australia remained, at 0.46, higher than the OECD average of 0.40.

The Victoria government started a number of programmes in 1983, including: energy information centres; advisory services for industrial and commercial energy users, developed in conjunction with the gas and electricity utilities; and a Home Energy Advisory Service (HEAS) to assist low-income households with energy efficiency. The New South Wales government ran a similar programme for welfare recipients in the mid-1980s.

HEAS was based on the UK's Neighbourhood Energy Action programme (see chapter 6) and was a joint initiative with the State Electricity Commission (the generation and transmission utility, which also acted as a distributor and supplier for some customers) and the local energy distribution/supply companies run by local authorities. The scheme involved a home energy audit and practical insulation work in the homes of people who qualified for certain state benefits and who also consumed relatively high levels of electricity.

Much of the impetus for HEAS came from one municipal utility in inner Melbourne – Brunswick Electricity – where the city electrical engineer, supported by key local councillors and environmental groups, had begun a series of environmental projects in the late 1970s to early 1980s. These included solar panels on the roof of the electricity supply department's offices and the conversion of adjacent land into an environmental park, including a low-energy demonstration house, a city farm, wind turbines and waste-recycling facilities. Discussions about an initiative to help low-income households to save energy between the city electrical engineer and some supportive officials in the Department of Energy during 1982 (one of whom had visited the UK and seen the NEA programme) led to the HEAS idea.

In 1986 the Victoria government launched a review of building and planning regulations that included consideration – for the first time in Australia – of the inclusion of minimum thermal insulation requirements for refurbished and new houses. At this time, however, the IEA noted that although the Australian climate is one of the warmest experienced by IEA member countries, the use of air conditioning was not nearly as extensive as in areas with similar climates such as California. Energy use in buildings was, thus, on the low side but with clear potential for a significant increase.

The Victoria and New South Wales governments published initial proposals in 1979 for labelling electrical appliances and, following several years of consultation, the state energy ministers agreed in 1983 that a voluntary labelling scheme, commencing with refrigerators and freezers, be implemented in early 1984. However, the proposal was abandoned due to strong opposition from Australian appliance manufacturers, who claimed that they would lose out to imports. In March 1985 the New South Wales Energy Minister decided to introduce a mandatory labelling scheme despite industry opposition, and the Victorian government joined in some time later. The main effect was that Australian manufacturers substantially improved the efficiency of the appliances they manufacture. There was an average efficiency improvement of 15% in Australian-made refrigerators in the first year of labelling. The experience with dishwasher labelling was even more dramatic: in anticipation of the labelling scheme, Australian manufacturers improved the efficiency of their models by 30% in the 12 months before the scheme's launch (*Energy Forum*, 1989).

Mandatory appliance labelling continues in New South Wales and Victoria, and South Australia also joined in the late 1980s. The products labelled vary from state to state – refrigerators and freezers (all states), dishwashers and air conditioners (Victoria and New South Wales), clothes-dryers and washing machines (Victoria only). Most other states also have labels on many of these appliances although labelling is not mandatory there.

The National Energy Management Program (NEMP; box 8.4), begun in 1985, was a joint Commonwealth and state initiative covering all sectors and involved expenditure of $560,000 in 1985–86. Similar programmes were launched in the mid-1980s to improve energy management in industry and in Commonwealth Government operations and buildings.

In March 1986 the Commonwealth Government launched Energy 2000, a national energy policy review, and held a major conference on the issue in September 1986. As a result the Government published the National Energy Policy Paper in spring 1988, which defined the key energy objectives as security of supply, development of exports and greater efficiency in the domestic energy sector.

Policy responses to climate change concerns

Like most other countries, Australia reduced its energy conservation policy initiatives in the late 1980s in response to lower energy prices. However, interest began to grow again in 1989 and early 1990 as concern about climate change increased. An environmental strategy

---

8.4 National Energy Management Program

Initiatives included:

- *The Energy Guide* – a booklet, produced with the Australian Consumers Association, explaining how to save energy in the home and delivered to every household in Australia during 1991
- Grants for energy audits in industry, commerce and public bodies
- Increased support for energy advice centres.

---

was outlined by the Prime Minister in July 1989, in which he stressed the importance of ecologically sustainable development and the Commonwealth Government's intention to strengthen energy efficiency through research and development, improved land-use planning, better use of public transport, more efficient building design and improvements in industry, and the use of renewable energy and clean coal. He also announced the development of a national energy conservation plan in co-operation with state and local governments. To take this forward a special working group on the greenhouse effect was established to identify sources of emissions and possible policy responses. This was one of nine separate working groups set up under the Ecologically Sustainable Development process, launched in 1990, which aimed to integrate environmental issues into economic development.

In October 1990 the Commonwealth Government announced a new National Energy Management Program, to be funded initially for three years and containing a number of measures deigned to improve energy efficiency and reduce greenhouse-gas emissions. In contrast to the previous few years, the energy efficiency programme's budget was doubled in 1989–90 and increased by a further 40% in 1990–91, although spending was still well below the early 1980s levels. It was also clear that Australia would have a tough job to reduce greenhouse-gas emissions as energy demand was forecast to grow at 2.5% per annum from 1988 to 2000.

In 1992 Australia agreed a target to stabilise greenhouse-gas emissions at 1988 levels by the year 2000 and to reduce them by 20% by the year 2005, provided that this did not endanger the competitiveness of Australian industry. In view of the fact that 1992 emissions were already 2% higher than in 1988 and that they were predicted to rise by 20% by 2000, this was likely to prove a challenging target.

In response to this the Council of Australian Governments agreed the National Greenhouse Response Strategy in December 1992 and the NEMP was renamed the National Energy Efficiency Program (NEEP). However, the Council noted that implementation of the strategy would depend on budget priorities and constraints within the national, state and local governments and that it could not bind its members and local authorities to act.

Environmental groups, including Greenpeace and the Nature Conservation Council, generally viewed the Commonwealth Government's stance in the early 1990s as positive. Effective lobbying by environmental groups since the early 1980s and an upsurge of interest in environmental issues – brought about particularly by the campaign of the Tasmanian Wilderness Society against development in Tasmania and concerns about tropical rainforest in Queensland – had put the environmental movement in a position of influence with the Labor government, a number of whose members were sympathetic. The election of 'green' councillors and MPs in several states, together with the appointment of some environmental activists as political advisers, reinforced this influence. As a result, by the early 1990s Australia was regarded internationally as one of the countries most committed to the cause of reducing greenhouse-gas emissions – albeit that the rhetoric was, so far, greater than the action.

By early 1995 it became clear that further measures would be required to achieve the target set for reducing emissions, and in March 1995 the Commonwealth Government announced its Greenhouse 21C (twenty-first century) Program, much of which consisted of measures designed to promote renewable energy. A key initiative was the Greenhouse Challenge Program, launched in October 1995, under which business and institutional energy users (particularly those which are energy-intensive) are encouraged to sign agreements to reduce their greenhouse-gas emissions.

Major firms have generally responded positively to the programme, with many developing comprehensive plans to reduce their emissions. Part of the enthusiasm may stem from the fact that the former Labor government reputedly encouraged industry to see the programme as a means of avoiding a carbon tax. However, the programme has been criticised by environmental groups as being complex, unclear and lacking proper means of evaluation. Their scepticism arises over a number of features, including: emission reductions required by the programme are calculated on the basis that companies would otherwise have made no energy efficiency improvements, which could exaggerate the claimed achievements of the programme as some savings would have been made anyway; and details of the agreements reached between the government and companies are treated as commercially confidential, so no independent evaluation is possible.

However, by late 1994 Australia's position on international action had begun to change, particularly in respect of calls for tougher targets than had been set at Rio. Australia was part of the JUSCANZ grouping (Japan, the US, Canada, Australia and New Zealand), which opposed the setting of post-2000 targets at the Berlin conference in March 1995. In 1996 a new Liberal Commonwealth government was elected and it decided to cut back many of the programmes initiated by its predecessor. The budget for the NEEP was cut from $4.7 million in 1996–97 to $1.9 million for 1997–98. The energy audit programme for industry was abolished entirely, along with the Energy Research and Development Corporation. Furthermore, the Liberal government has taken an even harder stance against new climate change targets set for after 2000 than the Labour government.

Australia's position stems from its heavy dependence on fossil fuels both as a source of energy and as a major export, along with many energy-intensive industries, particularly aluminium production. Economic growth has led to an increase in its use of fossil fuels in recent years, as a result of which it is unlikely to meet even the 2000 stabilisation target. In 1996 energy intensity in Australia remained higher than in most other IEA countries except the US, Canada, Turkey and Luxembourg. Thus, the government argued, uniform emission-reduction targets would impose a disproportionate economic burden on Australia compared to most other Annex 1 countries.* However, environmental groups argue that Australia has more scope to pursue cost-effective emission-reduction options than many other OECD countries as it has made so little progress so far in this field. Both ABARE (the Australian Bureau of Agricultural and Resource Economics – a government-funded research agency) and IEA studies have concluded that Australian industry has reduced its

* Western and Eastern Europe, the US, Canada, Australia, New Zealand and Japan.

energy intensity at about half the rate of the OECD average since the late 1970s, even taking into account differences in the nature of their industrial sectors.

Australia proposed that different targets be set for Annex 1 countries based on the economic costs incurred by strategies to reduce emissions, which would result in Australia being set less stringent targets than most other countries. Australia also wanted to see developing countries being set targets sooner rather than later, mainly because it fears a migration of some of its energy-intensive industries to developing countries in Asia if energy costs are perceived to be lower there.

In the final run-up to Kyoto, Prime Minister John Howard issued a statement (20 November 1997) on the country's position. Australia's dependence on fossil fuels looked likely to continue and its population was expected to grow by 30% from 1990 to 2020 compared to less than 3% in Europe. If no further action was taken, emissions were expected to increase by 28% from 1990 to 2010, and he therefore announced a range of measures (action on renewable energy and energy conservation) designed to reduce this emissions growth by around one-third. In the event, the outcome of Kyoto took account of Australia's concerns, allowing it an 8% increase in emissions from 1990 levels by 2012.

Efforts to introduce DSM

The concepts of demand-side management and integrated resource planning began to be discussed in Australia in 1988–89, and one early initiative was a report prepared by Amory Lovins for the Victorian Minister for Industry and Economic Planning in follow up to a seminar held in late 1989. The report (Lovins, 1990) made various recommendations on how US-style DSM could be introduced into the electricity industry in Victoria.

A number of mainly small-scale initiatives were developed in the early to mid-1990s, mainly in New South Wales and Victoria. Most of these were aimed at reducing peak demand for electricity to minimise the need for reinforcement or extension of distribution/ transmission networks. For example, the SEC in Victoria developed a number of lighting programmes, including rebates for businesses that installed low-energy lighting and information and discounts for households and schools on energy-efficient lighting. Schemes to stimulate the use of small-scale CHP in industry and commerce were developed in several states by the electricity utilities.

In 1993 the Australian and New Zealand Minerals and Energy Council established a committee to make a study of a national approach to demand management and least-cost planning. The committee decided to focus first on how IRP (its preferred term) could fit into the proposed competitive electricity market. In 1995 the committee published its report, which concluded that IRP was compatible with the proposed competitive electricity market, although it made a number of recommendations for action to make it work, including the need for incentive regulation to make DSM commercially attractive to electricity suppliers.

However, the fact that interest in DSM/IRP coincided with the beginnings of the restructuring of energy industries in Australia from 1990 onwards has affected its development. Although Australian electricity companies have undertaken some DSM and energy-saving activities, particularly in the light of the country's commitments on climate change, there has been a continuing debate on the extent to which DSM activity would be compatible with competition. The key question has been whether energy saving is a business opportunity for electricity and gas companies or a non-commercial community service obligation which the utilities will be obliged to undertake via regulation, levies, etc.

In Victoria the question was, effectively, sidelined, as the main emphasis there, for the Liberal government, was on securing the sales of the privatised electricity companies at the highest possible price. An emphasis on DSM/IRP or environmental matters might have been seen as detrimental to the Treasury's goal of securing a good price, although how much energy conservation or the environment were even considered during the privatisation process is open to some question. The end result, however, is that there are no environmental or energy conservation/efficiency obligations placed on Victorian companies or the industry regulator (the Regulator General). Furthermore, one company, Citipower – which wanted to continue with some of the initiatives on energy conservation and renewables previously undertaken by one of the municipal companies (Brunswick Electricity) which it absorbed in the reorganisation – has come up against a number of problems because the regulatory system does not allow for differentiated tariffs to reflect 'green energy' provision.

New South Wales

In New South Wales things have been done rather differently. By 1998 the electricity industry had not been privatised (although in late 1997 this had begun to be considered by the government, despite opposition to it within the Labor Party), but it had been corporatised and some competition was being introduced. Under the Electricity Supply Act 1995, retail suppliers' licences include obligations to develop strategies to reduce greenhouse emissions. Compliance with the retail licences is monitored by a four-member Licence Compliance Advisory Board. The board consists of one member nominated by the Nature Conservation Council and one nominated by the Australian Consumers Association, together with two members representing the Minister of Energy.

The Environmental Protection Authority will assess, every three years, the effectiveness of the greenhouse gas-reduction strategies and publish a report which will also be sent to the Licence Compliance Advisory Board and tabled in each house of parliament. The licence holders have to develop one-, three- and five-year plans for energy efficiency and demand management, along with strategies for the purchase of energy from sustainable sources of cogeneration and renewable energy. The EPA will audit both the overall greenhouse targets per licensee (those negotiated with the Minister) and the effectiveness of the specific strategies to increase purchases from sustainable energy sources. So purchases from low-emission fossil fuel sources (as well as measures to improve energy efficiency) will count towards achieving the targets.

However, the New South Wales government decided not just to rely on new obligations for suppliers to help achieve environmental targets. Under the Sustainable Energy Development Act 1995, it has established the Sustainable Energy Fund (SEF) and the Sustainable Energy Development Authority (SEDA; box 8.5) to help stimulate the integration of energy efficiency into the emerging competitive energy market. The government's view is that while structural reform will remove some of the old regulatory biases, the SEF is required to 'provide a specific stimulus to the energy efficiency and renewable energy industries which are needed for a true energy services market but which are still in their infancy'.

The first report from the Licence Compliance Advisory Board (October 1997) seemed to confirm that – in view of the time being

---

8.5 The Sustainable Energy Development Authority

- Established in February 1996
- Initial grant from the Sustainable Energy Fund of $7 million for 1996–97, $12 million for 1997–98 and $20 million for 1998–99.

Initial programmes of loans, grants, information and advice are targeted at a range of areas, including:
- Reducing energy use in public sector and commercial buildings and promoting the use of more energy-efficient office equipment
- Energy-efficient refrigerators for households
- Small-scale cogeneration.

---

taken to implement the licence requirements – the government had been wise to establish the SEF and SEDA and not to rely solely on restructuring in the electricity industry to deliver energy saving. The board found that the first year's reporting had been complicated by a range of timing and transitional issues and that relevant guidelines for licensees were not issued until July 1997. Many licensees found difficulty in understanding the reporting requirements and all the first reports failed to meet the requirements and had to be resubmitted.

The guidelines on greenhouse gas-reduction strategies established a CO_2 emissions benchmark of 7.87 tonnes per capita from the New South Wales electricity sector in July 1996. They require this level to be maintained in 1997–98 as a first step towards a reduction to 7.34 tonnes per capita by 2000–01. It will be in the 1998 report that the first assessment of progress in this area will be able to be undertaken. The 1-, 3- and 5-year plans are to be negotiated with and approved by the Minister of Energy by July 1998.

In effect, SEDA has a similar role to that of the UK's Energy Saving Trust, except that SEDA also covers renewable energy and that the Commonwealth Government has, through the Sustainable Energy Development Act, specific powers to fund the Authority, which may make its budget rather more secure than that of the Energy Saving Trust.

Why was there such a difference between the policy approaches adopted in New South Wales and Victoria? In part this was due to some of the lessons that had been learnt from Victoria, which led environmental groups (such as Greenpeace and the Nature Conservation Council), together with some supportive academics, to engage in some very effective lobbying in the lead-up to the 1995 Acts. Although the recent history of the Labor Party in Australia (particularly at national level) might have led one to expect that its attitude to competition and privatisation of the electricity industry would be similar to that of the Liberal Party in Victoria, environmental and consumer groups do seem to have found a more sympathetic ear for their concerns in New South Wales.

The prospects for energy saving were also significantly enhanced by a sympathetic attitude at Pacific Power (the corporatised state electricity commission), which had undertaken a considerable amount of work on DSM/IRP in the early 1990s. The manager of demand planning at Pacific Power (who had, in the early 1980s, worked for the Victorian state government on its energy-saving initiatives), was seconded to the state government to work on the electricity reform task force and led the work on proposals for the Sustainable Energy Fund. Clearly, however, an important factor was the fact that the industry was not being sold and, hence, that there were no concerns about the potential impact of energy-saving requirements on the valuation of the industry.

Conclusion

Australia has made very limited progress on energy conservation. It is a country with plentiful and relatively cheap fossil fuel resources, as a result of which it has developed many energy-intensive industries and has been experiencing rapid population and economic growth – all of which have contributed to increasing energy demand. The upsurge of interest in environmental matters and the consequent increase in power and influence of the environmental lobby during the 1980s and early 1990s led for a while to some increased action on energy conservation at national level. However, as it has become clear that Australia would face a major struggle to meet international targets due to its dependence on fossil fuels and increasing energy demand, there has been a tendency once again to dismiss energy conservation as a means of significantly altering the trend to rising energy consumption. Energy suppliers that have formed policy networks with government departments, with further support from energy-intensive industry (which also has close links with the industry department), have been able to sideline environmental interests.

However, in a federal country it is not just action and inaction at the national level that matter as the states have considerable power to develop and follow their own policies. Here we see that a number of initiatives were developed at state level in the 1980s – particularly in Victoria and New South Wales, where environmental and consumer interests were able to work closely with the relevant government departments. More recently, with the development of electricity privatisation and liberalisation there has been an interesting contrast between policies adopted in New South Wales and Victoria. The differences between the two states owe much to the different politics of the energy market reforms in each, but the role of policy networks is also part of the explanation.

In New South Wales the role of the secondee from Pacific Power to the state government to work on the energy market reforms was an example of a policy network working in favour of energy conservation, with both the key actors committed to the idea. In contrast, in Victoria the main enthusiasm for energy conservation was within one of the municipal energy companies. Local councils (mainly Labor-controlled) were not generally enthusiastic about losing control of local energy supply and distribution in the privatisation plans of the Liberal state government and so were not strongly influential in the policy process. For the State Electricity Commission (SECV), energy conservation was at best a marginal issue compared to its more weighty interests in the nature of the privatisation and the break-up of the corporation. This was a change from the situation in the 1980s, when the state government, the SECV and municipal suppliers had worked together on the Home Energy Advisory Service, forming an effective network for conservation.

For the future Australia faces a major challenge as its dependence on fossil fuels looks set to continue and a rising population and economic growth also mean that the buildings sector – where, historically, energy demand has been low – looks set for rapid increases in demand, particularly due to growth in the use of air conditioning.

9

Japan

Political and institutional background

Japan has a parliamentary system with a Cabinet headed by the Prime Minister and composed of twenty Ministers who are collectively responsible to the Diet, which consists of two houses. Cabinet must enjoy the formal confidence of the House of Representatives or resign *en masse* unless the House is dissolved and a general election called. One political party, the conservative Liberal Democratic Party (LDP), controlled the Diet and Cabinet for almost four decades until the 1993 general election. The new coalition government, formed in August 1993 after 38 years of LDP rule, came to power on the promise of political, administrative and economic reform, emphasising competition and deregulation.

In the late nineteenth century Japan 'adopted for its new political system a version of what Weber called "monarchic constitutionalism"' (Johnson, 1982: 36). Thus, bureaucrats were 'officials of the Emperor', appointed by and answerable only to him. This high status and 'right to authority' persists to a large extent today. Ex-bureaucrats dominate the Diet and the Cabinet. Most bills originate within the Ministries and the Cabinet acts on behalf of the bureaucrats to introduce them into the Diet. Before bills are sent to the Cabinet by the Ministries they are considered by 'deliberation councils', made up of outside experts selected by the Minister largely from business interests. These councils perform a much more important function than the Diet, which just rubber stamps and does not debate legislation.

Each Ministry has only one political appointee – the Minister, who is appointed by the Prime Minister and is a member of the Cabinet, although not necessarily a member of the Diet. The senior

official is the Vice Minister. The civil service is dominated by an elite
from Tokyo University, which also dominates the senior levels of
banking and business. For the elite, promotion to section chief is
virtually guaranteed, but not all the elite can go higher. Those who
are not promoted beyond section chief are compelled to resign –
'descend from heaven' (*amakaduri*) as the Japanese describe it –
when others from their year are promoted. Ultimately, all officials
have to 'descend' to create positions for the next class – the usual
retirement age for a vice minister is just over 50. They are usually
found board-level posts in industry.

The three most powerful and elite Ministries are Finance, the
Foreign Office, and the Ministry of International Trade and Industry
(MITI). The activities of the 'economic general staff', to use
Johnson's (1982) term, are perhaps best illustrated by MITI, whose
officials have used a wide range of devices to shape the economy as
they desired, handing some government functions to private and
semi-autonomous organisations.

Associations for specific industries are particularly powerful and
active in Japan. Successive Japanese governments have used these
associations for various purposes – for example, to run quality control systems, to undertake research and development and, particularly, to participate in the deliberation councils, which gives them a
key role in policy development. Their role as 'peak associations' is
therefore a strong one, but the ability of Japanese government
officials to deliver the co-operation of these associations should not
be underestimated.

The quango system is also popular in Japan, with such bodies
usually being established at the instigation of the bureaucracy. It is
seen as a cost-effective way of supplementing government activity by
mobilising private effort and providing a means of communication
with particular clientele constituencies. Quangos are thus a way for
the bureaucracy to finance entrepreneurial and propagandist activities that might attract political hostility if carried out directly by the
government. The quangos are also important in the 'descent' system
for older bureaucrats. Along with many of the private industries
with which each department has built up links, quangos provide
senior bureaucrats who are not going to progress further with a second, mid-life career, thus keeping the central bureaucracy young.

Another important point to remember is that Japan is a unitary
state. Despite constitutional provisions and structural arrangements

---

9.1 Key actors in Japan's energy policy community

Government departments
Ministry of International Trade and Industry (MITI)

Agencies
Agency of Natural Resources and Energy
Energy Conservation Centre (ECC)
Environmental Agency

Electricity industry
Pre-1996 Ten privately owned, vertically integrated generation, transmission, distribution and supply companies with monopoly franchises, plus fifty smaller generating companies owned by local authorities or large consumers.

Post-1996 The ten companies remain but competition is being opened up to allow smaller generators to develop new capacity and local distribution/supply.

Gas and district heating
A mix of private sector and local authority-owned distribution/supply companies.

---

for the autonomy of local governments (direct elections for councillors and chief executives, and the right to manage their own affairs), local government in practice remains very much under the control of central government. This is very different, for example, from the situation in most of western Europe apart from the UK.

Structure of the energy market

MITI has overall responsibility for energy policy in Japan, with its subsidiary body, the Agency of Natural Resources and Energy, responsible for administration of the energy industries and promotion of efficient energy use. Energy policy is developed through a consensual process in which the energy industries submit general plans to MITI for consideration by the Advisory Committee for Energy. This committee consists of government representatives plus members from industry, trade unions, consumer organisations and academics. It has a sub-committee for each energy source and one for energy conservation.

Most of Japan's energy industries, including electricity and gas supply and distribution, are in the private sector, although there are some municipally owned gas and district heating suppliers/distributors. However, there is a strong tradition of government regulation by MITI, particularly through the use of what is known as 'administrative guidance' (discussed in a later section), even though there were some moves towards deregulation in the 1980s.

Until January 1996 the electricity industry consisted of: 10 privately owned and vertically integrated generation, transmission, distribution and supply companies (EPCOs), each with a monopoly of supply in its service area and which between them are responsible for the generation of 75% of Japan's electricity; the Electric Power Development Co (EPDC) and the Japan Atomic Power Co (JAPC), which are joint ventures between the government and the EPCOs to develop electricity generation and nuclear power – the JAPC and EPDC are responsible for 6% of generation; and 34 municipal generating companies (all producing hydro-power) and 20 joint venture (between utilities and large electricity consumers) companies, which are responsible for the remaining 7% of generation.

The bulk of generation (60%) is from fossil fuels – oil, coal and liquefied natural gas (LNG) – with nuclear and hydroelectric responsible for 20% each. Oil's share of the fossil fuels portion has dropped considerably since 1973, when it accounted for 86%, but it remains at a significant 38% despite attempts to diversify into coal and LNG and away from fossil fuels altogether into nuclear and hydro generation. Environmental restrictions on coal use, public hostility to nuclear power and practical constraints on hydroelectricity generation mean that LNG is the favoured fuel to replace oil in urban areas, although new coal-fired plant is being built away from the major urban areas.

The structure outlined above was established by the Electric Utilities Industry Law in the 1960s. Consistent with the new coalition government's ethos of deregulation and economic reform, the Advisory Committee for Energy submitted a report to MITI in late 1993 calling for deregulation for the oil, electricity and natural gas industries. The Electric Utilities Industry Law was amended in 1995. The amendments, which came into effect in January 1996, divided the industry into the three categories of general, wholesale and special suppliers. A key change is the opening up of generation to competition and new market entrants, which had previously been tightly controlled. Wholesale suppliers are those who supply electricity to general suppliers – essentially, wholesalers are generators and general suppliers are suppliers/distributors. While the larger wholesalers will continue to face controls on the development of new capacity, smaller wholesalers will be exempt from these regulations to help foster competition. Special suppliers are essentially smaller-scale generators who will be allowed to supply electricity in limited, designated areas – these will mainly be industrial or other cogeneration plants which can supply not only their own site but also other buildings with heat and electricity in urban redevelopment areas.

Other changes included in the amended law include a bidding system to foster further competition in the generation sector and new controls on tariffs designed to promote efficiency and bring down electricity prices in response to criticism that Japan's energy prices are high compared to those of the rest of the world.

Japan applies taxes to almost all uses – domestic, electricity generation and industrial – of oil, electricity and gas, such taxes representing between 3 and 5.6% of the final price to consumers. Energy prices have been high in Japan because of the country's dependence on imported fuel and because its indigenous resources (renewable energy and coal) tend also to be high-cost. However, the prices of most things are high in Japan when compared to other countries – though when purchasing-power parity* is used to compare prices the difference is not so great. For example, in 1990 the price of industrial electricity was fifteen cents per kilowatt-hour in Japan, compared to seven cents in the UK. However, converted to a purchasing-power parity basis, the respective figures were nine cents for Japan and seven cents for the UK.

The Japanese developmental state

By any standards Japan's economic and industrial progress since the Second World War has been impressive, with the growth of its GDP

---

* Purchasing-power parities are rates of currency conversion that eliminate the differences in price levels between countries. Thus, a given sum of money, when converted into different currencies at these rates, will buy the same basket of goods and services in all countries.

substantially outstripping that of other OECD countries. Between 1950 and 1973, for example, Japan's annual rate of growth was nearly 10% compared to an average of 5% in all OECD countries – even that of Japan's nearest competitor, Germany, was only 6%. Clearly, Japan had some catching up to do given its late industrial-isation, but such achievements in such a short space of time can only be considered impressive. And while growth in all OECD countries (including Japan) fell in the 1970s following the oil price increases, Japan's remained higher than all except Norway for the remainder of that decade.

Johnson (1982) considers that it is the unique structural and insti-tutional features of Japan which are primarily responsible for the country's success. These include the 'descent' of retired bureaucrats into industry; the industrial groupings and conglomerates; public corporations; government-controlled financial institutions; and the nature of the civil service. Although these have grown up in an *ad hoc* and unplanned way, Johnson argues that they constitute a for-midable set of institutions for promoting economic growth.

By the early 1950s Japan had a range of institutions with the capacity and will to bend market forces in the pursuit of national goals. The elite of bureaucrats and managers, many of whom had been educated in the same institutions, set out to transform Japan into an advanced industrial power by formulating a public purpose rather than allowing the market to decide. The effect of the Japanese will to become a 'developmental state' on the role of the civil service, and on the interactions between the civil service and industry, has thus been highly significant.

The Ministry of Trade and Industry and 'administrative guidance'

After the creation of the Ministry of Commerce and Industry's (MCI) Resources Bureau in 1927, military economists used it to get laws enacted for particular strategic industries. The first such law was the Petroleum Industry Law of 1934, which MCI was given responsibility for administering. In 1943 the MCI was converted into the Ministry of Munitions and incorporated the Electric Power Bureau (EPB) and the Oil Bureau. The MITI Establishment Law of 1949 was designed to orient government effort towards interna-tional trade and the promotion of exports, which had fallen dramatically during the war.

Although the Japanese economic system rests on a legal foundation, the laws are short and very general. In Johnson's (1982) view, the key to MITI's success in industrial policy lies in its development of 'administrative guidance', a term that first appeared in a MITI annual report in 1962. Administrative guidance is not technically a law or even enforceable but exists as a set of unwritten rules allowing ministries to issue directives, warnings and encouragement to the enterprises or clients within the jurisdiction of a particular ministry.

While penalties for non-compliance are not spelt out, there are few objections when administrative guidance is presented as being in the national interest, according to Johnson. Furthermore, administrative guidance is often also implemented with an effective incentive to compliance – for example, the stipulation that those not complying will have their names made public or by not granting licenses immediately to those, such as builders, who do not comply (Shiono, 1984). Administrative guidance is usually complied with even when businesses do not agree with it, as they may feel that their relationships with the bureaucracy will be impaired if they do not (especially if they are seeking government subsidies).

However, the notion that MITI is all-powerful has been challenged – notably by Friedman, who feels that people have swallowed the bureaucratic regulation thesis because they have 'confused the promulgation of a policy with the policy's effectiveness' (Friedman, 1988: 203). Friedman's view is that Johnson's exclusive focus on MITI ignores the political dynamic, leading him to believe in the power of the 'absolutist state' in which the bureaucracy controls all decisions and is responsible for policy innovation, even though opposition from industry has often constrained what the state (via MITI) can do. For example, Friedman points out that private companies have frustrated attempts at greater state control of the oil industry before and since the Second World War.

A striking example of bureaucratic inability to control policy choice provided by Johnson is pollution – mercury poisoning of the sea, asthma suffered by people near petrochemical plants, air pollution in the major cities – in the 1960s. Considerable political pressure from consumers and residents persuaded the Diet to enact the Pollution Countermeasures Basic Law in 1967, which, MITI insisted, should be watered down so that anti-pollution measures should not harm the economy. However, in view of the public concern, the Diet overruled MITI in the famous 'pollution Diet' of 1970. Perhaps realising it had better make the best of a battle it had lost, MITI renamed its Mine Safety Bureau the Environmental Protection and Safety Bureau and increased the budget for dealing with pollution from 274 million yen in 1970 to 638 million yen in 1971. By the 1980s MITI was credited with having run 'one of the most effective industrial clean-up campaigns in history and, in the process, it also developed a thriving new industry in anti-pollution devices' (Johnson, 1982: 297).

Friedman's analysis supports a case against bureaucratic omnipotence in Japanese policy choice, but it neither proves nor disproves the effectiveness of the bureaucracy in Japan in delivering and developing economic policy within the constraints of policy choice. Johnson aims to show that MITI was indeed successful in developing and delivering policies, particularly through the technique of administrative guidance. By and large, his examples give some support to this – notably the system of priority production in the coal industry. As he says, 'priority production had an important effect on later bureaucratic attitudes as a precedent for bolder rather than more cautious fiscally responsible courses of action ... ' (Johnson, 1982: 186).

Johnson tends to assume a much more all-powerful role for the bureaucracy, particularly in policy choice, than even his own evidence would support, but his work is useful in illustrating those aspects of the Japanese bureaucratic system which make its role in policy development and implementation particularly effective. Friedman's work injects an important note of realism about the nature of policy choice in Japan.

Development of energy policy

The first government action on energy was the Petroleum Industry Law of 1934, which was the model for the Petroleum Industry Law of 1962. The Petroleum Industry Law gave the government licensing powers over the industry, required importers to store six months supply of oil in Japan and empowered the government to set quotas, fix prices and compulsorily purchase petroleum products. The Ministry of Commerce and Industry was put in charge of administering the law, which authorised the creation of a fuel section in the Mining Bureau. MITI was created in 1949, consolidating wartime moves to bring together aspects of energy policy that had previously been split between various ministries.

Japan made its first attempts to introduce energy conservation measures in the 1950s. The Heat Energy Control Law of 1951 was enacted because industrial reconstruction was threatened by the limited extent of indigenous energy resources and a shortage of foreign exchange to import fuels. This law, administered by MITI, required factories to employ heat-control technicians qualified to prescribed government standards. It remained in effect until 1979, although monitoring was relaxed in the cheap oil era of the 1960s. Thus we see a confident Ministry – realising that its main aims of boosting foreign trade and exports might be hampered by limited indigenous energy supplies – taking swift, early action to reduce energy demand. This seems to have set the scene for the later action which is outlined below.

MITI was reorganised in 1973 and a new external agency – the Natural Resources and Energy Agency (NREA) – was established, combining administration of oil, coal, energy conservation and public utilities (including nuclear) into one powerful unit. This reorganisation, coming three months before the oil shock, was to prove highly fortuitous. Japan was the world's largest oil importer and totally dependent on the Middle East, so it was hit hard by the oil shock. Eighty-nine per cent of its primary energy demand was met by imported oil – higher even than France (78%) and considerably higher than the UK, where over 50% of primary energy demand was met by indigenous resources in the mid-1970s, even before North Sea oil and gas came fully on stream. Given Japan's target of 5–6% annual economic growth for the 1980s, there was a clear need to reduce energy consumption (particularly of imported oil) per unit of GNP.

On 16 November 1973 the Cabinet enacted its Emergency Petroleum Countermeasures Policy of crash conservation programmes. According to Johnson (1982), the oil shock provided MITI with an opportunity to regain its previous authority. There were severe problems. Heating oil rose in price dramatically and then became scarce along with other items. Ministers were confronted with the sight of angry housewives unable to buy toilet paper and frustrated taxi drivers unable to obtain liquefied petroleum gas (LPG). The initial government response was to declare a state of emergency and a 15% reduction in electricity supply to industry. Two new laws –

the Emergency Measures Law for the Stabilisation of the People's Livelihood and the Petroleum Supply and Demand Normalisation Law – gave MITI considerable powers over wholesalers and retailers to ensure the supply of goods, to establish fixed prices for certain goods and to fine violators.

In 1977 the Supply and Demand sub-committee of MITI's Energy Council had revised its previous target of a 5.5% cut in energy consumption during the 1980s to 10.8% for 1985 and 13.5% for 1990. However, as the Conservation sub-committee reported in November 1977, actual demand (in energy use/output terms) was increasing; hence their proposals for various actions, including legislation. The 1951 Heat Energy Control Law was reinforced in the form of the new Law Concerning Rationalisation and the Use of Energy (referred to hereafter as the '1979 Law'), which was passed by both houses of the Diet in June 1979.

Energy conservation programmes

The 1979 Law (box 9.2) was concerned particularly with the use of energy by industry as that represented the major sector of energy use in Japan. In 1978 industry accounted for 57% of total energy use in Japan; by 1985 this had been reduced to 50%, but this is still high compared to many other OECD countries, where the industrial sector typically accounts for 30–40% of total energy use. All plants in manufacturing, mining, electricity, gas and heat supply that consume more than a specified amount of fuel are designated 'energy management factories'; such plants account for about 63% of total industrial energy demand in Japan.

Various depreciation allowances and loans and tax incentive schemes have been provided to industry to finance energy-saving measures. However, because the cost of borrowing is so low in Japan and because the qualification criteria for these loans are so stringent, take-up has been fairly minimal.

MITI had established a Comprehensive Energy Policy Research Council in 1965, made up of academics, business representatives and trade unions. The council did very little, however, until 1977, when it established a Conservation sub-committee. As we have seen, the quango system is very important in Japan. A key quango in the energy field is the Energy Conservation Centre (ECC), which was founded in October 1978 and inherited some staff and assets from

> **9.2 Law Concerning Rationalisation and the Use of Energy 1979**
>
> - Major energy users are designated 'energy management factories' and are required to have qualified energy managers – MITI specifies how many.
> - MITI prescribes the curriculum and sets the exam that energy managers have to pass. The courses and exams are run by the Energy Conservation Centre.
> - Energy managers have to maintain detailed records of: the purchase, internal generation, sale and use of fuels; measures to save energy; and the energy consumption ratings of all equipment.
> - MITI officials can ask to see these records and require an 'energy use rationalisation plan' to reduce consumption if performance is considered inadequate. Firms that produce inadequate plans or fail to implement them can be instructed to make changes.

a body set up in the 1950s – the Heat Managers Association. Around 24% of the ECC's costs are met by central government, the remainder coming from membership subscriptions paid by private firms, running courses, selling publications and income from the bicycle-race betting tote. Staff are drawn from MITI officials and private industry – senior people in second careers and more junior people on secondment. The ECC has a close working relationship with the Energy Conservation Measures Department of MITI, both centrally and in its branch offices.

Most of the ECC's work is with industry and its primary role is in relation to the 1979 Law. It publishes a monthly magazine for members and other publications, runs courses and competitions and promotes good practice. It also maintains a panel of consultant energy managers from firms which have won awards for energy saving who provide a free (paid for by MITI) energy audit for small companies. Here again MITI retains tight control by requiring a report on the audit and the recommendations made. On behalf of MITI, the ECC also runs many general information and education campaigns aimed at the general public and schools.

The ECC is a good example of how business and the government work closely together towards a common end. This general feature of the Japanese system of business–government policy networks has thus worked to the benefit of energy conservation.

Energy conservation in the household and commercial sector

As we have already seen, compared to most other OECD countries a much higher proportion of energy is used in the industrial sector and a much lower proportion in the household and commercial sector – and these differences were even more marked in the 1970s. It is therefore not surprising that most of Japan's efforts have been concentrated on the former rather than the latter. Insulation standards for new homes, for example, have lagged far behind those in most European countries. In commercial sector buildings standards have been largely voluntary and compliance has generally been low.

However, Japan did make some headway with the efficiency of domestic appliances in the early 1980s. Energy labelling was introduced (against some opposition from manufacturers, who held the scheme up for some time), but perhaps more important was the setting of minimum efficiency standards for 'designated' appliances. Refrigerators were designated in 1980, for example, with manufacturers and importers required to achieve an average efficiency improvement of 20% over the 1978 consumption rate by September 1983. This target was actually beaten, which led to designated status being removed from refrigerators, since when their average efficiency has not improved at all. Even those appliances which have remained designated or have since been designated (e.g. a number of office equipment items including photocopiers) have shown little improvement – and this cannot be said to be due to technical limitations as the efficiencies of many products in the Japanese market are well below the world's best. It is worth noting that appliance standards were implemented in the Japanese tradition of guidance – the standards are in the form of targets rather than mandatory regulations.

How much progress has Japan made as a result of these various programmes? From the late 1970s to the mid-1980s major improvements were made in the industrial sector, but IEA figures show that energy efficiency stopped improving in 1986 and that demand has risen since 1987. Japan's TPES/GDP ratio is about 40% below the IEA average and TFC per capita is about 43% below. From 1979 to 1987 energy intensity fell nearly 25%.

However, it was not just the energy-saving programmes which were responsible for the improvements through to the mid-1980s. Fuel switching from oil to nuclear power and gas was widely encouraged, with financial incentives to electricity generators to switch fuels. The share of natural gas in total energy consumption rose from 1.5% in 1973 to 9.6% by 1988, while that of nuclear power rose from 0.6% to 9% (Perkins, 1994). Industrial restructuring was also an important factor, with conscious government efforts and encouragement to shift capital and labour from energy-intensive to new, high-tech industries.

Although energy demand in the buildings sector has been low, it has been increasing rapidly since the mid-1980s as a result of increased commercial sector activity, greater use of central heating and air conditioning and an increase in the number of households. The lack of energy conservation in this sector is thus becoming much more significant for total energy use in Japan and accounts for a significant proportion of growth in use since the late 1980s.

The Japanese response to climate change concerns

In October 1990 the Council of Ministers decided on an Action Programme to Arrest Global Warming for 1991–2010. This set the aim of stabilising CO_2 emissions on a per capita basis in 2000 at the 1990 level. Japan signed the Framework Convention on Climate Change in 1992 and ratified it in 1993, but stuck to its per capita target rather than the absolute target of most countries. Actions to achieve the target include the promotion of CHP, energy conservation (including the use of tax incentives), natural gas and non-fossil fuels.

The Basic Environment Law was enacted in late 1993 and sets out principles for environmental conservation and sustainable economic development. It sets the framework for specific policies, such as those in the area of climate change. The law includes a provision relating to the use of economic instruments. One specific policy developed under the law, for example, has been an action plan on 'greening government operations' designed to improve efficiency in energy and water use in the public sector.

Japan is one of the countries that have come under criticism from environmental groups for a less than positive attitude to the setting of targets, particularly in respect of targets after 2000. The difficulties arise from Japan's desire to maintain its position as a leading economic power and from the power of the industrial lobby, including MITI, which opposes targets on the grounds that they would harm Japan's position. Japan also argues that it starts from a more energy-efficient baseline and lower CO_2/GDP ratio than many other countries – both claims are true if the first is taken on a per capita basis, but in absolute terms Japan's energy consumption and emissions are the second highest in the OECD after the US.

Attempts by the Ministry of Finance (which saw it as a useful potential source of revenue) and the Environmental Agency (which saw a way to increase its influence) to introduce a carbon tax during 1992 and 1993 were effectively opposed by MITI and the industry lobby, which saw the tax as a threat to the competitiveness of Japanese industry and warned that it could lead to many firms relocating from Japan to countries without such a tax. Despite efforts since 1973 to lessen dependence on oil imports, in 1996 80% of Japan's energy demand was still met by imports and 55% was still met by imported oil. The main energy policy concern for Japan thus remains security of supply rather than environmental considerations.

Japan was a member of the JUSCANZ (Japan, the US, Canada, Australia and New Zealand), which opposed the setting of targets at Berlin in 1995. In the lead up to Kyoto in 1997 it continued to oppose the setting of tough targets, such as the 15% reduction suggested by the EU, and proposed only a 5% target. In the event, the Kyoto agreement required Japan to reduce emissions by 6%, which is lower than the target set for the EU and the US.

Conclusion

There has been a tendency to praise Japan as one of the best examples of a country that has successfully decoupled GDP growth from growth in energy demand. The nation has made impressive improvements in energy intensity since the 1970s – although these have been a result of a combination of shifts in industrial mix as well as improvements in energy efficiency. However, the improvement rate slowed down from the late 1980s and, although the growth of GDP was considerably higher than the growth of electricity demand during the 1980s, this trend has halted since the early 1990s, with electricity demand increasing much faster than GDP growth – in 1994, for example, GDP growth was only 0.6% but electricity sales increased by 7.2%.

Industry's share of energy consumption will continue to fall as the household and commercial sector takes an increasing share due to structural change (a move from basic industries to commercial sector businesses) and growth in the use of heating, air conditioning and appliances in buildings. A key factor in this change is the increasing demand for air conditioning due to a number of very hot summers, with the result that the peak annual demand is in the daytime in summer.

During the 1970s and early to mid-1980s there was a fortunate coming together of several factors in Japan which put it in a good position to secure major energy efficiency and even energy conservation achievements. First, the need to reduce dependence on imported oil and to boost exports provided a strong sense of purpose that was shared by government and business. Second, a ministry that was well used to intervention was given an early responsibility (in 1951) for energy conservation policies and programmes which were well within its competence to administer.

The third factor was the experience MITI has of working closely with industry (the main target for its energy conservation programmes), of setting up effective joint industry–government organisations (in this case the ECC) and the existence of its own regional offices, which could all be involved in delivery. The Japanese propensity to form closed industry–government policy networks (environmental and consumer groups may be marginalised in many countries but they tend to be excluded completely in Japan) thus worked for energy conservation rather than against it, as has often been the experience in other countries. And finally, there was the existence of the tool of administrative guidance, through which industry compliance could be secured. Indeed, the use of various forms of regulation does seem to have been much more significant for Japan's success in energy conservation than grants and loans.

However, since the end of the 1980s this favourable position has changed. The first reason for this has been low energy prices, which dulled the conservation/efficiency effort in most countries. Second, much of the easy potential in industry has been realised and continued economic growth means that energy demand is likely to remain, at best, constant despite some continued efficiency improvements. Added to this is the fact that the MITI–industry policy network remains powerful and will continue to resist calls for new conservation efforts which industry may find more difficult to achieve. Third, the rise in demand is mainly in the household and commercial sectors, where the potential for growth is substantial. And fourth, government attitudes to the system of voluntary regulation have changed. Since the election, in 1993, of a government committed to deregulation, industry has begun to take administrative guidance and other similar forms of regulation much less seriously than it once did.

Finally, it has to be said that Japan may be a very energy-efficient country but it is also one with very high energy consumption in absolute terms and is thus, perhaps, a good illustration of the fact that improvements in energy efficiency do not necessarily lead to energy conservation.

10

The impact of conservation programmes and energy prices

Changes in energy intensity

All six countries featured in this book have made efforts to conserve energy since the 1973 oil crisis. What changes can we now see in energy intensity and consumption in specific sectors? How far are these due to energy conservation programmes involving regulation, incentives, information and/or exhortation, and what has been the effect of energy prices?

At one level, of course, enormous progress has been made since 1973 in terms of the way that energy is used in western countries. Buildings are better insulated, home and office appliances are more energy-efficient, industry uses more energy-efficient processes, and many older, energy-intensive industries have been replaced by less energy-intensive ones. Power stations are raising the level of efficiency at which they convert primary energy to electricity from around 30% in older coal- and oil-fired power stations to 50% plus in newer gas-fired, combined-cycle power stations.

As a result, the rate of growth in energy use has been much slower than that of gross domestic product. By the mid-1990s most countries used far less energy – as measured by total primary energy supply – per unit of GDP than they did in the early 1970s. As Table 10.1 shows, only Australia, of the countries studied in this book, has achieved a relatively low improvement in its energy intensity ratio.

However, although the western world is using energy much more efficiently in the late 1990s than it did in the early 1970s, it is using more energy now than it did then. The total energy demand of IEA countries rose from 3,494 Mtoe (million tonnes of oil equivalent) in 1973 to 4,315 Mtoe in 1994. The reasons for this are not hard to identify. Buildings may be better insulated and have more energy-

Table 10.1   *TPES/GDP (energy intensity) ratios*

	1973	1995	Change (%) 1973–95
Australia	0.32	0.28	−12
Denmark	0.21	0.14	−33
Japan	0.21	0.16	−23
Netherlands	0.32	0.23	−28
UK	0.32	0.21	−34
US	0.47	0.34	−28

Source: International Energy Agency (1997); percentage changes calculated by the author.

efficient heating systems than they did 25 years ago, but there are many more buildings now than then (particularly homes and offices), they are heated and air-conditioned much more, and they contain many more energy-using appliances and equipment. Power stations may be more efficient, but rising electricity demand for all those home and office appliances means there are more of them producing more electricity.

Just think of a typical home in 1973 compared to its counterpart in 1998. In 1973 it had one television set, one stereo system, a refrigerator, a washing machine and one central light in each room. In some countries – notably the UK – it might not have had central heating. In 1998 it has central heating, three TVs (one in the living room, one in the kitchen, one in a teenager's bedroom), a video recorder, two stereo systems (one for the teenager again), a computer and printer, a refrigerator, freezer, washing machine, tumble-drier, dishwasher and microwave oven, multiple lights in most rooms and numerous other small appliances.

If one adds in the growth in transport use – particularly growth in the use of cars – it is not hard to see why reductions in energy use (as opposed to using it more efficiently) have not been achieved over the last twenty-five years. However, even if one excludes transport, energy use has still been rising in most IEA countries, particularly in the residential and commercial sectors.

Thus, what the improvements in energy intensity may obscure is that four of the six countries (the exceptions being the UK and Denmark) were using significantly more energy in 1995 than they

Table 10.2   *TPES in 1973, 1995 and 2000*

	1973 (Mtoe)	1995 (Mtoe)	Change (%) 1973–95	2000 (forecast, Mtoe)	Forecast change (%) 1995–2000
Australia	58	94	+64	108	+15
Denmark	19.7	20.5	+4	19.6	−5
Japan	324	497	+53	494	−0.5
Netherlands	62	73	+17	71	−2.5
UK	221	222	+0.5	232	+5
US	1723	2078	+21	2251	+8

Source: International Energy Agency (1997); percentage changes calculated by the author.

were in 1973 – much more in the cases of Japan and Australia. Table 10.2 illustrates the extent of this growth in energy use. The table also shows that, while Denmark, Japan and the Netherlands are forecasting small reductions in TPES from 1995 to 2000, Australia, the UK and the US are predicting further increases.

Some countries have a much higher TPES than others owing to their higher population levels. Increased energy demand may also be due to population growth, and it is therefore also useful to look at changes in TPES per inhabitant.

The most striking feature revealed by this measure (Table 10.3) is the huge differential between the US and the other countries. Indeed,

Table 10.3   *TPES per inhabitant in 1973 and 1995 (toe per capita)*

	1973	1995	Change (%) 1973–95
Australia	4.27	5.22	+22
Denmark	3.93	3.92	0
Japan	2.98	3.96	+33
Netherlands	4.65	4.74	+2
UK	3.93	3.79	−4
US	8.13	7.90	−3

Source: International Energy Agency (1997); percentage changes calculated by the author.

of all OECD countries only Canada is close to the US level (7.85 toe
per capita in 1995) and only Luxembourg exceeds it (at 9.52 toe per
capita) due to its very special circumstances of having a small population and a lot of energy-intensive industry.

Turning to look at the *changes* in TPES, the figures for the UK
and Denmark suggest that in these two cases population change is of
limited significance. However, in the other four countries the change
in per capita consumption suggests that a proportion of the growth
in total TPES could be due to population growth. This is particularly
marked in the case of Australia (TPES up by 64%, per capita consumption up only 22%), which is, of course, one of the few western
countries still to encourage considerable immigration. The US and
the UK have made some modest progress in terms of energy use per
capita (albeit from a very high base), and Denmark has managed to
stabilise its per capita consumption. The small increase in the Netherlands may not be significant. However, for Australia and Japan this
measure further illustrates the problems they have with rising energy
use, which will make it difficult for them to meet even very modest
climate-change targets.

Changes in consumption in different sectors of the economy

The TPES measure covers all energy use. To find out what changes
there have been in specific sectors (such as transport or industry) we
need to look at the total final consumption measure. Data for the
changes in TFC over the period 1973–95 are given in Table 10.4.
Here we can see that only Denmark had a lower TFC in 1995

Table 10.4   *Percentage changes in TFC from 1973 to 1995*

	Total	Industry	Transport	Other
Australia	+57	+40	+87	+51
Denmark	−5	−20	+36	−13
Japan	+36	0	+102	+95
Netherlands	+17	+5	+70	+10
UK	+2	−33	+54	+19
US	+13	+7	+29	+4

Percentages derived from IEA statistics. 'Other' comprises domestic, commercial and
public sector buildings.

than it did in 1973. Much of the increase is down to transport – all countries show sizeable increases in TFC in this sector over the twenty-one-year period. The US increase was the lowest perhaps because it was already so much higher than that of other countries in 1973, but it may also owe something to efficiency standards for cars and the imposition of the low speed limit on US roads, both of which were introduced in the 1970s. In Japan's industrial sector TFC in 1995 was the same as in 1973, and in the Netherlands and the US it was slightly higher. In the UK and Denmark industrial TFC has decreased substantially, but in Australia TFC by industry increased by 40%. The 'other' sector (households, commerce and the public sector – i.e. buildings) shows a reduction only in Denmark, a significant increase in the UK, and major increases in Australia and Japan.

Changes in energy prices

As outlined in the chapters on individual countries, most, apart from Denmark, have made limited use of energy pricing or taxation to achieve energy conservation. Furthermore, some – notably the US and Australia – have provided substantial incentives for energy production, which have exacerbated the bias in favour of energy supply. Table 10.5 shows how energy prices have changed in the six countries since 1978.

The data indicate that the peak year for energy prices after 1978 was 1983, except in Australia and the Netherlands, where it was 1985. In particular, the US, the UK and Japan have experienced steadily declining prices since 1982, apart from short-term increases in 1991 due to the Gulf War. In the Netherlands prices remained

Table 10.5 *Indices of real energy prices for end-users (1990 = 100)*

	1978	1983	1985	1989	1992	1993	1994	1995
Australia	64.4	123.4	129.5	95.2	105.2	104.6	102.3	99.8
Denmark	82.4	143.8	135.8	104.9	106	111.2	106.2	106.5
Japan	118	156.9	143.7	95.3	94.2	91	88.2	82.3
Netherlands	89.7	142.6	147.7	92.8	99.6	104	104.2	104.3
UK	111.6	139.6	136.2	99.5	97.8	98.9	97.4	94.9
US	107.1	141	130.4	98	92	90.6	89.2	85.9

Source: International Energy Agency (1998).

broadly stable until 1993, then increased and remained at the same level through 1994 and 1995. Prices in Denmark fell from the 1983 peak until 1990 but increased in 1990–93, fell in 1994 and increased again in 1995. Prices fell in Australia from 1985 to 1990, then increased until 1992, and then fell through 1993–95. Thus, by 1995 energy prices were lower than they had been in 1990 in Japan, the UK and the US, while in Australia they remained at 1990 levels. In Denmark and the Netherlands energy prices were rather higher in 1995 than in 1990.

Energy conservation programmes versus energy pricing – the theories assessed

Do the changes in energy intensity for each country owe much to government action to stimulate energy conservation, or more to the level of energy prices or other factors? First, on energy prices, it is important to distinguish between absolute price levels and the effects of price changes. Industrialised countries with low energy prices tend to have high levels of energy intensity. For example, Japan had by far the highest electricity and gas prices of any of the six countries in 1995, with Denmark in second place, followed by the UK and the Netherlands, with the lowest prices in the US and Australia. These rankings correspond closely with their relative levels of energy intensity in 1995 as shown in Table 10.1.

However, what matters more over time is the trend of energy prices as, given the low price elasticity for much energy use (particularly in transport and by households), people tend to acclimatise themselves to prices whether high or low and it is price changes that are more likely to affect behaviour. We can also distinguish between sudden, large changes in prices (as happened after the oil price shocks) and more gradual changes – the latter being less likely to have an immediate impact although over several years the effect may be more noticeable.

Brookes (1990) and Greenhalgh (1990) have suggested that efforts to improve energy efficiency do not lead to significant energy savings because they make energy cheaper and people are able to afford more of it (e.g. by having a warmer home, using more appliances) or to buy more goods and services on which energy has been used (in production, delivery, etc.). In support of his argument, Brookes (1991) cited the US government's reluctance to raise taxes on oil in the 1970s. Instead, it introduced regulations to improve the fuel-efficiency of cars. The result, according to Brookes, was that the improved fuel-efficiency of cars increased oil use as more people could afford cars and to use them more often. Thus, Brookes argues that taxation is the main way to reduce energy consumption, rather than incentives and regulation which make energy cheaper.

Grubb (1990) disagreed with Brookes' scepticism about energy-saving regulations and incentives on two grounds. First, that saturation may be reached for certain energy-using goods and services; and second, that there is a fundamental difference between naturally arising efficiency improvements (such as occurred prior to 1973 in the desire to reduce costs and develop new markets and products) and those which are specifically engineered by government action. The former tend to encourage demand growth, whereas the latter can be targeted at sectors that are unresponsive to price but which are likely to have much unrealised technical potential for efficiency improvements.

Brookes' general thesis is based in sound economic theory – if you make something more efficient you make it cheaper to use and, hence, increase demand for it. Grubb's argument that specifically engineered energy efficiency measures can somehow buck this trend is contradicted even by his own examples, such as people maintaining a constant consumption level and taking the advantage of improved comfort in previously draughty buildings. Indeed, Grubb does acknowledge that the cost-reduction benefits of improved efficiency might lead to greater use if not countered by price rises.

However, Brookes seems to ignore the law of diminishing returns – whereby the marginal utility of an extra unit of energy may eventually become nil. His example of car fuel-efficiency illustrates this well. The demand for fuel to run cars is not infinite (even if every adult owned more than one car, they can only drive one at a time!), so making them more efficient will eventually be beneficial. Furthermore, greater fuel-efficiency was not the only reason why more people bought and used cars. Social trends such as rising incomes, smaller households and the baby-boom generation buying cars for the first time in the 1970s helped to stimulate demand and use. These trends encouraged more facilities to be geared to car-owners, creating an increasing spiral towards car-ownership and use. Thus it is quite feasible that car-ownership and use would have increased without the regulation but that the cars wouldn't have been as efficient. As has been found in many countries, car use has proved remarkably unresponsive to petrol tax increases.

Support for the energy pricing option also comes from von Weizsacker (1994), who argues for the ending of subsidies that encourage depletion of natural resources (in mining, agriculture, etc.) and the incorporation of externalities, via taxes, on non-renewable sources of energy, primary raw materials, water consumption, certain chemicals and land use. In von Weizsacker's vision such ecological tax reform would enable market solutions to be developed and stimulate technological innovation. This, he argues, is more likely to lead to substantial energy savings than bureaucratic measures such as efficiency standards, subsidies for investment in energy efficiency, etc. von Weizsacker has said of least-cost planning by US utilities that it 'will not reach beyond relatively superficial savings to reduce excessive waste of energy. Truly new energy efficient technologies ... are not to be expected as a result of local LCP, simply because energy prices are too low to make major changes profitable' (von Weizsacker, 1994: 255).

The relative effectiveness of energy conservation programmes and energy prices

What support does the evidence provide for these theories? Lucas (1985) points out that there is a historical trend to increased energy efficiency. In the past – especially in the 1960s – economies grew faster than the decline in specific energy consumption, with the result that energy demand continued to grow, even if at a slower rate than GDP. Since the early 1970s economic growth has been slower, resulting in a drop in total energy consumption. The trend to energy efficiency is the result of more efficient power generation, substitution of gas for coal and more fuel-efficient cars and appliances, each of which has occurred as a natural market trend even where governments have taken no action to mandate higher standards. Other trends, however, can militate against reductions in energy use (conservation) despite improvements in efficiency. Among these are the rapid growth in private car use, more appliances and air conditioning and substantial increases in industrial output or commercial activity. For example when the UK Department of Energy examined changes in energy intensity between 1982 and 1988 it found that, within the industry sector, around one-half of the savings were due to major industrial restructuring, with the remainder coming from rationalisation of plant, fuel switching and energy efficiency. In the domestic sector, fuel switching to gas for home heating resulted in significant savings, although some of this was cancelled out by increased electricity use for appliances and lighting.

The evidence on energy prices is also somewhat mixed and can be confusing because high or low energy prices may coincide with other changes – structural changes or changes in the level of economic activity – that can also affect energy use. Of course, such changes may themselves be driven by the level of energy prices, leaving one with a circular argument over cause and effect. Golove and Schipper (1997), examining changes in energy intensities in the US from 1973 to 1991, found that the rate of decline in energy intensities between 1979 and 1985 was the greatest, with lower rates from 1973 to 1979 and from 1985 to 1991. Looking in more detail at the period 1985–91, Golove and Schipper conclude that although a decline in activity (the recession) had slightly reduced energy consumption in 1990 and 1991, this was offset by a structural factor – the shift to a more energy-intensive mix between 1985 and 1991. They comment: 'that this increase occurred during a period of falling energy prices suggests (but does not prove) that some of the shift away from energy intensive production observed in the late 1970s and early 1980s was driven by higher energy prices' (Golove and Schipper, 1997: 810).

The sharp fall in oil prices (and consequent reductions in other fuel prices) in 1986 certainly seems to have had a depressing effect on trends to energy efficiency improvement in the US: in 1989 the IEA reported that the average efficiency of appliances had levelled off or fallen for the first time in more than a decade as consumers responded to lower prices by buying less efficient products. Coal prices were 20%, natural gas prices 38% and oil prices 52% lower in 1988 than they had been in 1985.

In Japan, domestic electricity customers have an incentive to conserve owing to the use of a three-tier pricing scale, whereby the rate per unit increases with consumption. This is operated by the electricity companies, at the instigation of the government, as a specific measure to encourage energy conservation. The main benefits of lower oil prices in recent years have thus been felt by industry. The Japanese Institute of Energy Economics found that energy conservation efforts by industry have been declining since 1987, which suggests that lower oil prices are indeed having the effect that economic theory would indicate (Taylor *et al.*, 1990).

As energy prices have risen and fallen in the UK, energy demand has risen and fallen in inverse proportion. In the 1960s, when energy prices were stable or falling in real terms, GDP growth of 3% a year was accompanied by rises in final energy demand of about 1.5% a year. When energy prices rose in the 1970s, economic growth of 1.75% a year coincided with an average annual drop in energy demand of 0.5%, despite the rise in consumption in the domestic sector due to the availability of relatively cheap North Sea gas. As energy prices fell in real terms in the 1980s, the average GDP growth of 2.5% a year between 1980 and 1988 was accompanied by an increase in energy demand of around 0.8% a year.

The evidence from previous studies thus tends to suggest that energy prices are a very important factor. Does the evidence assessed for the six countries studied in this book support this view? To assess the relative importance of energy prices, energy conservation programmes and other factors, it is interesting to compare the two periods 1973–90 and 1990–95. In the UK, TFC in industry showed a 35% decline during the first period but then increased by 5% between 1990 and 1995. Similarly, in the US industrial TFC declined by 7% between 1973 and 1990 but increased by 11% between 1990 and 1995. The decline in TFC in the first period can be assumed to be due to structural change away from energy-intensive heavy industry, probably encouraged by high energy prices in the 1970s combined with the effects of recession in the 1980s – particularly in the UK. The subsequent increase from 1990 to 1995 may be explained partly by the improving economy since around 1992, but it may also be due to lower and falling energy prices, which have been the trend in both countries (for all end-users but particularly for industry) since the mid-1980s.

In the buildings sector, falls in consumption between 1973 and 1990 in the US, Denmark and the Netherlands contrast with increases between 1990 and 1995. For example, in the US the sector showed a 4% decrease in TFC from 1973 to 1990 followed by an 8% increase from 1990 to 1995; in Denmark a 23% decrease in TFC from 1973 to 1990 contrasts with a 12% increase from 1990 to 1995; and in the Netherlands a 3% decrease from 1973 to 1990 contrasts with a 14% increase from 1990 to 1995. In the UK, Japan and Australia there are no such differences between the two periods – in all three cases consumption increased in both. Various factors could explain these recent increases in energy use in the buildings sector, but they may not all be related to low and falling energy prices.

The most significant factor is likely to be increasing electricity use in homes and offices for appliances, office equipment and air conditioning, which is due to rising living standards and expectations in which low energy prices play a part but may not be the sole explanation. In the household sector the trend to more and smaller households due to divorce and people living longer (factors that are unlikely to be caused by low energy prices) has also tended to increase electricity use. Given lower energy prices, there may have been less interest in energy saving on the part of households and businesses, manifested as lower investment in energy-saving measures and a weakening of energy efficiency standards for appliances. However, it is debatable how much difference higher energy prices since the late 1980s would have made. In Denmark prices to commercial users did increase between 1990 and 1995 (although prices to households fell), yet it too exhibited significant growth in this period – which suggests that structural trends can overwhelm pricing effects and that some energy use may be very inelastic to price changes. Despite falling energy prices in the late 1980s for households and commercial users, TFC in buildings in Denmark actually fell by 18% from 1987 to 1990, which suggests that an effective energy conservation programme (heat planning) can produce results despite low energy prices.

Australia consistently shows the worst performance on every measure, including energy intensity, and only perhaps half of its problem can be due to population growth. Significant factors here, which are likely to continue for the foreseeable future, are rapidly increasing private car use in a country where very long distances are frequently travelled; rapid growth in the commercial sector in terms of both number of buildings and use of air conditioning; new house building; considerable expansion in household central heating and air conditioning, both of which are still at fairly low levels of market penetration; and substantial industrial growth – much of it energy-intensive, which is unusual in a western country. Since 1973 Australia has made fewer attempts at energy conservation programmes than most western countries, but, given the size of these growth trends, it is debatable whether even a very aggressive conservation programme would have made much impact. However, it is interesting to note that Australia was facing rising energy prices during the mid-1980s and also saw price rises from 1990 to 1992, so falling energy prices cannot be the main reason for its rising energy consumption. Again this demonstrates that structural trends can overwhelm the effect of prices.

The fact that Japan's improvement in energy intensity between 1973 and 1995 turns out to be lower than that of the UK, the US, Denmark and the Netherlands is perhaps rather surprising, as too is the unchanged TFC in the industrial sector. However, if we break down this period it becomes clear that there is a marked difference between the period 1973–87 and what has happened since. TFC in Japanese industry fell by 19% between 1973 and 1987, about the same as Denmark (–20%) and less than the UK (–33%), but better than the US (–10%), Australia (+11%) and the Netherlands (+3%). Yet GDP growth was significantly higher in Japan (at an average of 3.6% per annum in the 1970s and 3.8% in the 1980s, compared to 2.5% and 2.8% in the US, 2.5% and 2% in Europe, and 2.8% and 3.3% in Australia) throughout this period. Furthermore, Japan, like all the other countries except Australia, experienced falling energy prices from 1982 to 1987 (albeit from a high starting point), which, once again, suggests that effective energy conservation programmes can work despite falling prices.

The relatively poor performance of Japan since the late 1980s can be assumed to be due partly to a winding down of energy conservation programmes in the industrial sector. Outside the industrial sector, the major factors accounting for the substantial increase in energy demand have been the growth in private transport plus a huge growth in consumption in the buildings sector. As we saw in chapter 9, most Japanese energy conservation programmes have been targeted at industry, with little effort to conserve energy in the domestic, commercial and public sectors (apart from efficiency standards for some domestic appliances).

In the Netherlands growth in the buildings sector has occurred mainly since 1990 and mirrors the trends in all the other countries. The major growth in energy use has been in the transport sector, the Netherlands coming third after Japan and Australia. The country exhibits fairly low growth in the industrial sector over the whole period (5%) despite its rather higher GDP growth than the European average (noticeably higher than the UK and Denmark). Furthermore, most of the growth in TFC occurred between 1973 and 1988, since when industrial TFC has not increased despite an average annual GDP growth of 2.6% from 1990 to 1995. This contrasts with the UK, where industrial sector TFC rose by 5% between 1990 and 1995 but average annual GDP growth was only 1.1%, and Denmark, where industrial TFC rose by 7% over the same period and average annual GDP growth was 2.1%. How important was the energy price factor? Looking specifically at prices to industry (which differ somewhat from those for all users given in Table 10.5), there was an 18% increase in the Netherlands from 1990 to 1995, compared to a 14% fall in the UK. However, industrial energy prices rose even more in Denmark – by 27% between 1990 and 1995.

It therefore seems reasonable to suggest that changes in energy prices may not be the sole reason for these differences between the UK, Denmark and the Netherlands. One reason for the difference could be the enormous increase in penetration of CHP in industry in the Netherlands since 1990. Clearly, rising industrial energy prices have been a stimulus for CHP, but there were also various government programmes to encourage its use. 2,300 MW of CHP was installed between 1991 and 1994, and by 1995 the country had 4,500 MW of CHP (25% of total electricity-generation capacity), 75% of which was in industry. This is a substantial figure for a small country – by 1995 the UK had only 3,500 MW of CHP (5% of overall generating capacity).

Denmark has done reasonably well – indeed, from 1973 until 1990 it required no increase in TPES). Part of this may be due to its policy of high energy prices, although prices fell during most of the 1980s. Furthermore, and paradoxically, the period since 1990 – when energy prices have been increasing – has seen TFC rise in all sectors, somewhat counteracting the achievements made mainly in the 1980s when prices were falling. Most of Denmark's efforts have been directed towards buildings, particularly those where most energy is used. These policies would seem to have been effective as Denmark is the only country to show a reduction in TFC in this sector over the whole period. Denmark's achievements can be seen even more clearly if we use a micro-level measure of space-heating intensity (the amount of heat input required to achieve a given room temperature). In the housing sector space-heating intensity declined by around 41% (from 220 kJ per square metre to 130 kJ per square metre) between 1973 and 1987; by comparison, in the UK it was still at roughly the same level (180 kJ per square metre) in 1987 as in 1973.

The small increase in TPES in Denmark is probably mainly due to a combination of greater use of coal for electricity generation and district heating at lower efficiencies than the oil it replaced, and an increase in the use of electricity for non-heating purposes in the household and commercial sector, particularly since 1990 (half of Denmark's worsening TFC/TPES ratio occurred between 1990 and 1995).

The increasing use of gas in the UK for both heating and power generation, together with the major decline of energy-intensive industry in the 1980s, are the main reasons why the UK alone has managed not to increase its TPES since 1973 despite the fact that energy prices have been low and falling since the early 1980s. Energy use in the buildings sector increased more rapidly in the five years from 1990 to 1995 than it did in the seventeen years from 1973 to 1990. This may be partly due to further price falls for commercial sector users since liberalisation of the energy market, but the main reason may be structural change – more and smaller households and the growth of the commercial sector since the late 1980s. From 1973 to 1990 certain factors constrained growth despite the low energy prices of the 1980s; these included not only the shift towards gas heating (more energy-efficient than coal or electric heating) but also the increased take-up of loft and cavity insulation and double glazing, which has helped to offset the increase in energy use due to more central heating. However, given that the government's only involvement was to provide grants for loft insulation, it cannot be said that government programmes made much impact in this period.

In the case of the US it is interesting to note that TFC in the buildings sector increased by only 4% from 1973 to 1995 and actually fell by 4% between 1973 and 1990 (again despite falling prices in the 1980s) – although from 1990 to 1995 it increased by 8%. Apart from the most recent years, the US displays a notable contrast to the trends in the UK, Japan and Australia. It is likely that much of the explanation for this is that the US reached saturation point in terms of growth in this sector much earlier than other countries, as indicated by the fact that per capita TPES was 8 toe in the US in 1973 compared to 3–5 toe in the other countries. However, it seems possible that part of the explanation for the US's limited growth in TFC in the buildings sector is the action that was taken to improve energy efficiency – notably the mandatory standards for household appliances in populous states like California and the DSM/LCP initiatives. Growth since 1990 in the buildings sector is due in large part to demographic changes – divorce and older people living longer resulting in more households – that are common to all industrialised countries.

Conclusion

In the end, therefore, it proves difficult in many cases to attribute changes in TFC in specific sectors, much less the broader measure of changes in energy intensity, to action or inaction on energy conservation, and particularly to ascribe changes to specific government programmes. The problem essentially is that energy conservation programmes tend to have an impact at the micro-level whereas changes in TFC and TPES are macro-level measures in which many variables, as well as energy conservation actions, have an effect. It is only when energy conservation programmes are large-scale and directed at major energy-using sectors (e.g. the industrial sector programmes in Japan from the late 1970s to the late 1980s, the heat planning programme in Denmark from the 1970s to the early 1990s, and possibly CHP in industry in the Netherlands since 1990) that their impact can be seen at these macro-levels.

This suggests two things. First, the need for more micro-level measures (such as space-heating intensity), which are more likely to reveal the effects of programmes. Second, that it might make sense to concentrate effort on some programmes rather than others. Improvements to the building fabric through insulation without making improvements to heating systems may result in consumers taking most of the benefits in higher heating standards as for the same expenditure they will now be able to get more useful heat. Improving the heating system as well as the building fabric – by installing a new boiler and/or heating controls or using CHP – will make it more likely that less fuel needs to be consumed to achieve the desired temperature. If the aim is to achieve the greatest energy conservation effect (or the greatest reduction in CO_2 emissions), it makes sense to look at all insulation and heating options (including CHP) rather than focusing exclusively on improvements to the building fabric as many government programmes have. A similar case might be made for improvements to the efficiency of those appliances (refrigeration for example) where improved energy efficiency is less likely to encourage more consumption.

It is also difficult to say with certainty that raising energy prices is more likely to lead to energy conservation than programmes involving regulation or incentives. The evidence of increasing energy use in the commercial, public and housing sectors since 1990 in all the countries considered may owe much to generally lower or falling energy prices since 1990. However, it is interesting to note that even in countries where energy prices have not fallen since 1990 (Australia, Denmark and the Netherlands) energy demand has been rising in these sectors.

The fact that prices sometimes seem to have limited impact on use may be due to prices being raised for sectors where demand is not growing very much but not being raised where price increases might take most effect – notably in the area of transport (although energy demand in transport may be even less elastic than many other uses). In a number of countries the brunt of energy taxation has fallen on households – for example in Denmark and Japan; this made sense in Denmark as that is where most energy is used, but not in Japan, where industry is the main user. There is also some evidence of a time lag whereby consumption may continue to fall for some time even when prices have begun to fall and may continue to rise even when prices have begun to increase.

While the evidence of the impact of prices on energy conservation is somewhat debatable, it does suggest that energy price levels and price trends affect conservation achievements. Although it is often difficult to separate the effects of price from other factors which have affected consumption, it seems clear that, in the absence of rising prices, other forms of intervention become more essential but may prove of limited effectiveness if there is no motivation to save money on bills. Indeed, a cynic might say that it is because raising energy prices is the best way of reducing demand that the energy industries are so opposed to such measures. Other measures can be regarded as mere tinkering which, at most, will reduce or slow down demand growth.

Two important points can be made in summing up. First, that energy demand is perhaps not quite as elastic and, hence, responsive to price changes as might sometimes be thought – a finding supported by much of the modelling work that has been done on the level of carbon taxes required to affect demand. The second is that effective energy conservation programmes (such as heat planning in Denmark) can produce results even if energy prices are low and/or falling – although higher energy prices would probably enable such programmes to achieve greater results at lower cost in terms of the need for incentives and regulation.

11

Factors affecting energy conservation policy

The reductions in energy intensity discussed in the previous chapter suggest that significant progress has been made since 1973 in terms of energy efficiency but not – apart from a few instances in some countries – in terms of energy conservation. However, to reduce greenhouse-gas emissions, the much tougher goal of energy conservation will have to be achieved.

As we have seen from the country chapters, energy conservation policies have developed in different ways and with varying degrees of success in the countries studied. These differences have been due to a number of factors, including differences in the structure of the energy-using sector, differences in government approach, the differing natures of the energy-supply industries, and different energy pricing policies. Significant changes over time from the first efforts following the 1973 oil crisis up to the late 1990s can also be observed – changes that have resulted from movements in world energy prices and differing perceptions of energy supply security between the 1970s and 1980s, major industrial restructuring in the 1980s and 1990s, the 1980s change of emphasis from conservation to efficiency, the rise of social welfare concerns in the 1980s, privatisation and liberalisation of the energy supply industries in the late 1980s and 1990s, and the new environmental imperative of climate change in the 1990s.

However, recurrent themes have been and continue to be, on the one hand, a conviction among energy conservation advocates that securing effective take-up requires government intervention, and, on the other hand, a reluctance of most governments to intervene to the extent considered necessary by the advocates. From the case studies we can identify a number of critical factors that appear to affect the development and implementation of energy conservation policies and programmes:

- the need for a sense of purpose
- a willingness to use intervention
- the role of policy communities and networks
- the role of departments and officials.

The need for a sense of purpose

To what extent can the failure to implement effective energy conservation (as opposed to energy efficiency) in most countries be attributed to the lack of a sense of purpose to save energy? It is certainly true to say that the sense of purpose for energy policy in most countries since the Second World War has been 'pile it high, sell it cheap', as is evident in the duty imposed on the gas and electricity industries to meet all demands for their fuels at prices that are considered politically acceptable. This has proved remarkably successful, at least, in terms of quantity – although fuel has never, in practice, turned out to be as cheap as was predicted in the 1950s and 1960s. This policy was challenged for a time in the 1970s, when most countries recognised that energy saving, as well as energy production, could be important. However, once energy prices began to fall in the 1980s any sense of purpose that might have been felt about energy saving diminished rapidly.

In the 1980s there was a change in terminology in many countries, including the UK, the US and Australia, from energy *conservation* to energy *efficiency*. This was more than a semantic change. It was an outward symptom of a change of emphasis that helped to frustrate any sense of purpose which had been developed in the 1970s through the 'Save It' message. In an era of relatively cheap energy prices (which the 1980s and early to mid-1990s were), it is unsurprising that households and businesses found the prospect of investing often significant sums of money in energy saving less than motivating. The poor take-up of energy-saving measures suggests that the majority of people are unconvinced that energy efficiency is in their interest, yet it is precisely this interest which most governments stressed during the 1980s and used as justification for not intervening further in the market.

The main exceptions, as far as the countries studied in this book are concerned, were Denmark and Japan, which were much more dependent on imported oil and therefore had a very clear public purpose – to reduce oil imports – setting the context for their energy conservation policies in the 1970s and 1980s. There was less reliance on exhorting consumers to act to save themselves money (although this was part of the motivation), and more on introducing regulations, incentives and other measures to ensure that action was taken which would benefit the country as a whole. However, in those areas where they had less sense of purpose – appliance use in Denmark, household energy use in general in Japan – they made limited progress.

It is, however, interesting that the US managed to achieve a small reduction in consumption in the buildings sector from 1973 to 1990 without ostensibly having the clear sense of purpose to do so that was present in Japan and Denmark. However, US per capita energy use was already much higher in these sectors in 1973 than in all other IEA countries except Canada. This was also true in the case of transport, where the US exhibited much lower growth in energy use from 1973 to 1990 than the other countries considered here. In effect, therefore, most other western countries have been through a catching-up process with North America, particularly in terms of energy use in household appliances, private cars and air conditioning. In the US there was considerable waste and therefore significant potential for relatively easy savings to be achieved through energy efficiency standards for appliances. In addition, the constraints on building new power plants in effect gave the utilities and their regulators a sense of purpose – the motivation to develop DSM initiatives to reduce growth in peak electricity demand.

The increasing concerns about climate since 1990 may be helping to create a new sense of purpose to save energy, although so far there is only limited evidence of such a change.

Willingness to use intervention and to challenge key interests

Reducing energy demand clearly challenges the interests of the fuel industries. For those in the public sector it would contradict their long-standing government-imposed aim of maximising production to meet demand. For those in the private sector it conflicts with the need to make a profit, which is dependent on maximising unit sales. With this context in mind it is worth examining how these conflicting interests were dealt with in the case of demand-side management as developed in the US.

Both the UK and US would generally be recognised as non-interventionist states with liberal political traditions. In neither country is there the strong belief in the ability of governments to run economies or plan 'in the public good' that one tends to find in developmental states like Japan, France and Germany. Despite this, the US managed, during the 1970s and 1980s, to introduce a remarkably interventionist energy conservation policy in the form of DSM by the energy (mainly electricity) utilities. The US does differ quite significantly from the UK, however, in the extent to which it uses regulation – for a market economy the US is, paradoxically it may seem, very heavily regulated. This is seen to stem from the fact that the US has *citizens*, protected by a written constitution and a bill of rights, which creates an expectation that the state will regulate to protect its citizens, whereas the UK consists of *subjects* (of the monarch) and has no written constitution, which leads to a presumption against formal regulation. In this respect the US might be considered rather more similar to many other European states (France, Germany and the Scandinavian countries, for example) than the UK.

First, it needs to be noted that DSM was developed at state rather than federal level, so it did not face the problems that beset attempts to develop federal energy policies. Second, it only operated in about half of US states and only very actively in about ten. These were mainly on the west and northeast coasts, where the pressure on peak demand (and hence the need for DSM) was high and there have been active environmental lobby groups that worked closely with the utilities and regulators to promote it. Third, as fuel consumers rather than taxpayers met the costs, this initiative did not run up against public expenditure constraints which would have been felt had the states themselves tried to mount similar programmes. Despite these qualifications, however, DSM was a significant policy initiative in those states where it was developed.

As outlined in chapter 7, most utilities were initially hostile to DSM, claiming that they would lose money by selling less electricity while having to spend money on which they would not earn a return. To get over this, most of the regulatory commissions introduced mechanisms whereby the utilities could pass on the costs of energy efficiency investment to their customers. These costs included a return to shareholders on the investment funded by customers. However, the utilities were facing difficulties constructing new capacity anyway. Add to that changes in price regulation that were making it difficult for utilities to achieve an adequate return on capital investment, and the argument that incentives were required to make them invest in DSM (at least, those forms which could be expected to reduce peak demand) begins to look rather thin.

Thus, at first sight DSM can look like an interventionist piece of regulation and a triumph for the environmental movement that utility businesses might be expected to resent. However, it can also be seen as yet another example of the effectiveness of the energy-supply policy network – this time managing to get the groups who had traditionally been their opponents to lobby for a form of DSM that best suited them. The utilities were able to ensure not only that DSM did not threaten their interests but that it was a pretty good deal given that they would have had difficulty building new power stations anyway. This is not to decry the achievements of DSM but rather to question whether the utilities needed such generous financial incentives to undertake it, with their consequent impact on consumer prices. These incentives can also be seen as sowing the seeds of DSM's destruction when the energy market was liberalised as they turned energy saving into an activity that was viewed by the utilities and many customers as costly and burdensome and something to be shed as soon as possible. DSM subsidies may therefore also have made it more difficult to sell energy conservation to consumers as something desirable that they would purchase for themselves.

It is perhaps the experience with energy pricing and taxation, however, that illustrates most effectively the importance of interest groups. The US is the classic example of the problems faced by governments in challenging the energy-supply interests – dating back to efforts by Nixon, Ford and Carter through to Clinton to impose energy price rises or taxation as a means of reducing energy demand. The actions of the Global Climate Coalition in the lead-up to the 1997 Kyoto climate conference indicate how powerful a lobby these groups remain. And it is not just industrial interests that have to be overcome because increased energy prices are not popular with the voters, as all politicians are well aware. The UK's experience with introducing VAT on household gas and electricity is a good example, and this experience has hardened attitudes in the UK against a carbon tax.

von Weizsacker (1994) suggests that there would be more gainers than losers if energy were taxed as taxes on employment could then be reduced. However, the 'losers' would include some powerful

interests – the energy suppliers, and heavy, energy-intensive industries such as paper, chemicals, aluminium smelting and steel
production, all of which tend to be large employers. Another problem is that every country is reluctant to be the first to move for fear
of reducing its industrial competitiveness relative to other countries.
von Weizsacker is optimistic about energy suppliers' ability to
restructure themselves into energy services companies and hence take
advantage of the new opportunities to sell energy saving, but the
problem is that the energy suppliers do not see it like this. They feel
threatened by talk of energy taxes, as evidenced by the extensive
lobbying undertaken by the European energy suppliers to block
attempts to introduce carbon taxes in the EU. A substantial culture
change is required of suppliers if they are to see environmental taxes
as an opportunity rather than a threat.

When we consider the energy companies with major upstream
interests (the oil, gas and coal producers, as opposed to the electricity and gas distribution companies), the perception of threat far
exceeds any perception of opportunity, and they have made extensive use of figures designed to frighten governments off such action.
Take, for example, the following quote from a vice president of
Texaco: 'A carbon tax of $100 a ton, according to US government
studies, could cost the average American family $1000 a year,
drag the US economy down by 1–3 per cent of GNP by the year 2000
and cost 600,000 jobs … . The US government recognized these
realities when, in response to the Rio conference, it adopted a policy
that entails taking sensible and realistic actions that slow down the
rate of greenhouse gas emissions … particularly the efficient use of
fossil fuels … ' (Malin, 1994: 171).

Turning to other areas of intervention and how they have been
handled, the UK case study of electrical appliance efficiency is
another example of failure to intervene and regulate due to an
unwillingness to challenge the interests of manufacturers. Similar
problems were also experienced for a time during the mid-1980s in
the US and Australia, although by the late 1980s they had been overcome, whereas it took the UK until the early 1990s – and even then
action was at the behest of a EU directive. By contrast, Japan has
been much more willing to intervene and require industry to behave
in certain ways, including by the setting of minimum appliance efficiency standards. The Japanese government has also been willing to
ask businesses to supply information about their energy use – rather

than viewing such activities as a 'burden on business', which has tended to be the view in the UK, for example.

In Denmark energy utilities have been actively 'encouraged' to opt for CHP as the government will not give final permission to build a power station until they have secured contracts for sale of the heat output. The Netherlands experience during the 1990s of CO_2-reduction targets agreed between the energy suppliers is another example of intervention used for environmental purposes, although in this case the neo-corporatist nature of the state meant that the energy suppliers were able to secure a levy on consumers to help fund these activities.

Reluctance to intervene has stemmed at least in part from a general government view in countries with a liberal tradition, particularly the UK, that compulsion is a 'last resort'. However, as Gilliat (1984) has pointed out, intervention that may seem quite impossible in some spheres may be acceptable in others because governments are more willing to challenge the autonomy of some groups than others. Thus, while policy choice constrains implementation, perceptions about the feasibility or legitimacy of certain forms of implementation also constrain policy choice.

However, it should be remembered that in Japan and the Netherlands regulations have tended not to be imposed but negotiated with industry. Shiono (1984) feels that Japanese administrative guidance works because business does not like regulation and prefers the negotiated nature of such 'guidance', often even requesting it and valuing the government's mediating role. There are signs that even states with a liberal tradition are beginning to see the value of regulatory negotiation – the US Environmental Protection Agency (EPA) has, since the mid-1990s, begun to engage in such negotiation over emissions trading, for example, which has benefits both for industry and the EPA. 'A major advantage of regulatory negotiation for the regulated industry is the promulgation of more considered regulations, whereas a major advantage for the EPA is the reduced risk of judicial challenge to its regulations' (Fogleman, 1994: 89).

For this style of consensus-seeking to be effective, though, industry needs to feel that the government has the will to regulate if adequate voluntary action is not forthcoming. In that respect the US to some extent, but perhaps the UK particularly, may find regulatory negotiation more difficult to operate than Japan and many other European countries.

The role of policy communities and policy networks

The development of policy networks and communities, made up of state institutions and external 'governing institutions' (Middlemas, 1979), can help to explain cases that seem to contradict the strong/weak state analysis (for example, effective interventionist policies in a state which is generally categorised as 'weak'). There are two theories about the relevance of this analysis for energy conservation policy.

First, there is the key role of the 'governing institutions' on the energy supply side – the nationalised or regulated gas and electricity industries, the oil and coal industries, and the energy supply unions – which have formed, together with the relevant divisions of energy ministries, effective policy networks for these interests. The power of these networks can be seen as an important factor in the marginalisation of energy conservation, which could be a threat to their interests.

Second, there is the absence of effective bodies (or the unwillingness of governments to take their interests seriously) to act as 'governing institutions' for energy conservation interests. The result has been to make those who lobby for energy conservation more marginal and has forced them to work as outsiders rather than inside the system, with the bureaucracy.

While the UK certainly could not generally be described as a developmental state, the way in which energy policy has evolved has aspects of the developmental state owing to the existence of the effective corporatist policy networks for each of the supply interests. The US can be viewed as rather similar to the UK: there the energy suppliers have developed long-standing and close relationships with the the relevant government departments and agencies to form effective policy networks at federal and state levels.

An important factor in Japan are the different levels of access to the government by different interest groups – the strategic industries have ready access, whereas consumer and conservation groups have less access to the established government–business networks. However, unlike the UK and the US, this does not seem to have worked against energy conservation because the energy conservation industry has managed to become one of the interests that has access. The Netherlands also provides an example of how a corporatist approach can be used to achieve environmental goals. In Australia environmental groups managed to enter the key policy making network in the 1980s and succeeded, for a time, in producing a positive government stance towards action on climate change. However, the energy supply network managed to reassert its influence by the mid-1990s – particularly following the change of government in 1996 – in the light of concerns about the potential impact of climate-change policies on energy-intensive industries and, hence, on the Australian economy.

In the field of energy policy, then, the issue of differential access for the insiders of the traditional energy supply industries versus the outsiders of the energy conservation and renewables industries is one of the keys to their markedly different treatment by successive governments. As Wilks and Wright (1987) say, what is kept off policy agendas is often as important as what is on them – influential members may be able to keep issues off the agenda that would challenge their power or interests. However, one has to identify how the supply interests have achieved this position of power and influence with the officials. Issues may remain off the agenda due to lack of organisation among those members whom one would expect to be advocates for such issues. Energy conservation's failure to move higher up the agenda during the 1980s and early 1990s was at least partly due to fragmentation and ineffectiveness within the conservation lobby. It is also true to say that the supply interests have worked themselves into a powerful position by making the officials' jobs easier by providing helpful briefings on a confidential basis rather than criticising them publicly, as much of the energy conservation lobby has done in countries such as the UK and US.

The historical nature of the energy policy community in most countries has thus been a cohesive network consisting of the energy ministry and a small number of monopolist or oligopolist energy suppliers (in many cases state-owned) inside a looser community which includes the energy conservation and renewable energy industry plus environmental and consumer organisations. One might draw a distinction between the essentially corporatist nature of the energy supply policy networks and the more pluralist energy conservation policy community. The main exceptions have been in parts of Europe – notably the Scandinavian countries, where the role of local authorities in energy supply gave a different perspective.

In those cases where energy conservation initiatives have been developed in circumstances that did not seem particularly favourable, this has tended to be due to the effectiveness of the energy conservation policy community (or parts of it) in adopting one of two main methods to secure its aims.

The first of these has been to work together and/or work with others (such as energy suppliers, local authorities or consumer groups) to argue their case and put pressure on the government. Examples include the development of DSM in the US in the 1970s and 1980s, where environmental groups worked with energy suppliers to make a case to the state regulatory commissions, and the work to secure the Home Energy Conservation Act in the UK in the 1990s, where the main energy conservation industry lobby group secured the support of local authorities, consumer groups and hundreds of backbench MPs in a two-year campaign to persuade the government to allow the bill to become law. These cases also underline the importance of the policy 'climate' – a factor identified by Heclo and Wildavsky (1981) in their study of the UK Treasury. Policy ideas which can seem unlikely to succeed in a certain 'climate' may fare very differently if this changes. For DSM in the 1970s and early 1980s, problems with building new supply capacity to meet peak demand made DSM an option to be considered. The Home Energy Conservation Act undoubtedly benefitted from the growing consensus on the need for action on environmental matters – particularly action that did not require substantial government expenditure.

The second approach was to build alliances with relevant and sympathetic officials in government departments, as well as building support among ministers and MPs, to help the officials argue the case for funding. Examples of the latter include National Energy Action in the UK, the Home Energy Advisory Service in Victoria, Australia, in the 1980s and the establishment of the Sustainable Energy Development Authority in New South Wales, Australia, in the 1990s. These cases also illustrate the importance of key individuals 'in the right place at the right time' – either within or outside government.

Energy conservation was generally not well served by state-owned or private sector old-style monopoly provision, where the emphasis was on supplying the maximum number of units to meet all demands. However, since the early 1990s these policy communities have been undergoing significant change due to corporatisation, privatisation and liberalisation of the energy supply industries and the fact that some countries have decided to abolish specific energy ministries.

Experience to date (mainly in the UK) suggests that liberalisation does not turn the energy market into a model of perfect competition. Monopolies, duopolies and oligopolies continue to exist, but where these once seemed immutable, they become subject to real challenge and new entrants can gain significant market share. As a result, incumbents are having to respond with new services to customers and better prices, and are finding it necessary to contract for cheaper and more efficient means of generation to keep down costs. Thus the dynamic or 'competitive process' model is more appropriate to the energy market than the static, perfect competition model.

What about the prospects for energy saving under liberalisation? It is unlikely to be offered by existing supply companies or new entrants who seek to compete primarily on the price per unit of gas or electricity with their established competitors. However, while this tends to be the initial focus of competition when supply is liberalised, as in other markets, price competition is likely to have its limitations. Eventually, price cutting reaches a level that is unsustainable and suppliers have to look to other means of product differentiation. As Schumpeter (1943: 84) said of the emphasis on marginal price changes in the perfect competition model: 'it is not that kind of competition which counts but the competition from the new commodity, the new technology, the new source of supply, the new type of organisation ... competition which commands a decisive cost or quality advantage and which strikes not at the margin of the profits and the outputs of the existing firms but at their foundations and their very lives'. This is the potential challenge that energy saving and what is coming to be called 'the energy services approach' could offer to the traditional gas and electricity markets.

The abolition of traditional energy ministries could also provide opportunities for energy conservation. The rationale for this has been particularly strong where energy companies are moving from state-ownership to the private sector – in which case, it is argued, the government's relationship with them should be no different from that with other industrial sectors and so can be undertaken within a general trade or industry ministry. A number of Republican US senators have made precisely this point in arguing for the abolition of the Department of Energy in debates on energy market liberalisation. Another motivation in abolishing energy ministries has been to integrate environmental considerations into energy policy. In the UK the Department of Energy was abolished in 1992 and its energy supply functions were taken on by the Department of Trade and Industry, while its energy conservation work went to the Department of the Environment. In Denmark the Ministry of Energy was merged with the Ministry of the Environment in 1994 to form the new Ministry of the Environment and Energy.

Energy market liberalisation and privatisation, together with the new political agenda in which the environment is taking a more prominent role, thus introduce the potential for destabilisation of the cohesive and exclusive policy networks that have developed between energy ministries and traditional energy suppliers and, hence, a potential for change, including closer relationships between energy conservation interests and ministries. However, as with any such change the outcome cannot be predicted, and much will depend on how energy ministries are reformed, where responsibilities go if they are abolished, the priorities and ideologies of governments, the effectiveness of energy suppliers in maintaining their key roles in the political process and the effectiveness of energy conservation interests in making use of the new opportunities.

In the UK, as the story of the Energy Saving Trust and attempts to build sustainability into energy regulation revealed, the changes do not so far seem to have helped the cause of energy conservation. The Department of Trade and Industry has retained the principal role in energy policy and, with no responsibility for energy conservation, its energy division has maintained the supply orientation of the old Department of Energy. The position may change, however, due to the commitments made by the new Labour government to sustainability, which have led to the increasing prominence and power of the new Department of the Environment, Transport and the Regions headed by the Deputy Prime Minister. In Denmark the decision to absorb the Department of Energy into the Department of the Environment may prove to be a positive move for energy conservation, as this Department clearly has environmental (rather than industrial) interests as its main priority.

Departments and officials

Energy conservation requires the use of a wide range of policy instruments – regulation, information, exhortation, incentives – that call for flexibility and innovation on the part of officials in dealing with a wide range of agencies. However, the main experience of energy ministries is in ensuring that a small number of statutory, quasi-autonomous or private sector bodies adhere to the rules laid down for them in legislation.

The supremacy of the generalist over the subject specialist in many civil services is also relevant. For energy conservation there are two aspects to this issue. The first is that where specialists are employed they have tended to be specialists in energy supply technologies rather than energy conservation technologies, leading to a supply bias by the specialists within an energy department. Second, and perhaps most crucially, however, is the fact that where energy ministries lack their own specialist expertise, particularly at senior levels, they have often relied heavily on the expertise of the supply industries. Patterson (1990) has pointed out that in the US and many other countries it was the traditional analysts – who did not question the link between growth in energy use and growth in GDP – who held sway with governments from the Second World War until the 1980s, either being directly employed by them or working on influential statutory bodies and quangos. The more innovative analysts who questioned these assumptions were largely based outside government in academic institutions or environmental organisations, with limited influence and no access to the closed energy policy network which existed until the mid- to late 1980s.

Thus, it is not so much that civil servants in energy ministries have been particularly biased towards supply but rather that, faced with policy areas where a considerable degree of technical and economic expertise is required, a generalist civil service is bound to rely heavily, for information and help in preparing advice to ministers, on experts it can trust. Unfortunately for the cause of energy conservation, most of these experts have been in the energy supply industries.

To what extent are the structure and powers of departments with energy conservation responsibilities relevant?

In Japan, the significance of placing energy conservation responsibilities within the Ministry of International Trade and Industry, a government department with high prestige, should not be underestimated. Another factor was that the oil crisis came at just the right time for MITI, which had, from 1965 to 1973–74, suffered a loss of purpose. It is not difficult to draw the conclusion that tackling this crisis through energy conservation measures offered MITI scope to develop a key role for itself again. Fortuitous factors can, thus, sometimes be important. A significant feature in Japan and Denmark is the existence of good local networks to implement policies and programmes and the fact that the relevant government departments have built up experience of working with them. In Japan this has been via the regional offices of MITI and the Energy Conservation Centre; in Denmark it has been through local authorities, which have had responsibility for energy planning and many of the other programmes.

In the Netherlands the lack of a central civil service and the close links between ministries and relevant interest groups enhance the tendency of officials to become technical experts and to identify closely with the external organisations with which they work. This reinforces the neo-corporatist approach of the Netherlands and helps account for way in which the energy distribution companies and the Ministry of Economic Affairs worked closely on the development of the industry's response to the National Environmental Policy Plan.

In the UK and US the Department of Energy developed relationships with a few, large, mainly statutory bodies in the energy supply field. Building relationships with many disparate and frequently small bodies in the conservation field was therefore a new experience and one which often proved difficult. Energy conservation has been a small and relatively new responsibility, requiring skills very different from those deployed in the Department's mainstream activities. It is perhaps not surprising, therefore, that officials find energy conservation difficult or that, as Lucas (1985) suggests, they are sceptical over whether energy conservation measures, undertaken by a wide range of small bodies, will deliver the outcomes their advocates suggest and prefer the comparative certainty of the supply options delivered by a few large bodies. The marginal nature of energy conservation has also made it more vulnerable in battles with treasury or finance departments over funding.

However, where the initiative has come from outside government departments – from an effective energy conservation group that has been able to work with the department – we can see examples of success, such as National Energy Action in the UK and the Home Energy Advice Service in Victoria. Many energy conservation programmes have thus been developed as a result of external initiative (by non-governmental organisations or local authorities, for example) rather than being initiated from within government departments.

The success of such groups has also been due to the fact that they were able to offer the government departments a ready-made delivery mechanism to help overcome the difficulties that officials face in working with disparate organisations.

Is government intervention the problem rather than the solution?

The four factors considered above suggest that the failure to achieve effective energy conservation is a failure of governments to introduce effective policies. As we have seen, governments face considerable problems in trying to develop energy conservation policies due to an unwillingness to stand up to certain interests and the nature of the energy policy networks. In the past there has also been a lack of sense of purpose and the nature of energy ministries has also been a barrier. Yet might part of the problem lie with the nature of government intervention itself? Is it possible that government subsidies (or those funded by utilities via regulator-mandated DSM programmes) have made it even more difficult to move energy conservation from the margins and into the mainstream?

It is usually argued that government or regulator-mandated subsidies send very effective signals to consumers – first, by signalling that 'this investment must be important if the government or regulator is prepared to give me this incentive for it'; and second, by drawing people's attention to investments that might otherwise not have occurred to them, or which they felt were too much trouble for the savings involved. Certainly many grant and loan schemes offered by governments and utilities have been very successful in terms of take-up, which seems to support these arguments.

However, there is something of a contradiction in a government running publicity campaigns to convince people that investment in energy efficiency will save them money yet at the same time providing a subsidy for such investment, which seems to imply that the measure will only be worth doing if you get a government subsidy. Not everyone will get a grant and programmes do not last forever, due to changing political priorities and budgetary constraints, so the effect tends to be a sharp downturn in take-up as soon as a grant ends or if it is reduced in value. In the UK, for example, the Energy Saving Trust found that take-up of its grants for condensing boilers fell dramatically when the grant was reduced from £200 to £100, and it was forced to put it back up to £200 to increase take-up again.

Although there was almost certainly a strong case for grants in the early days of energy conservation – in the 1970s and early 1980s as people came to understand what conservation was about – the fact that grants are still seen as so essential some twenty-five years after energy conservation was first talked about widely could be seen as a remarkable failure by the energy conservation industry to market its products effectively. After all, energy-saving measures should have strong appeal to consumers – in reducing fuel bills, improving comfort and convenience and, in this age of increasing environmental awareness and green consumerism, helping to protect the environment. However, the industry seems convinced that most consumers do not believe or are not interested in these messages and that without government incentives it is impossible to change their minds. Hence the self-fulfilling prophecy that 'we can't sell them and consumers will only buy them if the government subsidises them'. This is very different from many other industries, which would use persuasion and provide their own incentives to get consumers to buy.

It is interesting that probably the most commercially successful energy-saving measure – double glazing – is the most expensive and least cost-effective, with payback periods typically of twenty years or more. It is also a measure which has tended not to attract government-funded subsidies, such as grants, low-interest loans or tax relief, unlike loft and wall insulation. Double glazing has been sold not solely or even primarily as an energy- or money-saving measure, but also on the benefits of comfort, convenience and noise reduction, on the basis of which millions of households have spent considerable sums of money (£350 per window is about the average in the UK) on replacing adequate windows that could have been draught-proofed for a fraction of the cost. The double-glazing industry, in contrast to those producing other energy-saving measures, makes extensive use of active sales techniques, high-profile advertising and promotion. In essence, it is actually 'sold' to customers.

The energy conservation industry may well be right in its assessment that most energy-saving measures, unlike double glazing, cannot be sold to more than a small percentage of consumers. Hence, a key question for the late 1990s is whether energy conservation can be made into a viable business opportunity or whether it has to be funded from the public purse – either from taxation or perhaps as a community service obligation on energy suppliers to serve environmental and perhaps social (e.g. help for low-income households) goals.

12

Conclusions

Historically, the cause of energy conservation has suffered from five main problems. The first has been the confusion with energy efficiency and the potential conflict between this – which makes energy cheaper and therefore can encourage more use – and energy conservation, which requires the use of less energy. The change in terminology from energy conservation to energy efficiency is more than semantic as it has influenced the types of programmes that have been developed and operated and the very nature of the message and its influence.

Second, it has suffered from changing goals. Energy conservation and efficiency have been advocated at different times since 1973 for reasons as diverse as: security of supply; helping low-income households to achieve warmer homes; economic efficiency and avoidance of waste; and protection of the environment. Changing goals have made it difficult to formulate and maintain a clear and consistent message.

The third problem has been the supply ethos, built up over several decades in the post-war era when increasing supply was seen as the solution to energy shortages, to the complete exclusion (except in times of crisis, as in 1947 and the mid-1970s) of any effort to reduce demand. One can therefore talk of a 'mind set' among ministers, officials and the energy industries, orientated towards increasing supply and reinforced by the close relationship that developed in many countries between energy ministries and key members of the policy network – the major oil companies, the electricity and gas utilities, and the nuclear and coal industries – which became very much insiders in respect of policy formation.

For proponents of energy conservation to break into this circuit was always likely to be an uphill struggle, particularly as their interests would conflict directly with those of the energy suppliers. The supply ethos also meant that the main experience of many energy ministries was managing relationships with a few large energy suppliers, where the role of the department was largely regulatory. By contrast, the skills needed for energy conservation policies are flexibility and the ability to work with more diverse and fragmented networks. Energy conservation has tended to be successful where the government is used to working with networks that have been involved in energy conservation (in Japan, Denmark and the Netherlands) or where energy conservation groups have established their own effective network to make the task of the government department easier (such as National Energy Action in the UK).

Fourth, there has been the unwillingness of governments to use energy pricing or taxation to encourage conservation as these have been seen as against the interests not only of the powerful energy supply policy network but also of those of consumers (voters). Low prices need not be an absolute barrier to energy conservation and high prices are not an automatic guarantee that energy usage will be reduced – as chapter 10 shows there are trends in society (to more households, for example) that can overwhelm pricing effects and effective energy conservation programmes can work even when prices are low or falling. However, low or falling energy prices make investment in energy conservation less attractive and, hence, more difficult to market to consumers. Low prices also increase the need for regulation and incentives, thus potentially increasing the costs of energy conservation.

Finally, there is the failure of the energy conservation industry to market its products to consumers and, hence, the continued reliance on government subsidies, which have been limited and subject to cutbacks.

In addition to these five problems, one also has to consider the effects of the changing nature of energy demand on efforts to conserve energy. As chapter 10 illustrates, energy demand is very dependent on economic structure – as economies change, so does the nature of energy use. The trend to whole-house heating in countries where this had previously been rare (as in the UK and Australia) and the growth in the use of household appliances and energy-consuming office equipment have all been increasing the amount of energy used in buildings since the 1970s, and particularly since the late 1980s. On the other hand, the decline in many energy-intensive industries, such as iron and steel and shipbuilding, has led to reduced demand in the industrial sector.

Since the early 1990s there have been some changes in the traditional picture, some of which are positive, but one of which is largely negative. On the positive side, climate change has become the overriding motivation for energy conservation, giving a clear and consistent goal and one which looks likely to persist for the foreseeable future. Furthermore, most governments have accepted the need for action to tackle climate change and that energy conservation can play a significant role.

The liberalisation and privatisation of energy supply can also be seen as potentially helpful for energy conservation by introducing change into energy policy networks – through reorganisation of the major supply companies, new entrants and, in some countries, the abolition of energy departments. With change comes the potential for new approaches, which could include a greater role for energy conservation. There are signs of some interest in the provision of energy services by energy suppliers and new entrants in these changing markets. Many governments are not relying solely on the spontaneous development of competition in energy services but are taking active steps to encourage it – for example, some of the work of the Energy Saving Trust (EST) in the UK and the Sustainable Energy Development Authority in New South Wales.

But, in another sense, liberalisation can be seen as potentially harmful to energy conservation as it tends to drive energy prices down, making it even more difficult to interest people in spending money to save energy. The evidence from the first few years of liberalisation in the UK suggests that this negative effect is outweighing the benefits it might have brought for energy conservation.

Some things, however, have not changed and look likely to continue to hamper the cause of energy conservation. Despite the commitments to international targets to reduce greenhouse-gas emissions, even recent government initiatives on energy conservation are still mostly small-scale and action on energy efficiency standards continues to proceed slowly. As was seen in the run-up to Kyoto, energy suppliers are still powerful in energy policy networks and are effective lobbyists against tough action on climate change that might help energy conservation but could harm their interests. Partly because of the continuing influence of the suppliers, but also due to the unpopularity of taxes with ordinary voters, most governments remain unwilling to raise energy prices. Although there are exceptions – notably the Scandinavian and some other European countries – even in these cases the carbon/energy taxes are generally small and so may have fairly limited effect. Where liberalisation is being introduced its main selling point is that it will cut energy prices, and this may counteract the effect of any energy taxes that are introduced.

Most energy suppliers still see energy conservation as a threat to their profits and hence are unwilling to promote it. Where competition in supply is being developed, most suppliers are unconvinced that energy saving is of interest to customers and therefore of value as a means of attracting and retaining customers. Meanwhile, the energy conservation industry still feels that it cannot sell energy-saving measures without subsidies – a problem which is exacerbated by low and falling energy prices.

If energy conservation can be made attractive to consumers, then breaking down the monopolies of the gas and electricity utilities (as has already begun in the UK and the US) and the emphasis on competition to serve customers may help to shift the energy market to an integrated energy services approach. It is certainly true that the nature of the old monopolies was not conducive to energy saving (which they did not encourage except when coerced into action by regulators). Ending the old monopolies provides the opportunities that any major shake-up in markets provides for new products and services. Whether this benefits energy conservation or energy efficiency will depend both on the ingenuity of suppliers in terms of packaging and marketing and whether customers see such services as valuable.

In the late 1990s little confidence is being placed in the market approach alone, with the emphasis instead on public service obligation (such as California's Public Goods Charge and lobbying in the UK for similar funding to support the EST). The evidence from the UK – which in 1998 has gone the furthest in introducing competition – is not encouraging for the development of energy services by established energy suppliers. Although there has certainly been some development in services to industrial and commercial users (particularly CHP), no supplier has so far offered energy efficiency services in the domestic sector.

However, it is possible that the energy market could be transformed by the setting-up of bodies such as EST and the Sustainable Energy Development Authority (SEDA) in Australia or by action like that taken during the late 1990s phase of the initiative by energy suppliers in the Netherlands. These initiatives could help to stimulate the energy conservation industry and new entrants who can combine energy supply and energy saving to provide a more serious challenge to traditional energy suppliers. But low or falling energy prices – particularly as the introduction of competition in supply offers the prospect of even lower prices – is likely to act as a continued dampener on demand for energy-saving measures. Furthermore, it seems likely that there will be a continued emphasis on energy efficiency as a means of saving money, which may help to constrain demand growth but will not achieve the major cuts required to meet the Kyoto and beyond targets.

There is now nearly unanimous agreement between governments and the energy conservation/environment lobby about the goal of energy conservation policy – the reduction of CO_2 emissions – yet there is no consensus on the means. The energy conservation lobby would like greater regulation and more financial incentives or penalties, whereas most governments and industry are more in favour of 'voluntary action'. Some governments are interested in the use of economic instruments, such as energy taxes, but many more consider them too politically risky to be considered a serious option. It has also to be said that, in the UK, Australia and the US, where problems of fuel poverty have been a serious concern since the late 1970s, politicians have understandable worries about how taxes on household energy use can be made equitable or even effective. Middle- and higher-income households (which are the major energy users) may continue to consume at their current (1998) level even if prices go up as they may value the time not spent trying to save energy more than the extra money they have to spend on higher fuel bills. However, poorer households, which tend to use rather less energy and are more likely to live in homes that are difficult and expensive to heat, may have to economise – perhaps at risk to their health.

One of the means that has often been most vigorously rejected by many governments in energy conservation and many other policy areas – regulation – is, paradoxically, the one which traditional civil services are likely to be best equipped to develop and implement effectively. Regulatory mechanisms could include minimum efficiency standards, or heat planning as used in Denmark. However, it seems possible that there may be a resurgence in the use of regulation – particularly the negotiated form as has been used in Japan and the Netherlands – since it may prove to be more politically palatable than taxation and more feasible, in a period when all governments are trying to reduce public spending, than subsidies.

Perhaps also there is a need to learn from the examples of Denmark and Japan and, more recently, the Netherlands, where some significant energy savings have been achieved by concentrating effort in sectors where energy use is high and by using methods which can deliver large results more predictably. Crucial to this is the fact that, in each case, action has been required from only a small number of actors, each with control over major amounts of energy use – local authorities undertaking energy planning in Denmark or major industrial users in Japan and industrial/commercial users in the Netherlands who can make use of CHP. By contrast, dissipated efforts that rely on millions of households and businesses of all sizes each to deliver mostly quite small savings can produce results that are difficult to measure, may be counteracted by increased consumption (more appliances and office equipment) or may be largely taken up by improvements in comfort.

Another important lesson is the need to target efforts at sectors where demand is increasing – Japan, for example, has been very successful in reducing energy demand by industry but, for it and most other industrialised countries, the main growth in energy demand in the late 1990s and beyond (apart from transport) is likely to be in buildings (air conditioning and higher heating standards), household appliances and office equipment rather than in traditional industry.

For energy conservation, for the first time since the oil crisis of 1973, there is now a strong chance of an agreed sense of purpose – to tackle climate change – to guide action. The need now is to develop this agreement on purpose into an agreement on the means necessary to achieve it.

Bibliography

Andeweg, R. B. (1993), *Dutch Government and Politics* (Basingstoke: Macmillan).

Appleby, C., and Bessant, J. (1987), 'Adapting to Decline: Organisational Structures and Government Policy in the UK and W. German Foundry Sectors' in S. Wilks and M. Wright (eds) (1987), 188–225.

Bakken, J. (1995), 'Incentives and Disincentives for DSM in a Deregulated and Competitive Electricity Market', *Proceedings of the Fourth International Energy Efficiency and DSM Conference, Berlin, October 1995* (Bala, Cynwyd, PA: SRC International), 389–95.

Barrett, S., and Hill, M. (1984), 'Policy, Bargaining and Structure in Implementation Theory: Towards an Integrated Perspective', *Policy and Politics*, 12(3), 219–40.

Birch, S., and Krogboe, J. (1986), *Cost Benefit Efficiency of Energy Reports for Buildings. The Impact of Heat Survey Reports in Denmark since January 1, 1985* (Brussels: European Commission).

Boardman, B. (1991), *Fuel Poverty: from Cold Homes to Affordable Warmth* (London: Bellhaven).

Boyle, S. (1995a), *DSM Progress and Lessons in the Global Context* (London: International Institute for Energy Conservation).

Boyle, S. (1995b), 'Who Needs Government?', *Energy Economist*, 166, 2–8.

Brookes, L. G. (1990), 'The Greenhouse Effect: the Fallacies in the Energy Efficiency Solution', *Energy Policy*, 18(2), 199–201.

Brookes, L. G. (1991), 'Confusing the Issue on Energy Efficiency', *Energy Policy*, 19(2), 184–6.

Brookes, L. G. (1993), 'Energy Efficiency Fallacies: the Debate Concluded', *Energy Policy*, 21(4), 180–1.

Brown, I. (1990), *Least Cost Planning in the Gas Industry* (London: OFGAS).

Burch, M. (1989), 'The Energy Committee' in G. Drewry (ed.) (1989), 84–102.

Christensen, B., and Jensen-Butler, C. (1982), 'Energy and Urban Structure: Heat Planning in Denmark', *Progress in Planning*, 18(2), 57–132.

Cm 1200 (1990), *This Common Inheritance* (London: HMSO).

Cm 2068 (1992), *This Common Inheritance: the Second Year Report* (London: HMSO).

Cm 2235 (1993), *The Prospects for Coal: Conclusions of the Government's Coal Review* (London: HMSO).

Cm 2427 (1994), *Climate Change: the UK Programme. United Kingdom's Report under the Framework Convention on Climate Change* (London: HMSO).

Conservative Party (1992), *The Best Future for Britain: the Conservative Manifesto, 1992*.

Danish Ministry of Energy (1990), *Energy 2000: a Plan of Action for Sustainable Development* (Copenhagen: Ministry of Energy).

Dawkins, L. A. (1986), *The Politics of Energy Conservation – a Case Study for the Association for the Conservation of Energy* (unpublished).

Department of Energy (1990), *Energy Efficiency in Domestic Appliances. A study by the March Consulting Group on Behalf of ETSU for the EEO*, Energy Efficiency Series no. 13 (London: HMSO).

Department of the Environment (1992), *Climate Change: Our National Programme for CO_2 Emissions. A Discussion Document* (London: Department of the Environment).

Department of Trade and Industry (1992), *Energy Related Carbon Emissions in Possible Future Scenarios for the UK*, Energy Paper 59 (London: HMSO).

Department of Trade and Industry (1994), *The Energy Report: Markets in Transition* (London: HMSO).

Department of Trade and Industry (1995), *Energy Projections for the UK*, Energy Paper 65 (London: HMSO).

Department of Trade and Industry (1997), *The Energy Report: Shaping Change* (London: HMSO).

Department of Trade and Industry/OFGAS (1994), *Competition and Choice in the Domestic Gas Market: a Joint Consultation Document* (London: Department of Trade and Industry).

DIW (1994), *Comparability of the Results of the DIW Study 'Economic Effects of an Ecological Tax Reform' in Austria* DIW/EVA (Vienna: Austrian Energy Agency).

Dore, R. (1982), *Energy Conservation in Japanese Industry* (London: Policy Studies Institute).

Drewry, G. (ed.) (1989), *The New Select Committees: a Study of the 1979 Reforms*, 2nd edition (Oxford: Clarendon Press).

Dunsire, A. (1978), *The Execution Process, vol. 1. Implementation in a Bureaucracy* (Oxford: Martin Robertson).

Dyson, K. (1980), *The State Tradition in Western Europe* (Oxford: Martin Robertson).

Eikeland, P. O. (1993), 'US Energy Policy at a Crossroads?' *Energy Policy*, 21(4), 987–99.

Energy Forum (1989), 'Energy Labels Sticking Nationally and Transnationally', *Energy Forum*, 6(2), 8–10.

European Commission (1995a), *Proposal for a Council Directive to Introduce Rational Planning Techniques in the Electricity and Gas Distribution Sectors*, COM (95) 369 (Brussels: European Commission).

European Commission (1995b), *An Energy Policy for the European Union*, White Paper of the European Commission COM (95) 682 Final (Brussels: European Commission).

European Commission (1997), *Amended Proposal for a Council Directive to Introduce Rational Planning Techniques in the Gas and Electricity Distribution Sectors*, COM (97) 69 Final (Brussels: European Commission).

Finer, E. (1982), *How the Government Handles Energy Conservation*, Rayner Scrutiny (London: Department of Energy).

Fitzmaurice, J. (1981), *Politics in Denmark* (London: Hurst).

Fogleman, V. M. (1994), 'Economic Impacts of Environmental Law: the US Experience and its International Relevance' in N. Steen (ed.) (1994), 81–101.

Fraunhofer Institute (1985), *Employment Effects of Energy Conservation Investments in EC Countries* (Brussels: European Commission).

Friedman, D. (1988), *The Misunderstood Miracle: Industrial Development and Political Change in Japan* (Ithaca, NY: Cornell University Press).

Gaitskell, H. (1983), *The Diaries of Hugh Gaitskell*, edited by P. Williams (London: Jonathan Cape).

Gilliat, S. (1984), 'Public Policy Analysis and Conceptual Conservatism', *Policy and Politics*, 12(4), 345–67.

Golove, W. H., and Schipper, L. J. (1997), 'Restraining Carbon Emissions: Measuring Energy Use and Efficiency in the USA', *Energy Policy*, 25(7–9), 803–12.

Gore, A. (1992), *Earth in the Balance* (London: Earthscan).

Greenhalgh, G. (1990), 'Energy Conservation Policies', *Energy Policy*, 18(3), 293–9.

Greenpeace (1997a), *Industry and the Climate Debate: Membership and Positions of International Lobby Groups* (Amsterdam: Greenpeace International).

Greenpeace (1997b), *Climate Change E Mail Newsletter*, 17 December 1997.

Grubb, M. (1990), 'Energy Efficiency and Economic Fallacies', *Energy Policy*, 18(8), 783–5.

Haaland, H. O., and Wilhite, H. (1994), *DSM and De-regulation: Experiences from Norway* (Oslo: Ressurskonsult).

Hadley, S., and Hirst, E. (1995), *Utility DSM Programs from 1989 through 1998: Continuation or Crossroads?* (Oak Ridge, TN: Oak Ridge National Laboratory).

Haigh, N. (1996), 'Climate Change Policies and Politics in the European Community' in T. O'Riordan and J. Jager (eds) (1996), 155–85.

Hamilton, C. (1997), *Climate Change Policies in Australia* (Lyneham, ACT: The Australia Institute).

HC 401-I, 401-II (1982), House of Commons Energy Committee, Session 1981–82 (Fifth Report), *Energy Conservation in Buildings. Report Together with Appendices and Minutes of Proceedings* (London: HMSO).

HC 310 (1983), House of Commons Energy Committee, Session 1982–83, *Dr Elliot Finer, Minutes of Evidence, 30 March 1983* (London: HMSO).

HC 87 (1985), House of Commons Energy Committee, Session 1984–85 (Eighth Report), *The Energy Efficiency Office. Report, Proceedings of the Committee and Minutes of evidence* (London: HMSO).

HC 262 (1986), House of Commons Energy Committee, Session 1985–86 (Third Report), *The Government's Response to the Committee's Eighth Report (Session 1984–85) on the Energy Efficiency Office. Together with an Appendix and Minutes of Proceedings Relating to the Report* (London: HMSO).

HC 91-I (1990), House of Commons Energy Committee, Session 1990–91 (Third Report), *Energy Efficiency* (London: HMSO).

HC 91-I, 91-II, 91-III (1991), House of Commons Energy Committee, Session 1990–91 (Third Report), *Energy Efficiency. Report, Proceedings of the Committee, Minutes of Evidence and Memoranda* (London: HMSO).

HC 648-I, 648-II, 648-III (1993), House of Commons Environment Committee, Session 1992–93 (Fourth Report), *Energy Efficiency in Buildings Report, Minutes of Evidence + Appendices* (London: HMSO).

HC 185 (1994), House of Commons Trade and Industry Committee, Session 1993–94, *The Work of Ofgas, Minutes of Evidence, 25.1.94* (London: HMSO).

HC 328 (1994), House of Commons Environment Committee, Session 1993–94, *Energy Efficiency: the Role of OFGAS* (London: HMSO).

HC 229 (1995), House of Commons Environment Committee, Session 1994–95, *Energy Efficiency, Minutes of Evidence and Appendices* (London: HMSO).

HC Debates (1.11.94), *Energy Conservation Bill*, cols 1356–415.

Heclo, H., and Wildavsky, A. (1981), *The Private Government of Public Money*, 2nd edition (London: Macmillan).

Hirst, E., *et al.* (1995), *The Future of DSM in a Restructured US Electricity Industry* (Oak Ridge, TN: Oak Ridge National Laboratory).

HL 62-I (1991), House of Lords Select Committee on the European Communities, Session 1990–91 (13th Report), *Energy and the Environment. Report and Minutes of Evidence* (London: HMSO).

Hogwood, B. W., and Gunn, L. A. (1984), *Policy Analysis for the Real World* (Oxford: Oxford University Press).

Hutton, S., *et al.* (1985), *Energy Efficiency in Low Income Households: an Evaluation of Local Insulation Projects*, Energy Efficiency Series no. 4 (London: HMSO).

International Energy Agency (1995), *Energy Prices and Taxes* (Paris: OECD/IEA).

International Energy Agency (1997), *Energy Policies of IEA Countries: 1997 Review* (Paris: OECD/IEA).

Johnson, C. (1982), *MITI and the Japanese Miracle: the Growth of Industrial Policy 1925–75* (Stanford, CA: Stanford University Press).

Joskow, P., and Marron, D. (1992), 'What Does a Negawatt Really Cost?: Evidence from Utility Conservation Programs', *Energy Journal*, 1(4), 41–74.

Joskow, P., and Marron, D. (1993), 'What Does a Negawatt Really Cost?: Further Thoughts and Evidence', *Electricity Journal*, July, 25–7.

Keatinge, W. (1986), 'Seasonal Mortality among Elderly People with Unrestricted Home Heating', *British Medical Journal*, 293, 732–3.

King, M. (1992), *Cold Shouldered* (London: Winter Action on Cold Homes).

Krier, B., and Goodman, I. (1992), *Energy Efficiency: Opportunities for Employment* (Amsterdam: Greenpeace International).

Leach, G. (1977), *A Low Energy Strategy for the UK* (London: International Institute for Environment and Development).

Lindberg, J. (1977), *The Energy Syndrome* (Lexington, MA: Lexington Books).

Lindblom, C. E., (1968), *The Policy Making Process* (Englewood Cliffs, NJ: Prentice-Hall).

London Economics (1994), *Demand Side Management: a Survey of US Experience* (London: OFGAS).

Lovins, A. (1990), *Report to the Minister for Industry and Economic Planning on Matters Pertaining to Victorian Energy Policy* (Snowmass, CO: Rocky Mountain Institute).

Lucas, N. (1985), *Western European Energy Policies: a Comparative Study of the Influence of Institutional Structure on Technical Change* (London: Clarendon Press).

Malin, C. B. (1994), 'Politics, Economics and Environment: Experience of the US Oil and Gas Industries' in N. Steen (ed.) (1994), 157–74.

Marquand, D. (1988), *The Unprincipled Society: New Demands and Old Politics* (London: Fontana).

Middlemas, K. (1979), *Politics in Industrial Society: the Experience of the British System since 1911* (London: Deutsch).

National Consumer Council (1980), *Paying for Loft Insulation: a Review of the Homes Insulation Scheme 1978* (London: National Consumer Council).

OFFER (1994), *The Distribution Price Control Proposals* (Birmingham: OFFER).

OFFER (1995), *The Competitive Electricity Market from 1998* (Birmingham: OFFER).

OFGAS (1992), *Gas and Energy Efficiency: the E Factor* (London: OFGAS).

O'Riordan, T., and Jager, J. (eds) (1996), *Politics of Climate Change: a European Perspective* (London: Routledge).

Owen, G. (1994), *Energy Services Market: Will Competition Be Left to Chance?* (London: Energy Saving Trust/Gas Consumers Council).

Owen, G., and King, M. (1997), *A New World for Energy Services?* (London: Energy Saving Trust).

Patterson, W. (1990), *The Energy Alternative* (London: Boxtree).

Perkins, F. C. (1994), 'A Dynamic Analysis of Japanese Energy Policies', *Energy Policy*, 22(7), 595–607.

Pigou, A. C. (1920), *The Economics of Welfare* (London: Macmillan).

Pressman, J. L., and Wildavsky, A. (1979), *Implementation* (Berkeley, CA: University of California Press).

Robens, A., Lord (1972), *Ten Year Stint* (London: Cassell).

Rosenbaum, W. A. (1981), *Energy, Politics and Public Policy* (Washington, DC: Congressional Quarterly Press).

Rosenfeld, A. H., and Price, L. (1992), 'Incentives for Efficient Use of Energy', paper presented at the Conference on the Economics of Energy Conservation', University of California, Berkeley, 26 June 1992.

Schumpeter, J. A. (1943), *Capitalism, Socialism and Democracy* (London: Unwin University Books).

Shiono, H. (1984), 'Administrative Guidance' in K. Tsuji (ed.) (1984), 46–74.

Sioshansi, F. P. (1994), 'Restraining Energy Demand: the Stick, the Carrot or the Market?', *Energy Policy*, 22(5), 378–92.

Slingerland, R. J. (1997), 'Energy Conservation and Organisation of Electricity Supply in the Netherlands', *Energy Policy*, 25(2), 193–203.

Steen, N. (ed.) (1994), *Sustainable Development and the Energy Industries* (London: Earthscan).

Taylor, L., *et al.* (1990), *Lessons from Japan: Separating Economic Growth from Energy Demand* (London: Association for the Conservation of Energy).

Tsuji, K. (ed.) (1984), *Public Administration in Japan* (Tokyo: University of Tokyo Press).

Uslaner, E. M. (1987), 'Energy Politics in the USA and Canada', *Energy Policy*, 15(5), 432–40.

Vietor, R. H. K. (1984), *Energy Policy in America Since 1945: a Study of Business–Government Relations* (Cambridge: Cambridge University Press).

von Weizsacker, E. U. (1994), 'Sustainable Energy Policies: Political Engineering of a Long Lasting Consensus' in N. Steen (ed.) (1994), 249–63.

Walker, P. (1990), *Staying Power* (London: Bloomsbury).

Weinberg, C. (1994), 'The Restructuring of the Electricity Utility: Technology Forces, R & D and Sustainability' in N. Steen (ed.) (1994), 265– 301.

Wilks, S. (1987), 'Administrative Culture and Policy Making in the Department of the Environment', *Public Policy and Administration*, 2(1), 25–41.

Wilks, S., and Wright, M. (eds) (1987), *Comparative Government–Industry Relations. Western Europe, the United States and Japan* (London: Clarendon Press).

Wright, M. (1988), 'Policy Community, Policy Network and Comparative Industrial Policies', *Political Studies*, 36, 593–612.

Index